ISBN 978-1-334-59355-0
PIBN 10635760

This book is a reproduction of an important historical work. Forgotten Books uses state-of-the-art technology to digitally reconstruct the work, preserving the original format whilst repairing imperfections present in the aged copy. In rare cases, an imperfection in the original, such as a blemish or missing page, may be replicated in our edition. We do, however, repair the vast majority of imperfections successfully; any imperfections that remain are intentionally left to preserve the state of such historical works.

1 MONTH OF
FREE
READING

at

www.ForgottenBooks.com

By purchasing this book you are eligible for one month membership to ForgottenBooks.com, giving you unlimited access to our entire collection of over 700,000 titles via our web site and mobile apps.

To claim your free month visit:

www.forgottenbooks.com/free635760

English
Français
Deutsche
Italiano
Español
Português

www.forgottenbooks.com

Mythology Photography **Fiction**
Fishing Christianity **Art** Cooking
Essays Buddhism Freemasonry
Medicine **Biology** Music **Ancient
Egypt** Evolution Carpentry Physics
Dance Geology **Mathematics** Fitness
Shakespeare **Folklore** Yoga Marketing
Confidence Immortality Biographies
Poetry **Psychology** Witchcraft
Electronics Chemistry History **Law**
Accounting **Philosophy** Anthropology
Alchemy Drama Quantum Mechanics
Atheism Sexual Health **Ancient History**
Entrepreneurship Languages Sport
Paleontology Needlework Islam
Metaphysics Investment Archaeology
Parenting Statistics Criminology
Motivational

THE

CORONERS ACT, 1887,

𝔚𝔦𝔱𝔥 𝔉𝔬𝔯𝔪𝔰 𝔞𝔫𝔡 𝔓𝔯𝔢𝔠𝔢𝔡𝔢𝔫𝔱𝔰.

BY

RUDOLPH E. MELSHEIMER, Esq.,

OF THE INNER TEMPLE, BARRISTER-AT-LAW.

BEING THE

FIFTH EDITION

OF THE

TREATISE BY SIR JOHN JERVIS

ON THE

OFFICE AND DUTIES OF CORONERS.

LONDON :

H. SWEET AND SONS, 3, CHANCERY LANE ;

W. MAXWELL & SON, 8, BELL YARD, TEMPLE BAR ;

STEVENS AND SONS, 119, CHANCERY LANE,

𝔏𝔞𝔴 𝔓𝔲𝔟𝔩𝔦𝔰𝔥𝔢𝔯𝔰.

1888.

+195

PREFACE

TO THE FIFTH EDITION.

————•————

THE passing of the Act of 1887, to consolidate the law relating to Coroners, has rendered it desirable to rearrange the whole of Sir John Jervis's work, and to publish the present edition in the form of an edition of that Act. The original text has, however, as far as possible been preserved, subject to such amendments and alterations as have been necessitated by the legislation of the past sixty years during which the book has been before the public.

Since the above Act was passed a further important alteration in the law has been introduced by the Local Government Act of 1888, by which the election of county Coroners by the freeholders is abolished, and the appointment transferred to the County Council.

The valuable assistance given to the Editor by Mr. Hussey, Coroner of the City of Oxford, in the preparation of the last edition has been continued on the present occasion, and is gratefully acknowledged.

R. E. M.

2, PLOWDEN BUILDINGS, TEMPLE.
November, 1888.

EXTRACT FROM THE PREFACE

TO THE FIRST EDITION.

———•———

THAT the office of Coroner is of great antiquity, and was originally of high dignity, all writers agree; that it is of considerable practical utility, requires no further confirmation than what experience affords. In progress of time, however, in proportion to the advancement of the prerogative, and the augmented authority of the sheriff, the power of the Coroner decreased; and we now look in vain for the individual, who, in the language of Chaucer, was

> " Lord and sire,
> Full often time was knight of the shire,
> A schreve had been, and a Coronour : "

for the office, whether in consequence of the rust and relaxation inseparable from ancient institutions, or of the inefficiency of its officers, has fallen from its pristine dignity into the hands of those who are, in some instances, incompetent to the discharge of even their present limited authority.

A perfect restoration of this office, which undoubtedly contains the germ of vast public utility, is for the consideration of the legislature alone;

but the efficient discharge of its existing authority
may, in some measure, be facilitated by a simple
and lucid arrangement of the law applicable to the
duties at present incident to it. With this view the
present Treatise is submitted to the profession and
the public. How far this has been accomplished is
a question which, with unfeigned diffidence, the
Author submits to that tribunal. Conscious that
many inaccuracies and imperfections must of
necessity pervade a work upon an abstruse and difficult subject, he claims no further approbation than
that which labour and a studious attention to
accuracy may entitle him to.

J. J.

MIDDLE TEMPLE,
    March, 1829.

TABLE OF CONTENTS.

PART I.

LAW OF CORONERS.

INQUEST.

LIABILITIES OF CORONER.

APPOINTMENT AND PAYMENT OF COUNTY CORONER AND DEPUTY.

PART II.

SUPPLEMENTAL.

PROCEDURE.

MEDICAL WITNESSES AND POST-MORTEM EXAMINATIONS.

EXPENSES AND RETURNS OF INQUESTS.

TABLE OF CASES CITED.

—◆—

THE

OFFICE AND DUTIES

OF

CORONERS.

INTRODUCTION.

THE Coroner is so called à Coronâ, because he is an Origin. officer of the Crown, and had conusance of some pleas which were called placita Coronæ.[1] At different periods in the history of this country he has been variously denominated. He was called serviens regis[2] and Coronarius[3] in the reign of Henry the Second. In the reign of Richard the First he is styled custos placitorum Coronæ,[4] and in Magna Charta and subsequent statutes Coronator.

The office of Coroner is of so great antiquity, that its Antiquity. commencement is not known.[5] By some it is said to be coeval with that of sheriff, and to have been ordained, with the latter office, to keep the peace when the earls gave up the wardship of the county;[6] but this is doubted

---

[1] 2 Inst. 30 ; 4 Inst. 271 ; 1 Bl. Com. 346.
[2] Umfrev. Lex Cor. XX.
[3] Wilkins, Leg. Ang. Sax. 337.
[4] Ibid. 346.
[5] Per Dodderidge, J., 3 Bulst.

176.
[6] Spel. Vicecom. ; Lamb. Eiren. ; Mir. c. 1, s. 3 ; 2 Inst. 31 ; 1 Bl. Com. 347; and Greenwood's "Courts," p. 285, and the authorities there cited.

J.   B

by others,[1] and, as it seems, with reason, notwithstanding
the great authorities to the contrary; for, according to
Sir Edward Coke, the sheriff was more ancient than the
division of England into counties by king Alfred, and
existed in the time of the Romans in this country as an
officer of the consul,[2] at which period we find no allusion
to any officer whose duties corresponded with those of
the coroner. But, whatever may have been the commencement of the office, it is evident that coroners
existed in the time of Alfred, for that king punished with
death a judge who sentenced a party to suffer death upon
the coroner's record, without allowing the delinquent
liberty to traverse.[3] This officer is also mentioned in the
charter granted by king Athelstan to the monastery of
St. John of Beverley, A.D. 925.[4]

Conserva-
tors of the
peace.
County Coroners are conservators of the queen's peace,
and become magistrates by virtue of their election and
appointment.[5] This privilege, independently of their
mere official duties, they are entitled at this day to
exercise; and are empowered to cause felons to be apprehended, as well those that have been found guilty after
inquisition, as those suspected of guilt, or present at the
death, and not guilty; as also burglars and robbers, in
respect of whom no inquisition can be taken.[6] And this,
says Lord Hale,[7] appears evidently by the statutes
3 Edw. 1, c. 9, and 4 Edw. 1, Officium Coronatoris; and
with this agrees the common usage at this day; for
many times the inquest are long in their inquiry, and
the offender may escape, if the coroner stay until the
inquisition is delivered up. And the coroner may now

---

[1] Bac. on Gov. 66; 6 Vin.
Abr. 242.
[2] Co. Litt. 168 a.
[3] Bac. on Gov. 66; 6 Vin.
Abr. 242.
[4] Dugd. Monast. 171.
[5] See *Davis* v. *JJ. of Pem-
brokeshire*, 7 Q. B. D. 515,
where, however, it was only
held that the two offices are
not incompatible.
[6] Mir. c. 1, s. 13; 1 Brit. 8
(edition by Nichols); Lamb.
Eiren. 378.
[7] 2 Hale, P. C. 107.

bind any person to keep the peace who makes an affray in his presence.[1]

Coroners are exempt from serving offices which are inconsistent with the duties of coroner, and disqualified for election as aldermen or councillors in the counties or boroughs for which they are appointed. They are also privileged from being summoned on juries,[2] and from arrest while engaged in the execution of their duty. This latter question first arose incidentally at nisi prius, in an action against the sheriff of Staffordshire for not arresting a coroner. On behalf of the plaintiff, it was proposed to show that several inquests had been held by the coroner between the delivery of the writ to the sheriff and the return of the writ; when Gaselee, J., before whom the cause was tried, expressed his opinion that no coroner could be arrested eundo morando vel redeundo for the purpose of taking an inquest. It has since been directly held that a coroner when engaged in the discharge of his official duty is privileged from arrest;[3] and in a more recent case the privilege was extended to a deputy coroner, the court ordering his discharge forthwith, and without the drawing up of a rule.[4]

Exemption from serving offices, and from arrest.

Before the statute of Magna Charta, coroners held pleas of the crown; but by cap. 17 of that statute,[5] which enacts "quod nullus vicecomes, constabularius, coronator, vel alii ballivi nostri teneant placita coronæ," their power in proceeding to trial and judgment was taken away, and this disability is re-enacted in section 44 of the present Act.

Pleas of the crown.

The duty of taking inquests, one of the most important duties of the coroner, was regulated and defined by the statute De officio Coronatoris, 4 Edw. 1, st. 2, and

Inquests of death.

---

[1] 1 Bac. Abr. 491.
[2] 33 & 34 Vict. c. 77.
[3] *Callaghan* v. *Twiss*, 9 Ir. Law Rep. 422.
[4] *Ex parte the Deputy Coroner for Middlesex*, 6 H. & N. 501; *S. C.*, 7 Jur. N. S. 103.
[5] 25 Edw. 1; 2 Inst. 30.

it would seem from that statute that the authority of coroners with respect to felony was not limited to inquests of death only ; for they were directed to inquire of breakers of houses; and Britton, in his paraphrase upon that statute, treats of their duty with reference to inquiries concerning rape and prison breach.[1] It has also been said that they had authority to inquire of arsons,[2] and to hold inquests in cases of fire, but that question was decided in the negative in the case of *Reg.* v. *Herford*,[3] and is now provided against in section 44 of the present Act, which limits the authority of coroners to inquisitions of death. By that section their jurisdiction in inquests of royal fish and of wreck is also abolished.

The statute De officio Coronatoris was merely directory, and in affirmance of the common law, and did not restrain the coroner from any branch of his power, nor excuse him from the execution of any part of his duty not mentioned in the statute, and which was incident to his office at common law. This statute is now repealed, and the Coroner's duty on an inquest is to be gathered from the Coroners Act of 1887, 50 & 51 Vict. c. 71, which is set out in the following pages.

---

[1] 1 Britt. c. 2, s. 2 (edition by Nichols).
[2] Mirr. of Just., ch. 1, s. 13.

[3] 6 Jur. N. S. 750 ; 29 L. J., Q. B. 249.

THE CORONERS ACT 1887.

———+———

An Act to consolidate the Law relating to Coroners.

[16th September, 1887.

BE it enacted by the Queen's most Excellent Majesty, by and with the advice and consent of the Lords Spiritual and Temporal, and Commons, in this present Parliament assembled, and by the authority of the same, as follows ·

Preliminary.

1. This Act may be cited as the Coroners Act, 1887. Short title.

2. This Act shall not apply to Scotland or Ireland. Extent of Act.

PART I.

LAW OF CORONERS.

Inquest.

3.—(**1.**) Where a coroner is informed that the dead body of a person is lying within his jurisdiction, and there is reasonable cause to suspect that such person has died either a violent or an unnatural death, or has died a sudden death of which the cause is unknown, or that such person has died in prison, or in such place or under such circumstances as to require an inquest in pursuance of any Act, the coroner, whether the cause of death arose within his jurisdiction or not, shall, as soon as practicable, issue his warrant for summoning not less than twelve nor more than twenty-three

Summoning and swearing of jury by coroner.

S. 3 (1). good and lawful men to appear before him at a specified time and place, there to inquire as jurors touching the death of such person as aforesaid.

When held. In all cases of sudden death, or death under any circumstances of suspicion, where the duty of informing the coroner is not by statute imposed upon any particular person, it is the duty of those who are about the deceased to give immediate notice to the coroner or his officer, or to the nearest officer of police, who then communicates with the coroner. If possible notice should be given while the body is fresh, and while it remains in the same situation as when the death occurred.[1] If, in such cases, it is attempted to register the death in the ordinary way, it is the duty of the registrar, acting under his instructions from the Registrar-General, to refer the matter to the coroner. It is an indictable offence to bury a man who dies a violent death before the coroner's jury have sat,[2] or to otherwise dispose of a body in order to prevent an inquest being held.[3]

Lunatics. In certain cases the duty of sending notice of the death to the coroner is imposed by statute on particular persons ; thus, if a lunatic dies in any asylum or licensed house, or while under the care of any person, the superintendent, or person having the care of the lunatic, respectively, must get a statement prepared and signed by the medical persons who attended the patient during his last illness, and must within two days of the date of the death certify it, and transmit it to the coroner, who must hold an inquest if he thinks that any reasonable suspicion attends the cause and circumstances of the death.[4]

---

[1] 1 Salk. 377 ; 1 E. P. C. 378.
[2] *Per* Holt, C. J., Anon. 7 Mod. 10 ; 3 Hawk. P. C. c. 9, s. 23 ; Stra. 22, 167, 533, 1097 ; *R.* v. *Clark,* 1 Salk. 377. It is said that the township may be amerced, Bacon, Abr. ; Staunford, P. C. 51, G.
[3] See *post,* p. 83.
[4] 16 & 17 Vict. c. 96, s. 19 ; and 25 & 26 Vict. c. 111, s. 44.

Where an infant under the age of one year has been received into a house registered under the Infant Life Protection Act, 1872, the person registered must, if the infant dies, cause notice to be given to the coroner for the district within twenty-four hours after the death; and the coroner must hold an inquest on the body of every such infant unless a certificate under the hand of a registered medical practitioner is produced to him by the person registered, certifying that such practitioner has personally attended or examined the infant, and specifying the cause of its death, and the coroner is satisfied by the certificate that there is no ground for holding the inquest.[1]

S 3 (1). Infants dying in registered house.

Again, if a person dies in prison it is the duty of the gaoler to send for the coroner before the body is buried; if he neglect to do so he is liable to be amerced—and if judgment of death has been executed, the inquest must take place within twenty-four hours after the execution.[2]

Deaths in prisons.

And under the Habitual Drunkards Act,[3] "in case of the death of any person detained in any retreat, a statement of the cause of the death of such person, with the name of any person present at the death, shall be drawn up and signed by the principal medical attendant of such retreat, and a copy thereof duly certified by the licensee of such retreat shall be by him transmitted to the coroner."

Habitual Drunkards Act.

Upon receipt of information, which need not, as in the case of an information before a justice of the peace, be given upon oath, the coroner must consider whether it is necessary to hold an inquest under the above sub-section. He has no absolute right to hold inquests in every case in which he chooses to do so. It would be intolerable if he had power to intrude without adequate cause upon the privacy of a family in distress, and to interfere with their arrangements for a funeral. Nothing could justify

When inquest should be held.

---

[1] 35 & 36 Vict. c. 38, s. 8.   [3] 42 & 43 Vict. c. 19, s. 27.
[2] 31 & 32 Vict. c. 24, s. 5.

S. 3 (1). such interference except a reasonable suspicion that there may have been something peculiar in the death, that it may have been due to other causes than common illness.[1] He should not go, generally speaking, until he is sent for.[2] And coroners, when paid by fees, were frequently censured by the court[3] for holding inquests, for the sake of enhancing their emoluments, where there was no reasonable probability that the death occurred from unnatural causes. On the other hand, when the coroner receives from the proper police authorities information of a sudden death, in order that an inquest may be held, and when there is no medical certificate of death from any natural cause, or other ground on which he can reasonably form an opinion as to the actual cause of death, it is his duty to hold an inquest. He cannot, in such a case, properly exercise any discretion to the contrary, unless by inquiry or otherwise he has obtained such credible information as may be sufficient to satisfy a reasonable mind that death arose from illness, or some other cause rendering an inquest unnecessary.[4] In some cases there may be suspicion where a medical practitioner has been in attendance, and refuses to certify his opinion of the cause of death, or where there is reason to suspect that the real cause of death is not truly stated. And it has been suggested that notice of the death should be sent to the coroner, and an inquest held, in all cases of death in a public institution, where patients are treated among strangers, away from their friends ; but in the exercise of his discretion, the coroner will observe that, although it is desirable that the authorities or managers should clear themselves from any possible imputation of misconduct, still cases of suspicion may arise also among friends,

[1] *Per* Stephen, J., in *Reg.* v. *Price*, 12 Q. B. D. 247 ; and see 11 East, 229.
[2] *R.* v. *Clerk*, 1 Salk. 377 ;
Re Hull, 9 Q. B. D. 699.
[3] 1 East, P. C. 382.
[4] *Per* Lord Selborne, L. C., in *re Hull*, 9 Q. B. D. 700.

and improper practices may be found in private houses, **S. 3 (1)** under the eyes of relations. Again, suspicion will exist where the deceased dies in a house of ill-fame, or in a public-house (for his liquor may have been drugged), or in an empty house, or in an unfrequented place, or alone in a railway carriage, or where the place presents any unusual or noisome appearance. The coroner should therefore inquire as to the circumstances of the death ; where and when the deceased died or was found dead ; by whom he was last seen alive ; who was present, or who first saw the body after death ; whether any known illness existed ; whether any negligence or blame is alleged against anyone ; whether the deceased has been seen by any medical practitioner ; what is the supposed cause of death, either known or suspected ; whether the death was sudden ; whether caused by violence, as wounds, burns, ill-usage, poison, suicide ; and whether any mystery is attached. In cases of accident he should inquire who was present, or who first saw the deceased after the accident.

If, then, it appears to be necessary to hold an inquest, Delay. the coroner should proceed forthwith to issue his warrant to summon a jury. Delay on his part is punishable. For instance it has been held to be inconsistent with a coroner's duty to delay holding an inquest upon a body in a state of decomposition during so long a period as five days without special reason.[1] It must in all cases When held. be held within a reasonable time after the death, but no precise definite time can be specified within which the inquest can be held ; the body is part of the evidence, and it is essential that that should be in such a state that information may be derived from the inspection of it ; and by the state of the body alone can the period within which the inquisition may be held be

---

[1] *In re Hull*, 9 Q. B. D. 692.

S. 3 (1). determined. Where, however the body has been buried so long, that it may reasonably be presumed that the view of it could afford no information, the coroner ought not to disinter it.

Sundays.   The proceeding by inquisition is a judicial act, and should not therefore be held upon a Sunday, which is dies non juridicus, in which no judicial act ought to be done.[1] It has been determined that the execution of a writ of inquiry on a Sunday is void, even upon the evidence of the almanack, without being specially assigned for error.[2] For this reason it is, that the day upon which an indictment or inquisition is taken ought to appear in the caption; and if it appear to have been taken on a Sunday, it will be void.[3] But there is no objection to the performance of ministerial acts on Sunday; for example, the warrant for summoning a jury may be issued on that day.

Jury warrant.   By the common law the coroner might direct his precepts and warrants to the sheriff, for returning a jury before him, and might also assess and set a fine upon the sheriff for not returning a panel;[4] but in practice the jury warrant is now directed to the coroner's special officer, if he have one, or to the constables and peace officers of the parish, place, or precinct where the party lies dead,[5] and sometimes to others of the next adjoining parishes. It is delivered to the special officer, or peace officer of the place where the party lies dead, who thereupon makes out his under-precept or summons[6] to the peace officers of the other parishes specified in the coroner's warrant, to summon a particular number of inhabitant householders to appear at the time and place appointed for the inquiry. He also prepares the summonses

---

[1] 9 Rep. 66 b.
[2] 1 Str. 387
[3] 2 Saund. 290 ; 1 Vent. 107 ;
2 Keb. 731.
[4] Dalton, c. 100 ; 12 Por. Fines pur contempts.
[5] App. Form 14.
[6] App. Form 15.

for the jury,[1] and, together with the under-precept, transmits them to the peace officers of the different parishes. The jury are summoned by the officer of each parish, who should, if possible, serve them personally, or at least leave the summons at their dwelling-house with some member of their family.

The qualifications and exemptions of jurors are to be collected from the provisions of the County Juries Act, 1825,[2] and the Juries Act, 1870,[3] which are to be construed together. By section 9 of the latter Act the following persons are exempt from serving upon any inquests whatever : — peers, Members of Parliament, judges, clergymen, Roman Catholic priests, ministers of any congregation of Protestant Dissenters, and of Jews, whose place of meeting is duly registered, provided they follow no secular occupation except that of a schoolmaster ; serjeants, barristers, certificated conveyancers, and special pleaders, if actually practising ; members of the Society of Doctors of Law, and advocates of the Civil Law, if actually practising ; attornies, solicitors, and proctors, if actually practising, and having taken out their annual certificates, and their managing clerks, and notaries public in actual practice ; officers of the courts of Law and Equity, and of the Admiralty and Ecclesiastical Courts, including therein the Courts of Probate and Divorce, and the clerks of the peace or their deputies, if actually exercising the duties of their respective offices ; coroners ; gaolers, and keepers of houses of correction and all subordinate officers of the same; keepers in public lunatic asylums ; members and licentiates of the Royal College of Physicians of London if actually practising as physicians ; members of the Royal Colleges of Surgeons in London, Edinburgh, and Dublin, if actually practising as surgeons ; apothecaries certified by the Court of

Exemptions.

---

[1] App. Form 16.   [3] 33 & 34 Vict. c. 77.
[2] 6 Geo. 4, c. 50.

S. 3 (1).   Examiners of the Society of Apothecaries, and all registered medical practitioners, and registered pharmaceutical chemists, if actually practising as apothecaries,
medical practitioners, or pharmaceutical chemists respectively; officers of the army, navy, militia, and
yeomanry while on full pay ; the members of the Mersey
Docks and Harbour Board ; the master, wardens and
brethren of the Corporation of Trinity House of Deptford
Strond ; pilots licensed by the Trinity House of Deptford
Strond, Kingston-upon-Hull, or Newcastle-upon-Tyne,
and all masters of vessels in the buoy and light service
employed by either of those corporations, and all pilots
licensed under any Act of Parliament or charter for the
regulation of pilots ; the household servants of Her
Majesty, her heirs, and successors ; officers of the post
office, commissioners of customs, and officers, clerks, or
other persons acting in the management or collection of
the customs, commissioners of inland revenue, and officers
or persons appointed by the commissioners of inland
revenue, or employed by them or under their authority
or direction in any way relating to the duties of inland
revenue ; sheriffs' officers ; officers of the rural and
metropolitan police ; magistrates of the metropolitan
police courts, their clerks, ushers, doorkeepers, and
messengers ; members of the council of the municipal
corporation of any borough, and every justice of the
peace assigned to keep the peace therein, and the town
clerk and treasurer for the time being of every such
borough ; and officers of the Houses of Lords and
Commons. Numerous special Acts confer the same
exemption on various other classes of persons.[1]

---

[1] For example : registrars of
deaths, 7 W. 4, c. 22, s. 18 ;
officers of post office, 7 W. 4, c.
34, s. 12 ; constables, 2 & 3
Vict. c. 93, s. 10 ; officials of
bankruptcy court, 5 & 6 Vict.
c. 122, s. 63, and 12 & 13 Vict.
c. 106, s. 47 ; Chelsea pensioners,
6 & 7 Vict. c. 95, s. 54 ;
Greenwich out-pensioners, 9 &
10 Vict. c. 9 ; magistrates of
metropolitan police courts, their

No man who has been attainted of any treason or **S. 3 (1)** felony, or convicted of any crime that is infamous, unless Convicts. he shall have obtained a free pardon, nor any man who is under outlawry, is qualified to serve.[1]

Aliens are qualified to serve after having been domiciled Aliens. in England or Wales for ten years or upwards.[2]

No person whose name is in the jury book as a juror, Excuses. is entitled to be excused from attendance on the ground of any disqualification or exemption, other than illness, not claimed by him at or before the revision of the list by the justices of the peace.[3]

No person is liable to be summoned to serve on any jury or inquest (except a grand jury) more than once in any one year, unless all the jurors upon the list have been already summoned to serve during such year.[4]

By section 52 of the County Juries Act, 1825,[5] the Qualifi- qualification of county jurors in proceedings under a writ cation. of inquiry is the same as the qualification under section 50, for trials at nisi prius; but it is provided that nothing therein contained shall extend to any inquest to be taken by or before any coroner of a county by virtue of his office, or to any inquest or inquiry to be taken before any other coroner. County coroners when acting otherwise than under a writ of inquiry, and other coroners on all occasions, "may respectively take all inquests and inquiries by jurors of the same description as they have been used and accustomed to do," before the Act was passed. An opinion has prevailed, that the concluding words of this section gave power to the coroner to summon even those who, under the Juries Acts, are expressly exempted from serving on juries, but it would seem that the above proviso has reference only to the provisions of

clerks, ushers, doorkeepers and messengers, 2 & 3 Vict. c. 71, s. 4; medical practitioners, 21 & 22 Vict. c. 90, s. 35; dentists, 41 & 42 Vict. c. 33, s. 30.

[1] 33 & 34 Vict. c. 77, s. 10.
[2] Ib. sect. 8.
[3] Ib. sect. 12.
[4] Ib. sect. 19.
6 Geo. 4, c. 50.

the section itself, and is only intended to enable the coroner to summon as jurors, persons who are not qualified to be jurors on trials at nisi prius. The question does not seem to have been judicially decided, but in 1840 the Incorporated Law Society took the opinion of the then Law Officers (Sir John Campbell and Sir Thomas Wilde, both subsequently Chancellors) upon the liability of members of their profession to serve on coroners' juries, and that opinion was in accordance with the view above expressed.

Subject therefore to the above exemptions, all persons, of whatever age, who are summoned are bound to appear, but no particular qualification by estate is necessary. The jurors must however be good and lawful men, and should be able to write their names legibly upon the inquisition. Aliens, convicts, and outlaws are not " good and lawful," and it would seem that if any such were empanelled on the coroner's inquest, it would be a good plea to avoid the inquisition.[1] In the case of Sir William Withipole,[2] it was pleaded to the coroner's inquisition, upon the statute 11 Hen. 4, c. 9 (now repealed), that several of the jury were nominated by the foreman, and that two of them were outlawed in actions of debt; upon which it was agreed by several of the justices and barons, that the statute applied to inquests before the coroner, and that an outlaw in personal actions was not probus et legalis homo, to be sworn on an inquest, and might be challenged for that cause. The point was not, however, judicially determined, but it is deserving of consideration, inasmuch as it illustrates the meaning of the words " good and lawful." Jurors ought also to be householders of the county or place in which the inquest is held, and to be persons who are indifferent to the subject matter of the inquiry.[3] Their number is immate-

---

[1] 2 Hale, P. C. 60, 155 ; 33 & 34 Vict. c. 77, ss. 8 and 10.
[2] Cro. Car. 134, 147.
[3] Fort. de Laud. c. 25.

rial, provided twelve agree ; if there be less, the inquisition **S. 3 (2).** will be bad : [1] therefore where there is likely to be an adjournment, it is desirable to have at least more than twelve.

There is no express provision entitling the jurors to Remuneration. remuneration, but in many places the authorities have allowed a fee to be paid to them.

Though, by the repealed statute De officio Coronatoris,[2] County juries. the coroner was directed to summon his jury out of the four, five or six of the next adjacent townships, and, by the ancient practice, it was usually so expressed in the inquisition, yet, that statute being merely directory, an inquisition was considered good if purporting upon the face of it to have been taken by jurors from the county at large. It still seems necessary, however, that the jurors should be good and lawful men from within the jurisdiction of the coroner.

(2.) Where an inquest is held on the body of a prisoner who dies within a prison, an officer of the prison or a prisoner therein or a person engaged in any sort of trade or dealing with the prison shall not be a juror on such inquest.

This is a re-enactment of the provisions of similar Inquests in prisons. sections now repealed. The inquest on such a death must be held by the coroner having jurisdiction in the place to which the prison belongs.[3] Where a prison which belonged to the county at the commencement of the Prison Act, 1865, is locally situate within the limits of a borough, the jurisdiction to hold such inquests remains with the county coroner, notwithstanding the transfer of prisons to the Secretary of State by the Prison Act, 1877, unless rules

---

[1] *Cobat's case*, 1 Hale, P. C.   [2] 4 Edw. 1, st. 2.
161, n.   [3] 28 & 29 Vict. c. 126, s. 48.

S 3 (3). to the contrary are made under the latter Act by th
Secretary of State.[1]

(3.) When not less than twelve jurors are assembled they shall be sworn by or before the coroner
diligently to inquire touching the death of the person
on whose body the inquest is about to be held, and
a true verdict to give according to the evidence.

Return of
warrant.

When the time arrives at which the inquiry is to be
instituted, the coroner (or his deputy) proceeds to the
place appointed, when the officer of the parish where the
party lies dead returns his warrant, together with the
names of the jury summoned from his parish. The other
officers of the respective parishes also return the names of
the jurors summoned by them respectively, which the
coroner or deputy coroner annexes to the principal warrant, and indorses the return thereon,[2] which the different
officers subscribe. The warrant and return should be
kept by the coroner.

Opening of
court.

The court is then opened by proclamation,[3] and the
coroner proceeds to call over the names of the jury, beginning with those of the parish where the inquest is to
be taken, and the others in the order specified in the
warrant. As the jurors appear, their appearance should
be denoted by a mark against their names. If a sufficient
number do not appear, proclamation [4] should be again
made ; and if a full jury cannot be obtained, the coroner

Tales jury.

may forthwith summon so many other good and lawful
men then present or in the neighbourhood as may be
sufficient to form a jury ; the coroner should examine the
summoning officers upon the voir dire,[5] as to the mode by
which the jury have been respectively summoned ; and

[1] *Reg.* v. *Robinson*, 19 Q. B.
D. 322 ; and see under sect. 7,
sub-s. (2).
[2] App. Form 17.

[3] App. Form 18.
[4] App. Form 19
[5] App. Form 20.

with this view he ought not to discharge the summoning **S. 3 (3).**
officers until a full jury are in attendance.

Formerly the oath was administered super visum cor- Oath.
poris;[1] but it was since held to be no ground for quashing the inquisition that the jury were first sworn, and
afterwards viewed the body,[2] and this is now all that is
required. The oath should be administered in the first
instance to the foreman, who may either be the first
juryman called, or may be nominated by his fellows, to
whom afterwards the oath is administered, by three or
four at a time,[3] in their order upon the panel. It must,
if the usual form is not binding upon any individual, be
administered in such form and with such ceremonies as
he may declare to be binding upon him.[4] And by the
30 & 31 Vict. c. 35, s. 8, it is provided that if he "refuse Affirmation.
or be unwilling, from alleged conscientious motives, to
be sworn, it shall be lawful for the court or judge or
other presiding officer or person qualified to administer
an oath to a juror, upon being satisfied of the sincerity of
such objection, to permit such person instead of being sworn
to make his or her solemn affirmation or declaration,"[5]
which "shall be of the same force and effect, and if untrue
shall entail all the same consequences as if such person
had taken an oath in the usual form." It is by the same
section sufficient to state in the inquisition that the jurors
have been "sworn or affirmed," without specifying any
particular juror.

In the form of jurors' oath given in the schedule of the Form of
Act[6] the words "and to the best of your skill and know- oath.
ledge" are added. This is the old form of oath, and
survives no doubt from the time when the jury were
selected with special reference to their personal know-

---

[1] *R. v. Ferrand*, 3 B. & Ald. 260.
[2] *Reg. v. Ingham*, 5 B. & S. 257.
[3] App. Forms 2 & 21.
[4] 1 & 2 Vict. c. 105, which is declaratory of the Common Law merely.
[5] Form 21.
[6] Form 2.

J.   C

S. 3 (3). ledge of the matters to be inquired into. Under section
37, it seems that the form given should be used notwithstanding this sub-section. The difference between this
form of oath and that administered upon a trial is notice-
able as giving larger power to the jury in the former
case. It is their privilege, for example, at any time
during the investigation, to call back before them any
witness who has been examined, and to ask any question
that may suggest itself to their minds as elucidatory of
their inquiry. Or if in the opinion of a majority of them
the cause of death has not been satisfactorily explained
by the medical practitioner or other witnesses examined
in the first instance, they may, under section 21, suggest
some other medical man to the coroner, and require him
to summon him as a witness, and if desirable, to order
him to make a post-mortem examination.

The jury, having once been sworn, it would be irregular
to dismiss them without proceeding with the inquiry
A refusal on the part of the coroner without adequate
reason, or from improper motives, to continue the
inquest, amounts to misbehaviour for which he would be
liable to be removed from his office.[1] In the case cited it
was also proved that the coroner attended in a state of
intoxication, and the actual decision may have proceeded
upon that ground.

Who may
attend.
It has been the subject of much controversy, whether
the inquiry before the coroner is of a public nature, for
the purpose of ascertaining the cause of the death merely,
and such as takes place in the ordinary courts of justice
or on an inquest of office ; or whether it is an ex parte
and secret proceeding, analogous to that before grand
juries and magistrates for the purpose of accusation,
which is admitted to be private.[2]

[1] *In re Ward*, 4 L. T. N. S.   [2] *Cox* v. *Coleridge*, 2 D. & R.
458 ; 30 L. J. Ch. 775.   86 ; 1 B. & C. 37.

In support of the publicity of the proceedings, it is urged, first, that the duties of the coroner, and the obligations of the public towards him, show that the inquiry is public ; secondly, that individuals have in- terests with reference to the inquest which can only be exercised by a right of access ; and, lastly, the dicta of learned judges are adduced to show that the proceedings should be open and public.

In support of the first proposition, it is contended, that the inquiry before the coroner does not necessarily lead to accusation ; and that the possibility of its so terminating is not a ground sufficient for saying that it should be secret.

Publicity of proceedings

The Statute of Marlbridge[1] is also cited as a legislative declaration, that all persons of the age of twelve years were bound to be present at an inquest for the death of man. The former part of that chapter remedied the grievance before felt from amerciaments imposed upon townships because all persons of the age of twelve years did not attend the coroner's inquest on all occasions, and provided that there shall be no amerciament, if a sufficient number of those summoned come to take the inquest ; but it excepted expressly from that provision inquests for the death of man ; and, therefore, in such cases all were bound to attend. How otherwise, it was said, could the inquiry be conducted with effect ; for the coroner goes to the spot where the inquiry is to be instituted, knowing nothing of the occurrence, or who may or who may not be able to testify to the circum- stances of it ? Moreover, the form of proclamation used upon the inquiry implies that the general public have a right to attend. Sir T. Smith, in his History of the Commonwealth,[2] observes that " the impannelling of the coroner's inquest, and the view of the body, is commonly

---

[1] C. 25.   [2] Page 96.

S. 3 (3). in the street, in an open place, and in corona populi."
And in an anonymous case,[1] in which the court held that
an inquisition of felo de se was traversable, Lord Hale
distinguished it from a fugam fecit by observing, that
"all the parties that were present at the death of the
party are bound to attend the coroner's inquest, and
their not appearing there is a flying in law, and cannot
be contradicted."

Access of
parties
interested.

With reference to the second proposition, it being
admitted that the coroner must hear the evidence of
every person who knows anything material with reference
to the cause of death, how, it is said, can one who is not
present tell what evidence is given to criminate him, so
as to be enable to adduce evidence in answer? Again, a
subject has a right to move to set aside an inquisition for
irregularity; but of that he can have no knowledge unless
he be present.[2] The coroner's inquest partakes of the
nature of other offices of entitling,[3] at which the public
have a right to be present, that right being secured by
the statutes of escheators,[4] which, it is said, are but
declaratory of the common law. It is not similar to the
proceeding before a magistrate or grand jury. There, in
the first instance, a particular individual is accused;
before the coroner there is no accusation, but the inquiry
is to ascertain how the party came to his death. Grand
jurors are sworn to secrecy; by the oath of the coroner's
jury no such term is imposed. Depositions before grand
juries are not evidence; those before the coroner are;[5]
which must be because the party suspected or ultimately
accused has a right to be present to cross-examine the
witnesses.

---

[1] Freem. 419.
[2] 3 Mod. 80.
[3] 1 Burr. 17; and see Whar-
ton's Law Lexicon, "Inquest of
Office."
[4] 34 Edw. 3, c. 13; 36 Edw.
3, c. 13; 36 Hen. 6, c. 16; 1
Hen. 8, c. 8.
[5] 2 Phil. & Arn. Ev. 90;
Kel. 55; Jon. 53; 1 Lev. 180;
Gilb. Ev. 124.

Thirdly, the dicta of modern judges are adduced to show that the proceeding is public. Blackstone, J.,[1] speaking of a presentment of fugam fecit, says, "the reason given in some books why this inquest is not traversable, like other inquests of office, is because of the notoriety of the coroner's inquest super visum corporis, at which the inhabitants of all the neighbouring villages are bound to attend, and so the finding of the flight is in effect recording the absence of the party." Lord Mansfield[2] likens it to other inquests of office, which are open by express statutes; and Lord Kenyon[3] expressly says, that "the examination before the coroner is a transaction of notoriety, to which everyone has a right of access."

However strong these authorities and arguments may at first sight appear, they do not, upon examination, establish a universal right for all the public to be present; but, at most, extend only to such as are summoned, suspected, interested in the result of the inquiry, or are inhabitants of the vill where the body is found dead.

According to the best opinions, the coroner's inquisition is in no case conclusive, and the inquiry is therefore preliminary only. It appears from the commentary of Lord Coke[4] upon the Statute of Marlbridge, that the occasion of that statute was the custom of coroners to summon many townships, and sometimes a whole hundred, where twelve persons should serve to make the inquiry; and, if all did not attend, to present them before the justices in eyre; when the whole township or hundred were amerced, even though a sufficient number to make the inquiry did appear. It is true that inquests of death are excepted from this provision; but it would seem,

S. 3 (3).
Authorities.

Persons summoned.

[1] 3 W. Bl. 981.
[2] 1 Bur. 17.
[3] *R.* v. *Eriswell*, 3 T. R. at
p. 722.
[4] 2 Inst. 147.

S. 3 (3). from the commentary, that none were bound to appear, even in these cases, but such as were summoned; and at most, it can confer no right upon those who are not inhabitants of the vill. The ancient practice, as stated by Sir T. Smith, cannot decide the right; and the distinction taken by Lord Hale, with reference to a fugam fecit, may be correct, even though the parties at the death may have no right personally to be present during the inquiry of the coroner; for they may be bound to attend to give evidence if called upon, or to abide the result of the inquiry, and yet not be entitled to be actually present in the room, notwithstanding the coroner, the presiding officer, may in his discretion direct their removal.

Opportunity for cross-examination. It is clear that the coroner is bound to hear the evidence on both sides,[1] if indeed there can be said to be "sides" at all upon an inquiry of this nature. This, it is presumed, is not to protect the interests of those who may be suspected or ultimately accused; but because the inquiry, how the party came to his death, cannot be truly satisfied, unless all the witnesses who know anything of the death be examined. This will not confer the right of access upon the witnesses generally, contrary to the direction of the coroner; for it is the constant practice in Courts of justice, both in civil and criminal proceedings, to order the witnesses to leave the Court, and to examine each out of the hearing of the others, a mode best calculated to ensure the truth. But how, it is said, can the depositions taken before the coroner be evidence, unless the party against whom they are used be present, and have the opportunity of cross-examining the witnesses? It must be admitted that, ordinarily, where there can be no cross-examination, depositions are not admissible; but those taken before the coroner have been said to be an

---

[1] *Rex* v. *Scorey*, 1 Leach, C. L. 43 ; *Reg.* v. *Colmer*, 9 Cox, C. C. 506.

exception to this general rule. The coroner is an elective S. 3 (3). officer, appointed on behalf of the public, to make inquiry about the matter within his jurisdiction, and therefore the law presumes that the depositions made before him will be fairly and impartially taken.[1]

There is another argument adduced to show that the proceedings are public; for how, it is said, can any irregularity be taken advantage of, unless the party have a right to be present? It must be admitted that there are instances in which, from the gross misconduct of the coroner, or of the jury, inquisitions have been quashed; but there are none in which that course has been pursued for a mere irregularity. The coroner is a public elective officer, and the jurors are sworn to the just execution of their office, and are not bound to secrecy: each is a mutual check upon the other, and it is almost impossible that gross misconduct should exist, without the means of bringing it before the Court. But should such a case occur, without the possibility of disclosure, it must be remembered that the inquiry is but preliminary, and may be traversed; and the temporary interest of private individuals must yield to the public good, if it be necessary for the ends of justice that the inquiry should be conducted in secrecy. Other inquests of office are undoubtedly open to the public, and the parties interested have a right to cross-examine the witnesses; but such do not end in the possible accusation of any individual. There are, indeed, many inquiries before the coroner, which ultimately do not afford this distinction; but that cannot legitimately be ascertained until the inquiry has terminated, at which period it is too late to allow or disallow the presence of the public.

The statutes of escheators, which were made in conse- Statutes of quence of the misconduct of those officers, and require escheators.

Buller, N. P. 238. See also under section 5, sub-s. (3).

S. 3 (3).

that in future their inquests should be taken publicly, do not in any degree affect the inquests of coroners. When Lord Mansfield spoke of express statutes, he probablv alluded to these, for there are none applicable to coroners ; and Lord Kenyon's dictum may be referred to the same source, viz. a confounding of the statutory provisions relating to these inquests of office with coroners' inquisitions.

When secrecy necessary.

It is obvious, although the inquiry of the coroner is preliminary only, that it may, and frequently does, lead to accusation. Such an inquiry ought, for the purposes of justice, in some cases, to be conducted in secrecy. It may be requisite that the party suspected should not, in so early a stage, be informed of the suspicion that may be entertained against him, and of the evidence upon which that suspicion is founded, lest he should elude justice by flight, by tampering with the witnesses, or by any other means. Accusation may begin at the moment when the evidence commences. Cases may also occur, in which privacy may be requisite for the sake of decency ; others, in which it may be due to the family of the deceased. Many things may be disclosed to those who are to decide, the publication of which to the world at large would be productive of mischief, without any possibility of good. Even in cases in which absolute privacy may not be required, the exclusion of particular persons may be necessary and proper. Of the necessity of this privacy or exclusion the coroner is the judge. It is a power necessary to the due administration of justice ; and it is impossible that the proceedings should be conducted with due order and solemnity, and with the effect that justice demands, if the presiding officer have not the control of the proceedings. The coroner is therefore the proper person to exercise discretion as to the degree of publicity to be allowed in inquests held by him.[1]

---

[1] *Garnett* v. *Ferrand*, 6 B. & C. 611.

What interests may be represented by counsel or S. 3 (3).
solicitor upon the inquest is a matter entirely within the Counsel.
discretion of the coroner ; if it seems to him that the jury
are likely to be benefited by their assistance he ought to
allow them to be heard. It is usual to allow the family
of the deceased, and any person who is likely to be
accused by the verdict, to be represented by counsel if
they desire it ;[1] but it should always be borne in mind
that they have no right to address the jury or to put
questions to the witnesses except by permission of the
coroner. There is in this respect no analogy whatever
between a coroner's inquest and a trial of issues.

If the inquiry before the coroner terminates in the Publication
accusation of a particular individual, this leads to a second of proceed-
inquiry to be investigated by another jury. Nothing (it
has been said) is more important to the administration of
justice than that jurymen should come to the trial of
those persons on whose guilt or innocence they are to decide, with minds pure and unprejudiced. It is therefore
most mischievous to the temperate administration of
justice, that either during or before a judicial examination
a statement should be published of facts which are to be
made the subject of a subsequent trial ; and it is still
more mischievous when that statement is accompanied
by comments. For these reasons it has been held to be
illegal to publish in a newspaper a statement of the
evidence given before a coroner's jury, even though the
statement was correct, and it was not imputed that the
party publishing was actuated by malicious motives in the
publication.[2]

It must, however, be observed, that publications of this
sort, although they may in strictness be illegal, have a

---

[1] See Barclee's case, 2 Sid. 563 ; R. v. Lee, 5 Esp. 123 ;
90, 101. Duncan v. Thwaites, 3 B. & C.
[2] R. v. Fleet, 1 B. & Ald. 556 ; 5 D. & R. 447.
379 ; see R. v. Fisher, 2 Camp

S. 4 (1).   tendency to protect innocent persons by communicating
──────────── to their friends a knowledge of the accusation ; they are
calculated also, by exposure, to prevent the repetition of
crime, and above all, to aid in the detection of guilt.
And different notions now prevail upon this subject from
those expressed by the judges in the cases referred to,
the publication even of ex parte proceedings if made
honestly and fairly being no longer the subject of prosecution.

Proceedings   **4.**—(1.) The coroner and jury shall, at the first
at inquest—
evidence and sitting of the inquest, view the body, and the coroner
inquisition.
shall examine on oath touching the death all persons
who tender their evidence respecting the facts and
all persons having knowledge of the facts whom he
thinks it expedient to examine.

View.   The body need not actually be stripped for the view,
although in some cases this is necessary to look for marks
of violence. If possible, especially in criminal cases.
some person who can identify the body should always
accompany the jury to the place where the body lies. It
is not now necessary, as it appears formerly to have been,
that the body should lie before the jury during the whole
of the inquiry, nor is it any longer necessary for the
coroner and jury to view the body at the same time, nor
for the inquest to be taken at the same place where the
body was viewed.   But if there be no view, the inquisition
is void. Although the repealed statute de officio coronatoris did not say expressly that the coroner must take
his inquest on the view of the dead body, and that an
inquest otherwise taken by him was void, yet it was
clearly laid down by all the books that a coroner has no
authority to take an inquest of death without a view of
the body, and that if he do so, the inquisition is void, as

being an extrajudicial proceeding.[1] And the same S. 4 (1).
principle appears to be applicable under the present Act.

The view must be such as will be calculated to afford
information to the coroner and the jury ; and therefore,
where the skull of a man who had been dead five years
was dug up, which the coroner told the jury he could
identify, and the inquest proceeded, the Court refused to
file the inquisition.[2]

From the words of the statute de officio coronatoris,
which, after describing the mode of taking the inquest,
says, " and immediately upon these things being inquired,
the bodies of such persons being dead or slain shall be
buried," it would seem that anciently the body was lying
before the jury and coroner during the whole evidence.
In truth, the body itself is part of the evidence before the
jury ; and therefore, if they see it before, and not after
they are sworn, a material part of the evidence is given
when the jury are not upon oath. For this reason, a
gaoler or township may be indicted for a misdemeanor,
or amerced, if a body upon which an inquisition ought to
be taken be suffered to lie so long that it putrefy before
the coroner has viewed it ;[3] and, for the same reason, a
coroner may order a body to be disinterred within a
reasonable time after the death of the person, either for
the purpose of taking an original inquisition where none
has been taken, or a further inquisition where the first
was insufficient.[4] So, if an inquisition be quashed, the
body may, by order of the Court, upon motion, be disinterred for the purpose of taking a second inquisition ;[5]
but the Court will exercise a discretion in making or refusing the order, according to the circumstances of the

<hr>

[1] *R.* v. *Ferrand,* 3 B. & Ald. 260.
[2] 1 Str. 22.
[3] 1 Salk. 377 ; 7 Mod. 10 ; 2 Hawk. P. C. c. 9, s. 23.
[4] Staund. P. C. 51 ; Hale.

Sum. 170 ; 2 Hawk. P. C. c. 9, s. 23 ; Britton, Ch. II. (ed. by Nichols, 1865), p. 8.
[5] Str. 167, 533. See section 6, sub-s. (3).

S. 4 (1).   case, and the length of time the body has been buried.[1]
So essential is the view to the validity of the inquisition,
that if the body be not found, or have lain so long before
the view, that no information can be obtained from the
inspection of it, or if there be danger of infection by
digging it up, the inquest ought not to be taken by the
coroner, unless he have a special commission for that purpose: but as the proceeding before the coroner is one
only of several, application should be made, in such cases
to the magistrates, or justices authorized to inquire of
felonies, &c., who, without viewing the body, may take
the inquest by the testimony of witnesses.[2]   Indeed, it
would seem that coroners may be amerced for taking up
a body that has been buried so long, that, from its state
of decomposition, no information can result from the
view;[3] and that, in such a case, the Court into which
the inquisition is returned may, upon affidavit of the
circumstances, refuse to receive and file it.[4]

The view, and indeed all the proceedings connected
with the inquest, must take place within the jurisdiction
of the coroner within whose duty it falls to hold the
inquest under section 7 of this Act.[5]

Opening of
inquest.

After the jury are satisfied with the view, they usually
adjourn with the coroner to another room in the same
house, or to another place, where the coroner, having
called over the names of the jury, and taken care that
they are conveniently seated, separately from the by-
standers, and having ascertained that they are satisfied
with the view, details briefly to them the object of their
inquiry, viz. to ascertain by what means the deceased

---

[1] Salk. 377 ; Str. 22, 533.
[2] 5 Rep. 110 ; 2 R. Abr. 96 ; 2
Hawk. P. C. c. 9, s. 23.
[3] 2 Lev. 140.   Some poisons,
such as arsenic, have the effect
of preserving the body—cases
have occurred, (e.g. at Liverpool

in 1884) where under such circumstances a view has been
possible three years after burial.
[4] 1 Str. 22; 2 Hawk. P. C.
c. 9, s. 24.
[5] See Reg. v. Hinde 5 Q. B.
944.

came to his death, and draws their attention to any particulars which may call for observation.

This having been done, the officer makes proclamation [1] for the attendance of witnesses ; or, where the inquiry is conducted in secrecy, calls in separately such as know anything concerning the death. It is the duty of all persons who are acquainted with the circumstances attending the subject of the coroner's inquiry to appear before the inquest as witnesses. Should one of the jury happen to be able to give evidence he may be sworn and examined,[2] but the better way is for such a person to inform the coroner beforehand, in which case he would not be sworn upon the jury. The coroner, being guided by the information he has received, usually sends a message to those witnesses whom he thinks material. Should they neglect or refuse to attend, the coroner, as incident to his office of judge of a court of record, has authority to issue a summons [3] to compel their appearance where he has been credibly informed that they are able to give evidence, and he may if necessary issue a summons to the constable to bring them into court. If a witness refuses without sufficient reason to obey this summons, the coroner may fine him £2 under section 19 ; and if a witness refuses to give evidence when sworn, or otherwise misconducts himself in court, the coroner has power to commit him for contempt. The coroner has also power to issue a warrant against a witness for contempt of the summons, under which the constable may bring up the witness in custody.[4]

It is submitted, although no direct authority can be found for the proposition, that the coroner may direct the witness to bring with him any papers or documents in

---

[1] App. Form 22.
[2] 1 Salk. 405 ; Styl. 233 ; 1 Sid. 133.
[3] App. Form 26. As to

medical witnesses, see section 21.
[4] Form 27 ; and see further as to this under sect. 19, sub-s. (3).

S. 4 (1).

his possession which are, in the opinion of the coroner, likely to afford assistance on the inquiry—or if the witness is out of the coroner's jurisdiction a crown office subpœna duces tecum may be issued.[1]

Adjourn-
ment.

If, during the inquiry, it appear that there are persons whose testimony is material, and who are not in attend ance, the coroner may, in the same way, issue his sum- mons to compel their appearance. For this purpose, or where the jury suspect that undue influence has been used, the coroner may adjourn the inquest[2] to a future day, to the same or another place, taking the recog- nizances[3] of the jurors to attend at the time and place appointed, and notifying to the witnesses when and where the inquest will be proceeded with. A memorandum of this adjournment and of the recognizances should be entered on the depositions and signed by the coroner. Care should be taken to hold the Court on the day fixed, otherwise the proceedings would drop, and anything done subsequently would be *coram non judice*.[4]   In the use of this power of adjournment great discretion is necessary, for undue or frequent adjournment is matter and cause of complaint above, and the coroner should not practise it except upon absolutely real necessity.

Attendance
of medical
witnesses.

In all cases of sudden or violent death, and especially where it is likely that a criminal charge will be made against any person, it is desirable that a surgeon should be called as a witness,[5] and that a post-mortem examination should be made ; and if the deceased has been attended by a medical practitioner his attendance should be secured, care being taken that he is able to identify the body.   It is also very desirable that he should prepare himself to give the required evidence by making a careful examina- tion of the body, not only externally or of the supposed

---

[1] See under section 19. sub-s. (3)
[2] Umf. 179 ; 2 Hawk. P. C. c. 9, s. 25 ; Lat. 166 ; App. Form 35.
[3] App. Form 37.
[4] *R.* v. *Payn*, 34 L. J. Q B. 59.
[5] *R.* v. *Quinch*, 4 C. & P. 571. See under section 21.

seat of injury, but also of the different cavities, and the　S. 4 (1).
head, and by taking written notes of the appearances.　If
this is done before the sitting of the Court, time may be
saved, and the trouble and inconvenience of an adjournment avoided.

Where the evidence of any person who is in custody　Persons in
is material, and his attendance is desired, application　custody.
should be made under the 16 & 17 Vict. c. 30, s. 9, to the
Home Secretary, or to one of the judges of the High
Court at chambers,[1] who are empowered, in any case where
they " may see fit to do so, upon application by affidavit,
to issue a warrant or order for bringing up any prisoner
or person confined in any gaol, prison, or place under any
sentence or under commitment for trial or otherwise
(except under process in any civil action, suit, or proceeding) before any Court, judge, justice, or other
judicature, to be examined as a witness in any cause or
matter, civil or criminal, depending or to be inquired of,
or to be determined in or before such Court, judge, justice,
or judicature; and the person required by any such
warrant or order to be so brought before such Court,
judge, justice, or other judicature, shall be so brought
under the same care and custody, and be dealt with in
like manner in all respects, as a prisoner required by any
writ of habeas corpus awarded by any of her majesty's
superior courts of law at Westminster, to be brought
before such Court to be examined as a witness in any
cause or matter depending before such Court is now by
law required to be dealt with."

Under that section an order will generally be made if
the prisoner is not the party under accusation ; or, if he
is accused or suspected, then when he is desirous of making a statement, and perhaps also when his presence is
requisite for the purpose of identification.　Thus, in
Cooke's case,[2] an application was made to the Court of

---

[1] C. O. Rules of 1886, rr. 246
247.

[2] Ex p. Wakley, 7 Q. B. 653 ;
14 L. J. M. C. 188.

S. 4.(1).

Queen's Bench, at the instance of the coroner, for a writ to remove a man who stood committed to the custody of the governor of Newgate upon a charge of murder, and to bring him before the coroner and a jury of the county of Middlesex, on an inquest on the body of the deceased, in order to be identified by certain witnesses. The Court, apparently not entertaining any grave doubt of their power to issue the writ, declined to do so in the particular case, on the ground that no necessity for it existed, it not being shown that the identification could not be effected without producing the prisoner. Lord Denman said—"I have the greatest respect for the office of coroner, and I have always entertained the highest opinion of the services rendered by that office in preserving the lives of the subjects of her Majesty. We ought not, however, to exercise our power of interference, supposing such power to exist, except under a due sense of the danger that may ensue from taking a man out of custody to which he has been committed upon so grave a charge as that on which the present party is confined. Nevertheless, if the jury could not otherwise go on with their inquiry, I should consider anxiously the course which this Court ought to pursue, for the purpose of assisting an inferior tribunal. But here I see no difficulty in the party being identified on the same evidence by which he was identified when he appeared before the committing magistrates." And Williams, J., observed—"No case of inconvenience has existed in the coroner's Court for centuries, by reason of no such writ having been granted; consequently I do not see the weight of the argument as to inconvenience which will arise from our refusing to grant this writ now. No inconvenience can arise from a person going to Newgate to see the party there; but there is great inconvenience in letting a party in custody out of the close walls of a prison."

The witnesses must be examined upon oath. A peer

cannot be examined upon his honour. But by the Evidence Amendment Act of 1869,[1] if any person called to give evidence in any court of justice [2] shall object to take an oath, or shall be objected to as incompetent to take an oath, such person shall, if the presiding judge [2] is satisfied that the taking of an oath would have no binding effect on his conscience, make a solemn promise and declaration,[3] and then, if false evidence be corruptly and wilfully given by him he may be indicted for perjury. The oath must be administered in the form most binding upon the conscience of the witness; and he is in all cases bound by the oath administered, provided it have been administered in such form and with such ceremonies as he may declare to be binding.[4] A Jew is sworn upon the Pentateuch, a Turk upon the Koran, and each witness according to the peculiar form of his religion. It seems, however, to have been no ground for a certiorari to bring up and quash a coroner's inquisition that evidence not on oath was received;[5] nor can there be any objection to hearing statements not on oath, which, though not received as evidence, may assist the inquiry.

Idiots, madmen, and lunatics during the influence of the frenzy, are incompetent to give evidence; but during the lucid intervals, lunatics may be examined.[6] Persons deaf and dumb, if they are capable of communicating their ideas by signs, and have a due sense of the obligation of an oath, may be admitted as witnesses and examined through the intervention of an interpreter.[7] The competency of children depends not upon their age,

---

[1] 32 & 33 Vict. c. 68, s. 4; see also 24 & 25 Vict. c. 66. s. 1.

[2] These words include any person having by law authority to administer an oath for the taking of evidence; 33 & 34 Vict. c. 49, s. 1.

[3] Form No. 24.

[4] 1 & 2 Vict. c. 105.

[5] *Reg.* v. *Ingham,* 5 B. & S. 267; and see p. 42.

[6] 1 Stark. Ev. 114, 410, 512 n.; *R.* v. *Hill,* 2 Den. C. C. 255.

[7] 1 Phil. & Arn. Ev. 7; *Ruston's case,* 1 Leach, C. C. 408.

S. 4 (1).

for there is no fixed and settled age at which an infant may be sworn, but upon the degree of knowledge and understanding which, upon examination, they appear to possess.[1] Children cannot be examined except upon oath, and it is therefore not their general acquirements, but their knowledge of religion and a future state, which will determine their competency. Questions of competency are purely in the discretion of the Court: and for the purpose of ascertaining this, it is usual to examine children of tender age before the oath is administered to them.[2] In criminal cases it is desirable that these prefatory questions and answers should also be entered upon the depositions.[3]

Husband and wife.

It was an admitted rule of the common law that where a husband or wife was a party to the inquiry, the other was altogether incompetent, in either civil or criminal proceedings; even though they had been divorced, if the subject of the inquiry occurred during their coverture. And although now, by statute, husband and wife are competent and compellable to give evidence for or against each other in civil proceedings, their incompetency to do so in criminal cases is still maintained, except, of course, in cases where a crime has been committed by the one against the other. But, where neither was a party to the proceedings, either was and still is competent and compellable to prove any fact not tending directly to criminate the other,[4] and this rule seems to be applicable to all inquiries before coroners, inasmuch as there are no parties to the record, and in fact no record at all until the jury have returned their verdict.

Criminating evidence.

Evidence ought never to be excluded on the ground that it may criminate the witness. The proper course is

---

[1] 1 Hale, P. C. 302; 2 Hale, P. C. 278.
[2] 1 Stark. Ev. 117; 2 Str. 700; R. v. Powell, 1 Leach, C. L. 110; R. v. Brazier, Ib. 119;
R. v. Williams, 7 C. & P. 320.
[3] R. v. Painter, 2 C. & K. 320.
[4] R. v. All Saints, Worcester 6 M. & S. 200.

to tell him that he is not bound to criminate himself, and to allow him to make any statement he may wish.[1]

S. 4 (1).

It is the duty of the coroner to examine the witnesses himself, but he has a discretion, in cases where he thinks that it will be of any assistance, to allow questions to be put by, or on behalf of, persons interested. And after each witness has been examined, the coroner should inquire whether the jury wish any further questions to be put. This is essential to the due administration of justice ; the jury living in the neighbourhood being, most probably, acquainted with the circumstances better than the coroner.

Practice on examination of witnesses.

It sometimes happens that witnessess acquainted with the circumstances relative to the inquiry are foreigners, and are unacquainted with the English language : such must be examined through the medium of an interpreter, who must be sworn well and truly to interpret as well the oath as the questions which shall be put to the witnesses by the Court and jury, and the answers which the witnesses shall give.[2]

Interpreters.

It was formerly doubted whether a coroner was bound or ought in all cases to examine all the witnesses, as well against the interest of the Crown as for it. It was admitted to be the duty of the coroner, in cases of felo de se, to examine the witnesses as well against the king's interest as for it ; for in that case no one was to be condemned to death, but the fact only was to be inquired into.[3] And in one case, an inquisition of felo de se was quashed, and the coroner reprehended, because he refused to admit witnesses to prove that the party was non compos mentis, but shut them out, and only took witnesses for the king.[4] There seems, however, to be no reasonable distinction between this and other cases ; for

Witnesses for defence.

---

[1] *Wakley* v. *Cooke*, 4 Exch. 511 ; 19 L. J., Ex. 91.
[2] App. Form 25.

[3] 2 Hale, P. C. 60.
[4] *Barclee's case*, 2 Sid. 90, 101.

S. 4 (1). the cause of the death cannot legally be ascertained until all the witnesses are examined. It was, notwithstanding, formerly holden, that, where one was killed by another, and it was certainly known that he killed him, the jury must hear the evidence only for the king, and that, whether the killing were with or without malice, the inquest must find it murder; because the party shall be put to answer, and upon pleading not guilty, the whole matter will come to be tried by the jury, where the evidence of both sides may be openly heard in court, and such direction given as the nature of the case requires. But this practice, Lord Hale observes, was neither reasonable nor agreeable to law or ancient usage, but was a novelty as regards the coroner's inquest, though it might be reasonable and fit in case of an indictment by the grand inquest of the county.[1] And it seems now to be agreed, that the coroner's inquest must in all cases hear evidence as well for the party suspected as against him if it be offered.

Recognizances.

But the coroner has no power to bind over the witnesses for the defence to appear at the trial,[2] and for this reason in all cases where the coroner commits a person for trial it is the proper course for an investigation to take place before magistrates, in order that if the person charged wishes to call witnesses he may have them bound over to appear. The object of the 30 & 31 Vict. c. 35 was in all cases to give a prisoner an opportunity of having witnesses if he chose to call them, and it is only fair that the magistrates should inquire into the facts so that the prisoner may not be deprived of any assistance which the law gives him.[3]

Evidence

The general rules of evidence are applicable alike to civil and criminal proceedings; it being an universal

[1] 2 Hale, P. C. 60, 61.
[2] R. v. Taylor, 9 C. & P. 672; and section 5, sub-s. (1).
[3] R. v. Spoor, 11 Cox. C. C. 550. Per Blackburn, J.

maxim, that a fact must be established by the same evi-   **S. 4 (1).**
dence, whether it be followed by a criminal or civil consequence. It will, therefore, be unnecessary to do more
than refer the reader to the established treatises upon
this subject, and to observe that the inquiry of the
coroner is not fettered by any stated allegations in pleading, which require particular proof, and also that it may
frequently be desirable for the coroner to hear statements
which are not, strictly speaking, evidence, with the object
of affording a guide in the examination of subsequent
witnesses. But where this is done, care should be taken
to direct the jury to dismiss from their minds, in considering their verdict, all such inadmissible statements.
The general rule that the party accused must have had
an opportunity of answering a statement, by its being
made in his hearing, in order to render it admissible in
evidence, is clearly inapplicable to coroners' inquests, at
which there is no accused party. It would be a matter
for the discretion of the coroner how far to allow this rule
to operate in favour of a party suspected of a crime
although not yet technically charged with it.

    The admission in evidence of a dying declaration is an   Dying de-
exception to the rule of law that statements made behind   clarations.
the back of a prisoner cannot be given in evidence. A
dying declaration is admitted in evidence because it is
presumed that no person who is immediately going into
the presence of his Maker will do so with a lie on his lips.
But the person making the declaration must be proved
to have entertained a settled hopeless expectation of
immediate death.[1] If he thinks he will die to-morrow,
or that there is any chance of recovery, however small,
evidence of his statements should be rejected as hearsay.

    With respect to scientific witnesses, such as medical   Scientific
men, who are necessarily called in nearly every case which   evidence.

---

[1] *R.* v. *Osman*, 15 Cox, C. C. 1.

comes before the coroner's jury, it is to be observed that
they form an exception to the general rule of law which
confines witnesses to a statement of such facts only as are
within their knowledge. Scientific witnesses are allowed
to state their opinions upon a matter with which they
are conversant, and thus the opinions of medical men may
be admitted as to the cause of disease or death, or the
consequence of wounds, or with respect to the sane or
insane state of a person's mind as collected from a
number of circumstances. But the weight due to this as
well as to every other kind of evidence is to be determined
by the jury, who should form their own judgment on the
matters before them, and are not concluded by that of
any witness, however highly qualified or respectable.
Nor is this always an easy task ; there being no evidence
the value of which varies so immensely as this, and respecting which it is so difficult to lay down any rules
beforehand. There can be no doubt that testimony is
constantly received as scientific evidence to which it is
almost profanation to apply the term, and, in truth,
witnesses of this description are apt to presume largely
on the ignorance of their hearers with respect to the
subject of examination, and little dread prosecution for
perjury, an offence of which it is extremely difficult,
indeed, almost impossible, to convict a person who only
swears to his belief, particularly when that belief relates
to scientific matters. On the other hand, mistakes have
occasionaly arisen from not attaching sufficient weight to
scientific testimony. Discrimination should be exercised,
and the means inquired into which the witness has had
of forming a judgment. It must be conceded that our
practice is much too loose in this respect, in receiving all
who are called doctors as witnesses, not only physicians,
surgeons, and apothecaries, but hospital dressers, students,
and quacks. And, further, it often happens that men
distinguished in one branch of a science or profession

have but little knowledge of its other branches ; the most able physician or surgeon may know comparatively little of the mode of detecting poisons, or of other intricate branches of medical jurisprudence, so that a chemist or physiologist, immeasurably his inferior in every other respect, might prove a much more valuable witness in a case where that sort of knowledge is required.

S. 4 (3).

(**2.**) It shall be the duty of the coroner in a case of murder or manslaughter to put into writing the statement on oath of those who know the facts and circumstances of the case, or so much of such statement as is material, and any such deposition shall be signed by the witness and also by the coroner.

The coroner should where possible follow the precise expressions of the witnesses in the first person. The depositions are afterwards forwarded under section 5 to the proper officer of the court in which the trial is to be, and copies supplied, upon payment, to the person charged in the inquisition, if he requires them.

Depositions.

(**3.**) After viewing the body and hearing the evidence the jury shall give their verdict, and certify it by an inquisition in writing, setting forth, so far as such particulars have been proved to them, who the deceased was, and how, when, and where the deceased came by his death, and, if he came by his death by murder or manslaughter, the persons if any, whom the jury find to have been guilty of such murder or manslaughter, or of being accessories before the fact to such murder.

It is the duty of the coroner to sum up the evidence and to explain to the jury the law applicable to the case,

Summing up.

S. 4 (3). pointing out for instance the distinction between murder and manslaughter. The court being a court of record, the coroner cannot be made liable to any action for slander for words used by him in the course of his summing up.[1] It is peculiarly the province of the jury to investigate and determine the facts of the case ; they are neither to expect, nor should they be bound by, any specific or direct opinion of the coroner upon the whole of the case, except so far as regards the verdict which, in point of law, they ought to find as dependent and contingent upon their conclusions in point of fact. But in questions of law, juries ought to show the most respectful deference to the advice and recommendation of the coroner ; ad quæstionem facti non respondent judices, ad quæstionem legis non respondent juratores.[2] The verdict should be compounded of the facts as detailed to the jury by the witnesses, and of the law as stated to them by the Court.

How far jury bound by direction of coroner.

It has been much questioned, whether juries are bound by any moral obligation to submit implicitly to the direction of the Court in point of law,—and at no time to exercise their otherwise discretionary power to decide according to their consciences. By some it is contended that, by opposing and usurping the judicature of the Court, the jury, even supposing they happen to be right, do what is morally wrong, because it is done wrongly ;[3] while by others it is said to be only the exercise of a wholesome and beneficial power, vested in juries by the constitution.[4] It would seem, however, that if a jury are entitled, by any sort of right, to canvass what is laid down to them for law by the Court, it may be done

---

[1] *Thomas* v. *Churton,* 31 L. J., Q. B. 139 ; 2 B. & S. 475 ; and see the cases cited in *Henderson* v. *Bromhead,* 4 H. & N. 569. *Quære,* whether the 11 & 12 Vict. c. 44, protecting justices from vexatious actions, can be construed to extend to coroners.

[2] Vaugh. Rep. 160.

[3] *R.* v. *Dean of St. Asaph,* 3 T. R. 431 (*n*).

[4] Fort. de Laud. by Amos, 98 ; Russ. on Govern.

equally with regard to any statute of the realm, and thus they would possess a power of setting at nought not only the authority of the Court, but of the legislature also. Yet instances have not unfrequently occurred, in which juries have taken upon themselves to decide questions of law, and, according to Littleton, in which opinion Lord Coke concurs, " if the inquest will take upon them the knowledge of the law, they may give their verdict generally."[1] It is, however, impossible not to concur in the result of the observations of a learned commentator upon the passage referred to,[2] that the immediate and direct right of deciding upon questions of law is entrusted to the Court, while in the jury it is at most only incidental ; that in the exercise of this incidental right, the latter are not only placed under the superintendence of the former, but in some degree controllable by them, and therefore, that in all points of law arising during the investigation, the jury ought to show the most respectful deference to the advice and recommendation of the Court. But should the jury usurp to themselves the province of deciding contrary to the direction of the Court upon the law, there seems to be no means by which they can be punished, should the finding be improper. The coroner is bound to accept the presentment which the jury make.[3] The writ of attaint, even before the statute which abolished that proceeding,[4] was a mere sound in every case, and in many cases it did not even pretend to be a remedy ;[5] it did not extend to criminal cases, nor to inquests of office.[6] It has been said, indeed, that jurymen may in such cases be fined ;[7] but it would seem that, in the exercise of their judicial functions, they are not answerable to any power of the state.[8]

---

[1] Co. Litt. 228.
[2] Hargrave and Butler on Co. Litt. *ubi sup.*
[3] Comb. 386.
[4] 6 Geo. 4, c. 50, s. 62.
[5] 1 Burr. 290.
[6] Com. Dig. Attaint, B.
[7] 2 Hawk. P. C. c. 22, ss. 21, 22.
[8] Fort. de Laud. by Amos, 9 ; Vaugh. Rep. 198.

S. 4 (4).

Independent knowledge of jury.

By the form of oath required by the schedule to be administered to the jury, they are not, as upon the trial of issues in Courts of law, sworn to give their verdict in accordance with the evidence only ; they are invited to use their skill and knowledge also, and may therefore presumably give a valid verdict in cases where no evidence whatever is tendered.

When the jury retire to consider their verdict, the coroner should take care that no paper or writing, such as notes of evidence taken by any one of the jury, be referred to by them except such documents as have been given in evidence.[1]

Where jury disagree.

Where the jury are not unanimous the coroner should collect the voices, and provided twelve agree he takes the verdict according to the opinion of the majority. If twelve do not agree he should exercise his discretion in either detaining them or adjourning the inquest to the ensuing assizes.[2]

The particulars necessary in drawing up the inquisition are further considered under section 18.

(**4.**) They shall also inquire of and find the particulars for the time being required by the Registration Acts to be registered concerning the death.

Particulars for registration.

The particulars required are, the date and place of death, the name, surname, and sex of the deceased, with his age and rank or profession at the time of his death. These particulars should be ascertained and legibly recorded by the coroner in the form supplied by the registrar of births and deaths in the most precise manner possible under the circumstances of the case. They may also be added to the inquisition. It is of the first import-

---

[1] Trials per Pais, Cap. XV.   [2] See subsection 5.
p. 363 (8th ed. 1766).

S. 4 (5).

ance, in view of the great national and local uses to which the death registers are applicable, that the place of death should be so definitely stated as to show not merely the city, town or parish, but, whenever practicable, the street, and the number or name of the house, if any, in which the death occurred. In the case of public institutions, the precise name of the institution should invariably be stated. When the certificate has been filled up and signed by the coroner, or his deputy if the inquest has been held by a deputy, it must be sent within five days to the registrar of the sub-district in which the death occurred,[1] whose duty it is to register the death. The certificate may be sent by post.

(**5.**) In case twelve at least of the jury do not agree on a verdict, the coroner may adjourn the inquest to the next sessions of oyer and terminer or gaol delivery held for the county or place in which the inquest is held, and if after the jury have heard the charge of the judge or commissioner holding such sessions, twelve of them fail to agree on a verdict, the jury may be discharged by such judge or commissioner without giving a verdict.

The coroner has also in his discretion power to keep them, under the charge of a sworn officer, without meat, drink, or fire, until they return their verdict.[2] Even this may sometimes be ineffectual. No verdict can in such cases be taken by the coroner, but it has been said that the jury may be fined.[3] This, however, seems to be contrary to the principles of our constitution, for no man can be forced to give his verdict against his judgment and

Where jury disagree.

---

[1] 37 & 38 Vict. c. 88, s. 16, and see 18 (3) of this Act.
[2] Form of oath, App. Form 35.
[3] 3 Buls. 173.

conscience.[1] It is within the power of the coroner to detain them as long as he thinks fit, adjourning the sitting from place to place to suit his own convenience ; whether indeed the coroner had power to discharge the jury without their giving a verdict, seems to have been considered doubtful ; but, in a case before the present act, when the power of the coroner to adjourn the inquest to the assizes was itself not so clearly defined as it is now by statute, the learned judge on circuit is reported to have said that if the coroner had discharged them he would not have found fault with him.[2] The jury might in such a case be invited to find as much as they are able to agree upon. In all cases they could probably find the identity of the deceased. and when and where the death happened, and in most cases they can find how it happened, the difficulty generally arising upon the question whether the killing was felonious, which can always be left open.

Proceedings upon inquisition charging person with murder or manslaughter.

5.—(1.) Where a coroner's inquisition charges a person with the offence of murder or of manslaughter, or of being accessory before the fact to a murder, (which latter offence is in this Act included in the expression " murder,") the coroner shall issue his warrant [3] for arresting or detaining such person (if such warrant has not previously been issued) and shall bind by recognizance all such persons examined before him as know or declare anything material touching the said offence to appear at the next court of oyer and terminer or gaol delivery at which the trial is to be, then and there to prosecute or give evidence against the person so charged.

---

[1] 2 Hale, P. C. 297.
[2] *Per* Hawkins J., at Winchester, April 1880. See also

Ferrar's case, Raymond 84.
[3] See Forms 37—39.

The coroner has also, as incident to this authority, power to commit for contempt a witness who refuses to enter into a recognizance pursuant to the above provisions.[1]

S. 5 (2).
Committal.

There is no legislative provision entitling witnesses who have given evidence at the inquest to their costs of attendance at the assizes, although bound over to appear ; because the inquiry before the coroner is so much wider than where a direct accusation against a prisoner is under consideration, and the evidence of witnesses examined before the coroner may be immaterial. But if there is, as there should be in all cases of homicide, an inquiry before the magistrates, the witnesses who attend there would then, in the ordinary course, receive their fees. It is also usual for their names to be on the back of the bill presented to the grand jury. The costs of their attendance at the inquest are generally provided for by the local authorities and paid by the coroner, but are not allowed as part of the costs of getting up the prosecution on taxation after the trial.[2]

Expenses.

(2.) Where the offence is manslaughter, the coroner may, if he thinks fit, accept bail by recognizance with sufficient sureties for the appearance of the person charged at the next court of oyer and terminer or gaol delivery at which the trial is to be, and thereupon such person if in the custody of an officer of the coroner's court or under a warrant of commitment issued by such coroner shall be discharged therefrom.

On admitting to bail the coroner is, under section 16, entitled to the same fee as a clerk to justices. The re-

Bail.

---

1 App. Form 34.
2 R. v. Lewen, 2 Lew. C. C.

161 ; R. v. Taylor, 5 C. & P.
301 ; R. v. Rees, Ib. 302.

S. 5 (2). cognizances should be in the form [1] in the schedule, and notice must be given to every person bound under section 18, subs. (4).

Formerly, where a person committed by the coroner for murder or manslaughter was advised that his commitment was illegal, and that he was entitled to his discharge, or to be bailed, his sole remedy was by application to the Court of Queen's Bench, which, as the supreme criminal tribunal in this kingdom, had an absolute and uncontrollable authority to bail offenders, whether in cases of treason, murder, or any other species of crime. In cases of manslaughter the power of bailing the accused person is now shared by the coroner, but where the jury have found a verdict of murder, application must still be made to the Court.

Discretionary power of court. The power of the High Court to admit a prisoner to bail is discretionary,[2] but is nevertheless exercised in conformity with the acknowledged rules adopted by other criminal jurisdictions, unless there be circumstances to induce them to deviate from that established course.[3]

In the exercise of this discretion the Court is guided, not by the finding of the jury, nor by the commitment, but by the facts and circumstances of the case as disclosed upon the depositions.[4] Where the offence appears from the depositions to be no more than manslaughter, the Court will in general accede to the application of the accused,[5] and even where the inquisition is for murder, they will look into the depositions, and exercise their discretion whether the offence amounts to murder or manslaughter, and refuse or accept bail accordingly.[6] On the other hand, it is not a sufficient reason to induce the Court to bail in cases of murder, that the offence has been

[1] See Form 4.
[2] T. Jones, 222.
[3] Bac. Abr. "Bail," D.
[4] Cald. 295.
[5] R. v. Magrath, 2 Str. 1242.
[6] R. v. Dalton, 2 Str. 911.

found by the coroner's jury to amount to manslaughter
only,[1] or even to a lower denomination of crime.[2]

This relief is obtained by writ of habeas corpus[3] at
common law, directed to the gaoler in whose custody the
prisoner is, to bring him before the High Court, and at
the same time the depositions and inquisition taken
before the coroner are brought up by writ of certiorari.[4]
In some cases, however, where from poverty the party
accused is unable to defray the expense of his removal,
the writ of habeas corpus may be dispensed with, and the
Court, upon looking into the depositions returned by the
coroner upon certiorari, will permit the bail to be taken
by a magistrate of the county.[5] So, where a party charged
with an offence is at large, he may give notice of his surrender before a judge, and of his intention at the same
time to offer bail for his appearance at the assizes. An
inquisition having been found before one of the coroners
for the county of Cornwall, against two officers of excise,
acting in the execution of their duty, for the murder of a
person unknown, they, to avoid being taken, came to London, and made an affadavit of the circumstances, which was
laid before Le Blanc, J., who thereupon granted a certiorari directed to the coroner, to remove the inquisition and
depositions, returnable immediately, before the Lord
Chief Justice Kenyon, at his chambers : notice was given
by the solicitor of excise to the coroner, the deceased
being unknown, of the intention of the defendants to
apply to Lord Kenyon to be bailed, and of the names of
the bail : the inquisition and depositions were returned ;
upon reading which, and the affidavit of the circumstances,
the defendants were admitted to bail, themselves in 80*l.*
and four sureties in 40*l.* each, for their appearance at the

---

[1] Comb. 111, 298.
[2] Comb. 298.
[3] See 31 Car. 2, c. 2. App.
Form 46.
[4] App. Form 42.

[5] *R.* v. *Jones*, 1 B. & Ald.
209 ; 1 Gude's Pract. 275, 276.
See *R.* v. *Massey*, 6 M. & Sel.
108.

S. 5 (2).   ensuing assizes, and a supersedeas was granted for each defendant.[1]

Habeas corpus, how obtained.   The writ of habeas corpus, although a writ of right, is not a writ of course,[2] and the granting and issuing of the writ, although the right to it existed at common law, is regulated by the Habeas Corpus Act[3] and subsequent statutes.[4] It can now be obtained either, during sittings, on motion in the Divisonal Court by counsel,[5] and, if the Court so direct, they may grant an order nisi, or an order absolute in the first instance ; or, the application may be made, as is now the regular practice, to a judge in chambers, who also may either order the writ to issue ex parte in the first instance, or may direct a summons for the writ to issue.[6] The application must be supported by affidavits, accompanied with a copy of the warrant, or an affidavit that such copy has been refused ;[7] and it should be supported by other evidence than the affidavit of the accused, upon which it is said the Court will not act.[8] When the application is granted the clerk makes out the writ or summons, which is signed by the judge, and also the certiorari, and delivers them to the solicitor of the applicant, who serves them upon the persons to whom they are directed.[9] A reasonable notice must be given to the coroner and the parties interested in the prosecution of the intended application, and of the bail, which must consist of four at the least,[10] in order to afford them an opportunity of inquiring into the sufficiency of the bail, and, if they should think proper of opposing the application when the party is brought up. Where the application is made to the Court, the day upon which the application

---

[1] 1 Gude's Pract. 276, 277.
[2] *Hobhouse's case*, 3 B. & Ald. 420 ; 2 Chit. Rep. 207.
[3] 31 Car. 2, c. 2, s. 3.
[4] 56 Geo. 3, c. 100 ; 1 & 2 Vict. c. 45, s. 1.
[5] *In re Newton*, 16 C. B. 99 ;

24 L. J. C. P. 148.
[6] C. O. Rules, rr. 236, 237.
[7] Hands. Pract. 73.
[8] 1 Chit. C. L. 125.
[9] C. O. Rules, r. 239.
[10] *R.* v. *Shaw*, 6 D. & R. 154.

is to be made should be specified : if at chambers, the **S. 5 (2).**
hour and place should be mentioned.[1]

The party to whom the writ is directed is bound, under *Return.*
the penalty of an attachment upon the first refusal,[2] to
pay obedience to the writ, and to return the body within
a reasonable time.[3] The gaoler is entitled to his expenses
in bringing up the body, not exceeding one shilling per
mile, which ought to be regularly paid or tendered when
the writ is served ; but it is no ground for refusing com-
pliance with the requisition of the writ that the prisoner
has not paid the costs of his conveyance, for the Court
will allow them on the return,[4] referring the amount to
the taxation of the master.[5] The coroner, in obedience
to the certiorari, returns the inquisition and depositions
into the Crown Office ; and after the case is disposed of,
they are transmitted to the clerk of assize for the county
where the inquisition was holden.

The usual practice is for the Court, in the exercise *Practice.*
of their discretion, to direct an order to be drawn
up for the prisoner's discharge or remand into custody
on the argument of the order nisi, instead of waiting
for the return of the writ, and such order is a
sufficient warrant to the goaler or constable for the
discharge of the prisoner.[6] Thus if the bail are not
in attendance, or the Court or judge require time
for consideration, the prisoner may be remanded to the
same gaol from whence he came, to be brought up again
under the same writ, or he may be committed to custody
until a future day, when the bail may be in attendance,
or the Court may have arrived at a decision.[7] Where

---

[1] 1 Gude's Pract. 278.
[2] *R.* v. *Winton,* 5 T. R. 89 ;
Bac. Abr. *Hab. Corp.* (B) 8 ; 2
Ld. Ken. 289 ; C. O. Rules, r.
240.
[3] See 31 Car. 2, c. 2, s. 2.
The time within which the
writ, under the statute, is

returnable, is 3 days if within
20 miles ; 10 days if within
100 miles ; and 20 days if
within any greater distance.
[4] Bac. Abr. *Hab. Corp.* (B) 8.
[5] *R.* v. *Jones,* M. T. 3 Geo. 4.
[6] C. O. Rules, r. 244.
[7] Bac. Abr. *Hab. Corp.* (B)13.

J.   E

S. 5 (3). the party is not entitled to be bailed, but the commitment is defective, it is usual to discharge him from the
imprisonment by virtue of that warrant, and to re-commit
him for the offence.[1]

(3.) The coroner shall deliver the inquisition,
depositions and recognizances, with a certificate
under his hand that the same have been taken
before him, to the proper officer of the Court in
which the trial is to be, before or at the opening of
the Court.

Practice. Failure to comply with these provisions renders the
coroner liable to be fined under section 9. At the assizes
the proper officer would be the clerk of assize, and at the
Central Criminal Court the clerk of arraigns. In practice, there is also in most cases a bill preferred before the
grand jury, and, if they find a true bill, the indictment
and inquisition are usually given in charge to the jury
at the same time; if the bill is thrown out, it is not
usual to offer any evidence upon the inquisition.[2]

The depositions ought regularly to be returned to the
clerk of assize at the opening of the commission; or if
possible before, so as to enable the learned judge who
presides to examine the facts of each case, that he may
explain to the grand jury, in his charge, any difficulty
that may exist, and state to them the law as applicable
to the facts. Coroners have frequently been censured
for remissness in this respect.

The Court into which the inquisition is returned may,
upon affidavit of circumstances showing it to have been
irregularly taken, refuse to receive and file it.[3]

Verge. This sub-section does not apply to the coroner of the

---

[1] 3 East, 166.
[2] See also under sect. 18, sub-s. (1.)
[3] 1 Str. 22; 2 Hawk. P.C. c. 9, s. 24.

Queen's Household, who, under section 29, sub-s. (5), **S. 5 (3).**
must deliver the inquisition to the Lord Steward.

Formerly inquisitions taken before an Admiralty Admiralty.
coroner were returned to the Admiralty, but now by
section 30, sub-s. (4), this sub-section will be applicable
to them also, and they must accordingly be delivered to
the Court in which the trial is to be.

The depositions are rendered admissible as secondary Admissibility in
evidence by virtue of the above section.[1] It seems that evidence.
they ought to be proved either by calling the coroner
who subscribed them, or by proving his signature, and
showing by his clerk or some one who was present at the
inquiry, that all the forms of law have been duly complied with.[2] Although formerly much doubted, the
better opinion now appears to be, that it is essential to
their admissibility that they should have been taken in
the presence of the party accused.[3]

It is also the duty of the coroner to be himself present Attendance
in court.
in Court when any case is tried upon an inquisition taken
before him; if he be not present the Court may fine
him.[4] By the precept for summoning sessions of oyer
and terminer, it was commanded to the sheriff " quod
scire faciat omnibus coronatoribus quod sint tunc ibi "—
and the names of the county coroners used formerly to
be called from the roll when the commission was opened.
The sheriff now sends a printed notice of the assizes to
all coroners within the jurisdiction.

In cases other than murder or manslaughter the in- Custody of
inquisitions.
quisition remains in the custody of the coroner, unless
required by the clerk of the peace as a voucher. And
if the director of public prosecutions gives notice to the

---

[1] See *Sith* v. *Brown*, 9 C. &
P. 601.
[2] See *R.* v. *Wilshaw*, C. &
Marsh. 145.
[3] *R.* v. *Rigg.* 4. F. & F. 1085;
and see *R.* v. *Wall*, 2 Russ. C.

& M. 893, n. (c).
[4] *In re Urwin* at the Old
Bailey, 1827, Carrington's Supplement to the Modern Treatises
on the Criminal Law, 3rd Ed. p.
17.

S. 6 (1). coroner that he has undertaken criminal proceedings, he must transmit the inquisition to him.[1] By a circular from the Home Office in September 1884, coroners were requested, in all cases in which a verdict of manslaughter or murder should be returned, to send a copy of the depositions to the director of public prosecutions with or without any remarks which the coroner might think fit to offer. Where an inquest has been held upon the body of any offender upon whom judgment of death has been executed, the inquisition must be in duplicate, one of the originals being delivered to the sheriff.[2]

Ordering ot coroner to hold inquest.

6.—(1.) Where Her Majesty's High Court of Justice, upon application made by or under the authority of the Attorney General, is satisfied either—

(a.) that a coroner refuses or neglects to hold an inquest which ought to be held ; or

(b.) where an inquest has been held by a coroner that by reason of fraud, rejection of evidence, irregularity of proceedings, insufficiency of inquiry, or otherwise, it is necessary or desirable, in the interests of justice, that another inquest should be held,

the Court may order an inquest to be held touching the said death, and may, if the Court think it just, order the said coroner to pay such costs of and incidental to the application as to the Court may seem just, and where an inquest has been already held may quash the inquisition on that inquest.

---

[1] 42 & 43 Vict. c. 22, s. 5.   [2] 31 & 32 Vict. c. 24, s. 5.

(**2**.) The Court may order that such inquest shall be held either by the said coroner, or if the said coroner is a coroner for a county, by any other coroner for the county, or if he is a coroner of a borough or for a franchise then by a coroner for the county in which such borough or franchise is situate, or for a county to which it adjoins, and the coroner ordered to hold the inquest shall for that purpose have the same powers and jurisdiction as, and be deemed to be, the said coroner.

(**3**.) Upon any such inquest, if the case be one of death, it shall not be necessary, unless the Court otherwise order, to view the body, but save as afore said the inquest shall be held in like manner in all respects as any other inquest under this Act.

(**4**.) Any power vested by this section in Her Majesty's High Court of Justice may, subject to any rules of court made in pursuance of the Supreme Court of Judicature Act, 1875, and the Acts amending the same, be exercised by any judge of that Court.

If an inquisition is sought to be quashed at the instance of any person otherwise than by authority of the Attorney General, application may be made to the Court,[1] and in the case of a person upon his trial on an inquisition which is on the face of it defective, the application could be to the Court before whom the trial is, and should be made before plea pleaded.[2] In the case of an inquisition not containing the subject matter of accusation, the application must be to remove the inquisition into the High Court to be quashed. This application is made by motion

Quashing at instance of private person.

---

[1] 20 Q. B. D 410.
[2] Fost. C. L. 231 ; Holt, 684 ; 4 St. Tr. 677.

in the Divisional Court, upon affidavits setting out the facts and the name of the person at whose instance the motion is made, for a certiorari, coupled with a rule nisi calling on the coroner to show cause why the inquisition should not be quashed. Such an inquisition may be be quashed on the ground that the coroner had no juris-diction,[1] or for objections apparent upon the face of it,[2] or on the ground of misconduct of either the coroner or the jury.[3] As, for instance, where the coroner fraudulently misdirected the jury to find a verdict of felo de se, telling them that it was in effect the same as a finding of lunacy, the Court quashed the inquisition.[4] And in another case the inquisition was quashed, where the coroner took some of the jury off the inquest, in order that he might induce the others to find a particular verdict.[5] So the Court will quash an inquisition taken without a view of the body ; for the view ascertains the cause of the death, and is an essential part of the evidence ; and in like manner, where, from the decomposition of the body no information can be derived from the view, the inquisition may be quashed upon an affidavit of the circumstances.[6] So also where there has been a miscarriage in consequence of the exclu-sion of evidence which might have thrown light upon the subject.[7] But it is no objection to the validity of an in-quisition that evidence was received not upon oath, there being no mala praxis, and the jury having found their verdict on the other evidence only ;[8] nor will the Court interpose on account of alleged misdirection of the jury by the coroner,[9] or on account merely of the finding of the jury being incomplete,[8] or on the ground that there was

---

[1] *Foxhall* v. *Barrett*, 23 L. J., Q. B. 7 ; *R.* v. *Robinson*, 19 Q. B. D. 322.
[2] 20 Q. B. D. 410.
[3] 3 Mod. 80.
[4] *R.* v. *Wakefield*, 1 Str. 69.
[5] *R.* v. *Stukely*, 12 Mod. 493 ; Holt, 167.
[6] *R.* v. *Bond*, 5 Str. 22 ; 2 Hawk. P. C. c. 9, s. 24.
[7] *Reg.* v. *Carter*, 45 L. J., Q. B. 711.
[8] *Reg.* v. *Ingham*, 5 B. & S. 257 ; *S.C.*, 10 Jur., N.S. 257 ; *Reg.* v. *The Coroner of Stafford-shire*, 10 L. T. 650.
[9] *Reg.* v. *Ingham*, *supra*; *Reg.* v. *M'Intosh*, 7 W. R. 52.

no evidence to warrant the finding of the jury.[1] But the Court will not issue a certiorari to bring up an inquisition to be quashed which has been taken before a totally unauthorized person, and so is a mere nullity.[2]

Where the inquisition is quashed, otherwise than under the above section of the Act, a new inquiry may, by leave of the Court,[3] be instituted by the coroner,[4] with a fresh jury, and, if thought desirable, with the assistance of an assessor, the body being disinterred by order of the Court; which will exercise a discretion in making or refusing the order, according to the circumstances of the case, and the length of time the body has been buried.[5] A coroner who has held an inquisition and recorded the verdict cannot hold a second inquisition unless the first be quashed, or a melius inquirendum has been awarded, and he be set in motion by the Court; and if he do hold such a second inquisition without authority it will be quashed.[6] But where there is any imputation upon the coroner he may be prohibited from again interfering in the inquiry; and under such circumstances the authority of the Attorney General would generally be obtained under this section; but by the common law a melius inquirendum may be awarded to take a new inquisition by special commissioners, who may proceed by the testimony of witnesses without viewing the body.[7]

7.—(1.) The coroner only within whose jurisdiction the body of a person upon whose death an inquest ought to be holden is lying shall hold the

(marginal notes: S. 7 (1). Melius inquirendum. Local jurisdiction of coroner.)

---

[1] *Reg.* v. *Ingham*, 5 B. & S. 257; *S. C.*, 10 Jur., N.S. 257; *Reg.* v. *The Coroner of Staffordshire*, 10 L T. 650.

[2] *Ex parte Daws*, 8 A. & E. 936; 1 P. & D. 146.

[3] *R.* v. *Saunders*, 1 Str. 167.

[4] *R.* v. *Hethersal*, 3 Mod. 80;

Reg. v. *White*, 6 Jur., N. S. 868; *R.* v. *Carter*, 45 L. J., Q. B. 711.

[5] *R.* v. *Clerk*, 1 Salk. 377; *R.* v. *Bond*, 1 Str. 22, 533.

[6] *Reg.* v. *White*, 3 E. & E. 137; 29 L. J., Q. B. 257.

[7] *R.* v. *Bunney*, 1 Salk. 190.

S. 7 (1). inquest, and where a body is found dead in the sea, or any creek, river, or navigable canal within the flowing of the sea where there is no deputy coroner for the jurisdiction of the Admiralty of England the inquest shall be held only by the coroner having jurisdiction in the place where the body is first brought to land.

Franchise coroners. As to the jurisdiction of the Admiralty coroners, and other franchise coroners, see under section 30.

Districts of counties. An inquisition super visum corporis might at common law be taken by one, although there were several coroners in the county;[1] for, wherever coroners are authorized to act as judges, the act of one, who first proceeds in the inquiry, and perfects it, is of equal authority as if all had joined. But after the proceeding has been instituted and concluded by one, the act of any other will be void.[2]

And upon the division of counties into districts by the 7 & 8 Vict. c. 92, it was provided (by sect. 19) that every coroner elected under the authority of that Act "although such coroner may be designated as the coroner for any particular district of a county, and may be elected by the electors of such district, and not by the freeholders of the county at large, shall for all purposes whatsoever, except as hereinafter mentioned, be considered as a coroner for the whole county, and shall have the same jurisdiction rights powers and authorities throughout the said county as if he had been elected one of the coroners of the said county by the freeholders of the county at large."

But by section 20 of that statute it is enacted " that except as aforesaid, every coroner for any county, or any

---

[1] 2 Hale, P. C. 50 ; Staund.　　　[2] 2 Hale, P. C. 59.
P. C. 53 a.

district thereof, or his deputy, after he shall, in pursuance ~~~~~~~~~~~~~~~ **S. 7 (2).**
of the provisions of this Act, have been assigned to or
elected by the electors of any particular district, shall,
except during illness or incapacity, or unavoidable absence
of any coroner for any other district, or during a vacancy
in the office of coroner for any other district, hold inquests
only within the district to or for which he shall have been
assigned or elected : provided always, that the coroner
who shall, by himself or deputy, hold any inquest in any
other district save that to which he shall have been
assigned or elected as aforesaid, shall in his inquisition to
be returned on such inquest certify the cause of his attendance and holding such inquest ; which certificate
shall be conclusive evidence of the illness or incapacity,
or unavoidable absence as aforesaid of the coroner in
whose stead he shall so attend, or of there being a vacancy
in the office of coroner for the district in which such inquest shall be holden."

And by section 43 of the present Act, and section 5 of
the Local Government Act of 1888, the rights and duties
of coroners as respects such districts are preserved.

(2.) In a borough with a separate court of quarter
sessions,[1] no coroner, save as is otherwise provided
by this Act, shall hold an inquest belonging to the
office of coroner, except the coroner of the borough,
or a coroner or deputy coroner for the jurisdiction
of the Admiralty of England.

The jurisdiction of the deputy borough coroner is pre- Deputy.
served by section 33. A further exception may be added
in the case of a prison situate in a borough, by reason of
the provisions of the Prison Act, 1865,[2] which enacts that County
prisons.

---

[1] This must now be read to
mean a "borough having a

coroner ; " see under section 33.
[2] 28 & 29 Vict. c. 126, s. 48.

S. 8 (1).   "it shall be the duty of the coroner having jurisdiction
            in the place to which the prison belongs to hold an in-
            quest on the body of every prisoner who may die within
            the prison," and that "every prison wheresoever situate
            shall be deemed to be within the limits of the place for
            which it is used as a prison."[1] It was accordingly held in
            a recent case [2] that notwithstanding the transfer of prisons
            to the Secretary of State by the Prison Act, 1877,[3] a
            prison, as to which no rules have been made under sect. 30
            of that Act, and which at the commencement of the
            Prison Act, 1865, was a prison belonging to a county, is
            still the county prison, although locally situate within
            the limits of a city, and therefore the jurisdiction to hold
            inquests on prisoners dying in such prison is in the
            coroner for the county, and not in the coroner for the
            city, and such jurisdiction is not affected by the above
            sub-section of the present Act.

Execution   Nor does this sub-section affect the rights of coroners
of process. when acting otherwise than in holding an inquest, as for
            instance where a county coroner is acting under process
            directed to him in the place of a sheriff.

               (3.) In a borough which has not a separate court
            of quarter sessions no coroner, save as is otherwise
            provided by this Act, shall hold an inquest belonging
            to the office of coroner except a coroner for the
            county, or a coroner or a deputy coroner for the
            jurisdiction of the Admiralty of England.

                        Liabilities of Coroner.

Removal   8.—(1.) The Lord Chancellor may, if he thinks
and punish-
ment of   fit, remove any coroner from his office for inability
coroner.   or misbehaviour in the discharge of his duty.

---

[1] 28 & 29 Vict. c. 126, s. 57.   D. 322.
[2] *Reg.* v. *Robinson,* 19 Q. B.   [3] 40 & 41 Vict. c. 21.

What amounts to inability or misbehaviour is a matter entirely within the discretion of the Chancellor. Unnecessary delay, or refusal without adequate reason or from improper motives to hold an inquest,[1] intoxication,[2] and the use of corrupt influence over the jury,[3] have afforded instances of misbehaviour. In the case of Rex v. Scory,[4] the coroner charged the jury to find the prisoner guilty of murder; they, however, returned a verdict of accidental death, which the coroner recorded, but committed the prisoner to gaol for murder; upon which the Court granted a rule nisi for a criminal information against the coroner. In another case, the coroner told the jury that a verdict of felo de se and of lunacy were in effect the same, and that the finding of felo de se was but a matter of course. Persuaded by this charge, the jury found a verdict of felo de se, and the inquisition was drawn up accordingly; but having been afterwards informed of the consequences of that finding, the jury applied to the coroner, telling him that they were satisfied that the man was a lunatic, and desired him so to take the verdict; whereupon he drew up a second inquisition, to which the jury set their hands and seals. He afterwards, upon a certiorari, returned the first inquisition, which the Court refused to file, and committed him.[5] Where the coroner, after the jury had been sworn, took some of them off the inquest, in order that the others might find the deceased non compos mentis, the Court granted a criminal information against him, and quashed the inquisition.[6] In Lord Buckhurst's case,[7] a coroner was amoved, and fined 100l., for favouring the prisoner, by keeping the inquisition in his pocket, and

S. 8 (1).

Misbehaviour.

---

[1] In re Ward, 30 L. J. Ch. 775; In re Hull, 9 Q. B. D. 689.
[2] In re Ward, 30 L. J., Ch. 775.

[3] R. v. Coates, Dick. J. P. 515.
[4] Leach, C. L. 43.
[5] 1 Str. 69.
[6] 12 Mod. 493.
[7] 1 Keb. 280.

S. 8 (1). not returning it at the next gaol delivery. In the case
of Rex *v.* Harrison,[1] the same punishment was imposed,
with the addition of six months' imprisonment, upon a
coroner who had accepted a sum of money for not holding an inquest, although it was not thought to be a case
in which an inquest ought rightly to have been held.

Neglect to
view.

If a coroner take an inquisition without viewing the
body, he is criminally to blame, for the view ascertains the
cause of the death, and an inquisition can be taken super
visum corporis only. An instance is mentioned in the
books,[2] in which the coroner was committed to prison,
and fined forty shillings, because he refused to view a
body, unless he was paid, for himself six shillings and
eightpence, and for his clerk two shillings. But if the
body has been so long buried that no information can be
obtained from the view, the coroner will not be justified
in causing it to be disinterred ; and if he do so, it would
seem that he may be fined.[3]

Forgery.

Where a coroner inserted in the inquisition, that three
persons had been found guilty of murder by the jury, who
had in fact found but one guilty, he was adjudged to have
committed forgery, and, being indicted, was found guilty.

Inability.

Again, if a coroner be so much engaged on other public
business in the county that he has no leisure to attend
to his office of coroner ; or if he be disabled and broken
with age, or incapacitated by reason of permanent
illness ; or if he dwell in the extreme parts of the county,
so that he cannot conveniently exercise the duties of
his office ; or if he be chosen into any other office which
is incompatible with that of coroner, as sheriff or ver-
derer ; or if he be unfit to execute his office ; or have not
lands and tenements sufficient within the county to
maintain the state and dignity of his office [5] : for these or

---

[1] 3 Inst. 149.
[2] 2 East, P. C. 382.
[3] 2 Lev. 140.
[4] 3 Salk. 172.
[5] See section 12.

either of these grounds he may be removed.[1] Lying in prison for twelve months has been adjudged to be a good ground for removing a coroner, even though the duties of his office were during that time discharged by another coroner of the county.[2] So a common merchant, who had been elected a coroner, was removed upon the ground that he was " communis mercator ; "[3] which probably means that his business took up too much of his time.

Formerly the practice was to present a petition, which, **Practice.** as in the case of a petition for a writ de coronatore eligendo upon a vacancy occurring by death, was signed by freeholders of the county, or by some recognised authority such as the justices at quarter sessions. But it is in the discretion of the Chancellor to entertain an application at the instance of any individual ; and the present practice is to move before him upon affidavits for a rule nisi calling on the coroner to show cause why he should not be removed from his office. If the rule be made absolute a copy of it is forwarded to the authority with whom the appointment lies ; and, if necessary, as in the case of county councils, who have no power of their own motion to discharge their coroners, a writ issues de **Issue** coronatore exonerando, which commands the council to **writ.** discharge him. Thereupon a writ de coronatore eligendo issues, which recites the ground upon which the former coroner was removed, and commands them to elect a new coroner in his stead. In practice both these writs issue together,[4] and although both are not tested on the same day, the fiat is put to both at the same time. But the writ de coronatore exonerando must be executed first.[5] By the appointment

---

[1] F. N. B. 163 ; S. P. C. 48 ; 2 Inst. 132.

[2] *Ex parte Parnell*, 1 J. & W. 451.

[3] 2 Inst. 32 ; Close Roll, 5 Edw. 3, part 1, mem. 21.

[4] *In re Ward*, 30 L. J., Ch. 775.

[5] *Ex parte Parnell*, 1 J. & W. 454.

of a new coroner, the authority of the old coroner is ipso
facto determined.[1]

(2.) A coroner who is guilty of extortion or of
corruption or of wilful neglect of his duty or of mis
behaviour in the discharge of his duty shall be guilty
of a misdemeanor, and in addition to any other
punishment may, unless his office of coroner is
annexed to any other office, be adjudged by the
Court before whom he is so convicted to be removed
from his office, and to be disqualified for acting as
coroner, and if he is a coroner for a county, a writ
shall issue for an election of another coroner, and if
he is a coroner of a borough, the council of the
borough, and if he is a coroner for a franchise the
lord or other person or persons entitled to the
appointment of the coroner, shall forthwith proceed
to appoint another coroner as in the case of any
other vacancy.

By section 35 this provision is not to prejudice or affect
the existing jurisdiction of the Court or a judge in relation
to or over a coroner or his duties.

Actions
against
coroner.
The Court of the coroner is a Court of record, of which
the coroner is judge ; and it is a general rule, of great
antiquity, that no action will lie against a judge of
record for any matter done by him in the exercise of his
judicial functions, and not exceeding the limits of his
jurisdiction.[2] This immunity from actions or questions

[1] Gobd. 105.
[2] 12 Rep 24 ; Lutw. 935,
1560 ; 1 Ld. Raym. 454 ; 1
Mod. 184 ; 3 Mod. 218 ;
Thomas v. *Churton*, 2 B. &. S.
475 ; 31 L. J., Q. B. 139 ;

Garnett v. *Ferrand*, 6 B. & C.
611. *Quære*, whether the 11
& 12 Vict. c. 44, protecting
justices from vexatious actions,
may not in some cases apply to
coroners.

at the suit of an individual is given by the law to the judges, not so much for the sake of the judges, as for that of the public, that the judges, being free from actions, may be free in thought and independent in judgment. Were it otherwise, no one would act at the peril of being harassed by a multiplicity of actions, and of having his motives and reasons weighed and tried by juries at the suit of individuals who may be dissatisfied with his conduct. There are few who would not prefer rather to admit disorder and confusion, and all the evil consequences that would follow from the indiscriminate admission of those who might choose to intrude, than to place themselves in a situation of so great jeopardy. It is not to be presumed that those who are selected for the administration of justice will make an ill use of the authority vested in them. In the imperfection of human nature, it is better even that an individual should occasionally suffer a wrong, than that the general course of justice should be impeded and fettered by constant and perpetual restraint and apprehensions on the part of those who are to administer it. Corruption, misconduct, or neglect of duty are quite a different consideration; for these there is a due course of punishment by criminal prosecution. And for acts done in excess of his jurisdiction the coroner is, of course, liable to an action at the suit of any party injured.[1]

9. If a coroner fails to comply with the provisions of this Act with respect to the delivery of the inquisition, or to the taking and delivery of the depositions and recognizances, in the case of murder or man-

Fine on coroner for neglect as to inquisition, depositions, and recognizances, &c.

---

[1] In *Foxhall v. Barnett*, 23 L. J., Q. B. 7, the plaintiff had been committed upon an inquisition taken without jurisdiction, and recovered as special damage against the coroner the costs of quashing the inquisition in order to obtain his release from custody.

S. 10, 11. slaughter, the Court to whose officer the inquisition, depositions, and recognizances ought to have been delivered may, upon proof of the said non-compliance, in a summary manner, impose such fine upon the coroner as to the Court seems meet.

The provisions referred to are contained in section 5.

Coroner not to act as solicitor and as coroner in same case. **10.—(1.)** A coroner shall not by himself or his partner, directly or indirectly, act as solicitor, in the prosecution or defence of a person for an offence for which such person is charged by an inquisition taken before him as coroner, whether such person is tried on that inquisition or on any bill of indictment found by a grand jury.

(2.) If a coroner acts in contravention of this section, he shall be deemed guilty of misbehaviour in the discharge of his duty

(3.) Moreover, the Court before whom such person is tried may impose on a coroner appearing to the Court to act in contravention of this section such fine not exceeding fifty pounds as to the Court seems fit.

In addition to this fine of £50 the High Court would have power under section 35 to treat the offence as a contempt of Court, and further, under section 8 the Lord Chancellor would have power to remove the coroner from his office.

Appointment and Payment of County Coroner and Deputy.

Election of county coroner. **11.**—A coroner for a county shall continue to be elected, until Parliament otherwise directs, by the

freeholders of that county, and in the case of a   **S. 11**
county divided into districts, by the persons residing
within that district who are at the time of election
qualified to vote at an election for coroners for the
county.

This section is repealed by the Local Government Act
of 1888,[1] which abolishes the ancient form of election of
county coroners by the votes of the freeholders at the
sheriff's county court, and relieves the candidates from
the expenses inseparable from a contested election and the
sheriff from a task involving considerable difficulty and
responsibility.   That a person should be elected to
judicial office by a popular vote had long been regarded
as an anomaly, and the appointment of county coroners
is accordingly now vested in the county council, following
the analogy of the previously existing practice in the case
of borough coroners.

These provisions are contained in the fifth section of   Appoint-
the Local Government Act of 1888, by which it is enacted   ment of
that "after the appointed day[2] a coroner for a county   by county
shall not be elected by the freeholders of the county, and   council.
on any vacancy occurring in the office of a coroner for a
county, who is elected to that office in pursuance of a
writ de coronatore eligendo, a like writ for the election of
a successor shall be directed to the county council of the
county instead of to the sheriff, and the county council
shall thereupon appoint a fit person[3] not being a county
alderman or county councillor, to fill such office, and in
the case of a county divided into coroners' districts shall
assign him a district ; and any person so appointed shall
have like powers and duties, and be entitled to like

---

[1] 51 & 52 Vict. c. 41, s. 5.   Local Government Board ; sect.
[2] 1st April, 1889, unless   109.
otherwise appointed by the   [3] See p. 73.

remuneration, as if he had been elected coroner for the
county by the freeholders thereof."

"(2.) Where the district of any such coroner is situate
wholly within any administrative county, the council of
that county shall, subject as herein-after mentioned,
appoint the coroner."

"(3.) Where the district of any such coroner is situate
partly in one and partly in another administrative county
forming part of an entire county, the joint committee for
the entire county may arrange for the alteration in
manner provided by law of the district, so that, on the
next avoidance of the office of coroner of that district, or
at any earlier time fixed by the joint committee when the
alteration is made, the coroner's district shall not be
situate in more than one administrative county "

"(4.) Until such arrangement is made, the joint
committee for the entire county shall appoint the
coroner for the said district, and the amount payable in
respect of the salary, fees, and expenses of such coroner
shall be defrayed in like manner as costs of the joint
committee are directed by this Act to be defrayed."

"(5.) Nothing in this Act respecting the appointment
of a coroner shall alter the jurisdiction of a coroner for
the entire county,[1] or any power of removing such
coroner, whether by writ de coronatore exonerando or
otherwise,[2] and all writs for the election or removal of a
coroner shall be altered so as to give effect to this
section."

"(6.) Sections eleven and fourteen and the First
Schedule of the Coroners Act, 1887, and any other
enactment relating to the election of a coroner for a
county by the freeholders of such county or any district
thereof, are hereby repealed as from the appointed day,
without prejudice to anything done or suffered, or any

---

[1] See under section 43.   [2] See under section 8.

legal proceeding commenced or penalty incurred before such repeal takes effect."

" (7.) A person who holds the office of coroner shall not be qualified to be elected as a county alderman or county councillor for the county for which he is a coroner."

The first step to be taken on the occurring of a vacancy is still, as formerly, to sue out a writ de coronatore eligendo, although under the similar powers of appointment already conferred by the legislature on borough councils, this formality was not considered necessary, except in a case of removal of a coroner.[1]

Writ de coronatore eligendo.

Therefore upon a vacancy caused by the death or resignation of a county coroner, a petition should be directed to the lord chancellor, subscribed by at least twelve of the freeholders of the county, stating the facts, and praying that the clerk of the petty bag may be directed to issue a writ de coronatore eligendo.[2] This petition, together with a certificate of burial of the late coroner, in case of death, must be lodged with the lord chancellor's principal secretary. Thereupon the fiat is made out, and delivered to the clerk of the petty bag, by whom the writ is issued.[3]

The only ground upon which the execution of this writ can be stayed appears to be that there has been fraud in obtaining it. Thus where an application to stay was made on the ground that the justices intended at the next quarter sessions to propose a division of the county, the motion was refused by the court.[4]

Extension of time.

It would seem as though by the use of the same words as are used in the Municipal Corporations Act, 1882, giving the council power to appoint a " fit person," it was the intention of the legislature to give to the county

Qualification.

---

[1] See p. 61.
[2] See App., Form 5.
[3] See App., Form 6.

[4] *In re the Coroner of Salop,* 1 Mac. & G. 377.

S. 11. council the same unfettered discretion respecting the
qualification of the candidate as is enjoyed by the
borough councils; but by the next following section of
the Coroners Act their choice is limited to freeholders
of the county.

Declaration of office.

It has always been the practice for county coroners to
take an oath or declaration of office, and although by
virtue of his appointment he is at once in full possession
of his office, it appears to be intended that the form [1]
given in the schedule to the Act should be subscribed by
both county and borough coroners before entering upon
their duties.

Borough coroners.

The further alterations introduced by the Local
Government Act of 1888 may conveniently be set out in
this place. There is a division of boroughs into three
classes according to their population; first, the county
boroughs, as set out in a schedule, being those with a
population of 50,000 and upwards; secondly, the larger
quarter sessions boroughs, containing according to the
census of 1881 a population of 10,000 or upwards; and
thirdly, the smaller quarter sessions boroughs.

County boroughs.

The county boroughs form administrative counties of
themselves, and to them the Act does not apply with
respect to the appointment of coroners. They therefore
continue to appoint their own coroners, with the proviso
in section 34, sub-s. (4), " that where the district of any
county coroner is wholly situate within a county borough,
the coroner for that district shall be appointed by the
council of that borough, and the writ for his election
may be issued to that council instead of to the county
council, and where the district of any county coroner is
situate partly within and partly without a county
borough, the writ for the election of such coroner shall
be issued to the county council, but if there is a joint

---

[1] App., Form 1.

committee of the county and borough councils for the purpose, the question of the person to be elected shall be referred to that joint committee, and the county council shall appoint the person recommended by the majority of such committee."

S. 11.

And by sub-s. (5), "if the council of a county borough so require, a joint committee shall from time to time be appointed for the purposes of coroners, consisting of such number of members of the county and borough councils as may be agreed upon, or in default of agreement may be determined by a Secretary of State."

The larger quarter sessions boroughs form part of the county in which they are situate, but, under section 35, they retain the power of appointing their own coroners under the provisions of the Municipal Corporations Act of 1882.[1]

Larger quarter sessions boroughs.

The smaller quarter sessions boroughs are practically merged into the counties, and will no longer have separate coroners of their own. Every such borough is under section 38, sub-s. (5), for all administrative purposes of the county council "included in the county, as if the borough had not a separate court of quarter sessions, and accordingly shall be subject to the authority of the county council and the county coroners, and may be annexed by the county council to a coroner's district of the county, and the parishes in the borough shall be liable to be assessed to all county contributions."

Smaller quarter sessions boroughs.

By section 114 it is provided that "the persons who at the passing of this Act are coroners for any districts which become wholly or partly by virtue of this Act part of the county of London, shall continue to act for such districts until otherwise directed as herein-after mentioned, and while so continuing to act shall, as respects

Metropolitan coroners.

---

[1] See p. 107.

S. 11. such part of their districts as is within the county of London, be deemed to be coroners for the county of London, and the amount payable in respect of the salaries, fees, and expenses of any such coroner, where the district is partly within and partly without the county of London, shall be apportioned between the counties in which such district is situate."

"In the case of any coroner's district being situate partly within and partly without the county of London, the county councils of the counties in which such district is situate shall arrange for the alteration in manner provided by law of the district, so that on the next avoidance of the office of coroner, or any earlier date fixed when the alteration is made, the coroners' districts shall not be situate in more than one county."

Preservation of existing interests.

The transfer of these powers of appointment of county coroners to the county councils will not of itself affect the tenure of office, or the terms and conditions upon which it is held by the coroners, but the council may redistribute the business, or abolish the office of any existing officer which they may deem unnecessary, but under section 119 such officer is entitled to compensation, and by section 114, sub-s. (3), the coroners are included as "officers" of the quarter sessions of the county for which they are coroners.

Compensation to existing officers.

Accordingly by section 120, a coroner "who by virtue of this Act, or anything done in pursuance of or in consequence of this Act, suffers any direct pecuniary loss by abolition of office or by diminution or loss of fees or salary, shall be entitled to have compensation paid to him for such pecuniary loss by the county council, to whom the powers of the authority, whose officer he was, are transferred under this Act, regard being had to the conditions on which his appointment was made, to the nature of his office or employment, to the duration of his

service, to any additional emoluments which he acquires
by virtue of this Act or of anything done in pursuance of
or in consequence of this Act, and to the emoluments
which he might have acquired if he had not refused to
accept any office offered by any council or other body
acting under this Act, and to all the other circumstances of
the case, and the compensation shall not exceed the amount
which, under the Acts and rules relating to Her Majesty's
Civil Service, is paid to a person on abolition of office."

"(2.) Every person who is entitled to compensation, as
above mentioned, shall deliver to the county council a
claim under his hand setting forth the whole amount
received and expended by him or his predecessors in
office, in every year during the period of five years next
before the passing of this Act, on account of the
emoluments for which he claims compensation, dis-
tinguishing the offices in respect of which the same have
been received, and accompanied by a statutory declaration under the Statutory Declaration Act, 1835, that the
same is a true statement according to the best of his
knowledge, information, and belief."

"(3.) Such statement shall be submitted to the county
council, who shall forthwith take the same into consideration, and assess the just amount of compensation (if any),
and shall forthwith inform the claimant of their decision."

"(4.) If a claimant is aggrieved by the refusal of the
county council to grant any compensation, or by the
amount of compensation assessed, or if not less than one-
third of the members of such council subscribe a protest
against the amount of the compensation as being
excessive, the claimant or any subscriber to such protest
(as the case may be) may, within three months after the
decision of the council, appeal to the Treasury, who shall
consider the case and determine whether any compensation, and if so, what amount ought to be granted to the
claimant, and such determination shall be final."

"(5.) Any claimant under this section, if so required by any member of the county council, shall attend at a meeting of the council and answer upon oath, which any justice present may administer, all questions asked by any member of the council touching the matters set forth in his claim, and shall further produce all books, papers, and documents in his possession or under his control relating to such claim."

"(6.) The sum payable as compensation to any person in pursuance of this section shall commence to be payable at the date fixed by the council on granting the compensation, or, in case of appeal, by the Treasury, and shall be a specialty debt due to him from ths county council, and may be enforced accordingly in like manner as if the council had entered into a bond to pay the same."

"(7.) If a person receiving compensation in pursuance of this section is appointed to any office under the same or any other county council, or by virtue of this Act, or anything done in pursuance of or in consequence of this Act, receive any increase of emoluments of the office held by him, he shall not, while receiving the emoluments of that office, receive any greater amount of his compensation, if any, than, with the emoluments of the said office, is equal to the emoluments for which compensation was granted to him, and if the emoluments of the office he holds are equal to or greater than the emoluments for which compensation was granted, his compensation shall be suspended while he holds such office."

"(8.) All expenses incurred by a county council in pursuance of this section shall be paid out of the county fund, as a payment for general county purposes."

Qualifica-
tion of
county
coroner.

12. Every coroner for a county shall be a fit person having land in fee sufficient in the same county whereof he may answer to all manner of people.

This is practically a re-enactment of the 14 Edw. 3, S 12. st. 1, c. 8, which, in consequence of no precise amount of land being mentioned, has never been very strictly enforced, and indeed the opinion has prevailed that if a coroner were a person of substance, the amount of land which he might hold in the county would be immaterial. It must now, however, be taken to be intended to be enforced, and that at least a substantial holding of land is an essential qualification. It is moreover to be observed that the Local Government Act of 1888,[1] while repealing the 11th and 14th sections of this Act and empowering the county council to appoint a " fit person," has left the limitation imposed by this section untouched. On the other hand, the consequences of an infringement of this provision are no longer of the same importance since the abolition of the election of county coroners by the votes of freeholders, when it was open to an opposing candidate to rely upon the absence of the property qualification as a bar to the nomination, or as vitiating [the sheriff's return to the writ. If now a person is appointed by the council who is otherwise fit, but not a freeholder, it would be necessary to make application to the High Court, or to the Lord Chancellor, who would exercise their discretion as to the removal of the nominee of the council.

In his official capacity a coroner is not, like a sheriff, under frequent pecuniary liability to all manner of people, therefore from practical considerations but little assistance can be derived ; while, owing to the great change in the value of money since the time of Edward III., it is difficult to deduce any conclusion from the analogy of that period.

At common law, confirmed by statute,[2] every man of

---

[1] 51 & 52 Vict. c. 41, s. 5. [2] 1 Edw. 2, c. 1, De militibus.

S. 12.   full age, and possessing a knight's fee,[1] was compellable
to take upon himself the degree of knighthood, pour
faire service al roy, et al realme in course de justice;
from which prerogative arose a principal source of the
revenue of the Crown.   In consequence of this usage, all
or the greater part of the public officers, under the degree
of barons, were milites; from which class of persons, by
the statute of 3 Edw. 1, c. 10,[2] the coroners for counties
were chosen.[3]   But as the sheriffs, who required of such
as were of age and sufficiency to take the degree of
knighthood, were empowered also to receive for the use
of the crown pecuniary commutations or aids from those
who were desirous of purchasing their redemption or
respite from that service,[4] this so far decreased the
number of persons compellable to assume the degree of
knighthood, that at length there was a deficiency of
knights to fill the public offices.   This probably was the
reason why the Statute of Westminster, above referred
to, fell into disuse, and gave rise to the statute 28 Edw.
3, c. 6, which enacted that coroners should be elected of
"the most meet and lawful people that shall be found in
the said counties to execute the said office."

Knight-
hood.
  The Statute of Merton (20 Hen. 3, c. 3), which was
passed nearly forty years before the Statute of Westminster, appears to assume that all coroners were knights;
and it is observable, that the latter statute, which
enacted that none under the degree of knighthood should
be chosen a coroner, is only now repealed, although long
fallen into disuse.   The chief intent of that statute was

---

[1] A knight's fee, in the time
of Edward 2, amounted to 20l.
arising out of land, or, according to Cay, as from the Cotton
MS., 40l.   The larger sum
appears from 16 Car. 1, s. 20,
rendering knighthood no longer
compulsory, to be the correct
one.

[2] "Of the most wise and
discreet knights which know,
will, and may best attend upon
such offices," &c.
[3] 4 Inst. 271.
[4] Seld. Tit. Hon. 1; Britton,
88 (Edition by Nichols); Bract.
117; Fleta, 1, c. 20, s. 94

to prevent the election of persons of mean ability, and was sufficiently answered by choosing men of good substance and credit.

But although the degree of knighthood ceased to be an essential qualification for the office of coroner, yet candidates for that office must, it was said, have land sufficient to take upon themselves that degree, whether they be really knighted or not,[1] and must be possessed of an estate in fee within the county over which, if elected, their jurisdiction would extend. The statute 14 Edw. 3, st. 1, c. 8, first enacted "that no coroner be chosen unless he have land in fee sufficient in the same county, whereof he may answer to all manner of people," which was considered to mean that he ought to have sufficient property to maintain the dignity of his office, and to answer any fine that may be set upon him for his misbehaviour. But if, having an estate in fee within the county, it were insufficient to answer his fines, that would not operate as a disqualification, or be a ground for his removal, if he were of sufficient estate to execute his office ; for the county, upon his default, is liable to the fine, as a punishment for having elected an insufficient officer.[2] On the other hand, if he had not land sufficient within the county to maintain the state and dignity of his office, it is suggested by Fitzherbert (De Natura Brevium [3]), in the form given by him of the writ de coronatore exonerando, that it would be a ground of removal. No instance is, however, to be found of a coroner being actually removed from his office for this reason.

Land.

13.—(1.) A coroner for a county shall from time to time appoint by writing under his hand a fit person approved by the Lord Chancellor to be

Appointment of deputy coroner in county.

---

[1] F. N. B. 163, 164 ; 1 Bl. Com. 347.

[2] 2 Hale, P. C. 74 ; 2 Inst. 175.
[3] P. 163.

S. 13 (2). his deputy, and may at any time revoke such appointment.

Practice. At common law, in the absence of prescription, the judicial duties of the coroner must have been discharged by the coroner himself, and could not be deputed.[1] The practice is for the person so appointed to forward to the lord chancellor a testimonial signed by at least twelve of the principal residents in the locality, showing his fitness for the office ; and it is usually further required that the deputy be a properly qualified legal or medical practitioner of at least twenty-seven years of age.

Counties of towns. Under section 38, the expression " county," unless there is something inconsistent in the context, does not include a county of a city, or a county of a town. It seems doubtful therefore whether a coroner of such a county has any power whatever to appoint a deputy.

Boroughs. As to deputies of borough coroners, see under section 33.

Franchises. Franchise coroners have by prescription in many cases the power to appoint a deputy, provided generally that the consent of the lord of the franchise be first obtained. Others possess the power by the express terms of their patent.

(2.) A deputy shall not act for a coroner except during the illness of such coroner or during his absence from any lawful or reasonable cause, or except on any inquest which he is disqualified, under this Act, for holding.

Cause of absence. It has been held to be a sufficient cause for the appointment of a deputy, that the coroner himself was engaged in holding another inquest.[2] If the jury are sworn and

---

[1] Cromp. Just. 227a; 2 Hale, P. C. 57 ; 1 East, P. C. 383.
[2] R. v. Perkin, 7 Q. B. 175.

the proceedings begin before the deputy of a county coroner, the deputy has power to finish them, though the coroner be present in the course of holding the inquest; but it is otherwise in the case of a borough coroner, for the words of the statute, 45 & 46 Vict. c. 50, s. 172, which deals with deputies of borough coroners, are narrower, and only empower the deputy to act during the illness or unavoidable absence of his principal. The inquisition is properly signed in the name of the principal coroner, "by A. B., his deputy;" and is properly described as having been taken before the principal coroner.[1]

Upon the death of the coroner the authority of his deputy is of course determined.

(3.) A duplicate of every appointment of a deputy shall be sent to the clerk of the peace of the county and kept by him amongst the records thereof.

(4.) For the purpose of an inquest or other act which a deputy coroner is authorised to hold or do the deputy coroner shall be deemed to be the coroner whose deputy he is, and have the same jurisdiction, and powers, and be subject to the same obligations, liabilities, and disqualifications as that coroner, and he shall generally be subject to the provisions of this Act and to the law relating to coroners, in like manner as that coroner.

14. The sheriff, in accordance with the rules contained in the First Schedule to this Act shall hold a court for the election of a coroner for a county, &c.

S. 14.

Death of coroner.

Proceedings for election of county coroner.

---

[1] *R.* v. *Perkin,* 7 Q. B. 175.

S. 15. This section is, together with the rules, repealed by the Local Government Act of 1888,[1] and the present practice on appointment of county coroners will be found under section 11.

Payment of coroners when they act for sheriffs.

15. Where any writ, process, or extent whatsoever is directed to and executed by a coroner for a county in the place of a sheriff, the coroner shall, in addition to any salary to which he is entitled, receive the same poundage fees or other compensation or reward for executing the writ, process, or extent, and have the same right to retain, and all other remedies for the recovery of the fees, compensation, or reward, as the sheriff would have been entitled to and had in whose place such coroner was substituted ; and if the fees or compensation payable to the sheriffs are at any time after the passing of this Act increased by Act of Parliament or otherwise, the coroner shall be entitled to such increased fees or compensation.

Writs are directed to the county coroners when any just exception is taken to the sheriff.[2] The coroner is in such cases in all respects considered as the immediate officer of the Court in place of the sheriff, and may do all lawful acts which the sheriff might have done, if not under any challenge or incapacity, and may even take the posse comitatus.[3]

If there be but one sheriff, who is either a party or interested in the suit, the writ should be directed to the coroners.[4] But if there be two sheriffs, and the objection of interest applies to one only, the writ should be directed to the other, and not to the coroner.[5] The process is

---

[1] 51 & 52 Vict. c. 41, s. 5.   [4] 1 W. Bl. 506.
[2] 4 Inst. 271.   [5] 5 M. & S. 144 ; Salk. 152 ;
[3] Hob. 85.   4 Mod. 65 ; 12 Id. 22 ; Carth.

not, however, awarded to the coroner in the case of the death of the sheriff, but to the under-sheriff, who by statute is empowered to act until another sheriff is appointed.

S. 15.

Coroners are open to the same objection as sheriffs, and if they be incapacitated by interest or otherwise, the process is directed to elisors, appointed by the officers of the Court.[1] But where there are several coroners, some of whom only are interested, the process must be directed to and executed by the others.[2]

Elisors.

Where the process is awarded to the coroners, the sheriff is no longer considered as an officer of the Court in respect of that particular action, and is expressly forbidden to act.[3]

The practice of awarding judicial process to the coroners is of great antiquity, instances occurring so early as the Year Books ; but that of directing to them the first process by original, in real actions, seems to have been first introduced 6 Edw. 6,[4] where, in writ of assize, the process was directed to and executed by five out of six coroners, one having been challenged on account of consanguinity to one of the defendants. Over was craved of the writ and return, and after argument on demurrer, a respondeat ouster was awarded.

Judicial writs follow the course of their original, and where the first process is awarded to the coroners, the execution must be directed to them also,[5] even though a new sheriff be in the meantime appointed ;[6] but the Court will not direct the final process to the coroners, upon a suggestion of interest in the sheriff, who has executed the other proceedings in the suit, although, if the

---

214 ; Comb. 191 ; 1 Show. 317 ; 2 Id. 262, 286 ; Lil. Ent. 483.

[1] 2 W. Bl. 911.

[2] 2 Show. 286.

[3] Cro. Eliz. 894.

[4] Plowd. 73.

[5] 2 H. 6, 21a ; Bro. Exon. 110 ; 18 Ed. 4, 7 b ; 14 H. 8, 316.

[6] Com. Dig. Officer, G. 13.

interest of the sheriff be made to appear, the Court will award the venire to the coroners.

Process improperly awarded to the sheriff will not be aided after verdict by the stat. 32 Hen. 8, c. 30 ; but that statute does apply to process which has improperly been awarded to coroners.[1]

In all proceedings against the sheriff, the process should be directed to and executed by the coroners.[2]

Where coroners act ministerially, although one may execute the writ,[3] the return must be in the name of all.[4] In Rex *v.* Dolby,[5] the coroners were directed to return a special jury, which they did ; but a tales being required, it was returned by one coroner who happened to be in Court. It was objected that the return must be by all, the act of one coroner being insufficient, where they were only empowered to act ministerially ; and the validity of the objection was admitted. A writ directed corona-toribus, where there are more than two coroners in the county, may be executed by the survivors, although one die before the return ; for so long as more than one coroner survives, the return will be good, but if one only survive, he can neither execute nor return the writ, until another be elected.[6]

Coroners are also liable in their ministerial character to an action for an escape,[7] for a false return,[8] or to an attachment,[9] according to the circumstances of the case. And if in that character they be guilty of malpractice, the Court will exercise summary jurisdiction over them.[10]

Acts of co-coroners. Where any act may be legally done by one coroner, as in the taking of an inquisition super visum corporis, his acts will not bind his co-coroners, and they will not be

---

[1] Ib. Dyer, 367 a.
[2] 7 H. 6, 36 a.
[3] 2 Hale, P. C. 56.
[4] 2 Hawk, P. C. c. 9, s. 45.
[5] Cited Umf. Lex Cor. 144.
[6] 2 Hale, P. C. 56 ; F. N. B.

163 ; Cro. Jac. 383.
[7] 3 Lev. 399 ; 6 Mod. 37.
[8] Freem. 191.
[9] 2 Bl. 911, 1218.
[10] 8 Mod. 192.

answerable for his default. But when coroners act ministerially, as in the execution of process, which is directed to all the coroners of the county, all will be responsible for the acts of each civilly by action, although a different rule applies with respect to a criminal liability.[1] No criminal responsibility can attach upon one who is constructively only a participator in the abuse ; and, therefore, where one coroner gave to another general authority to act in his name, it was held that he was not responsible criminally for an abuse of that authority, committed without his concurrence or participation.

S. 18.

16. Where a coroner admits a person charged with manslaughter to bail, he shall be entitled to the like fee as a clerk to a justice of the peace is entitled to on the admission to bail of a person so charged.

Fees on recognizances.

17. Save as is authorised by this or any other Act, a coroner shall not take any fee or remuneration in respect of anything done by him in the execution of his office.

Prohibition on coroner taking fee.

The remuneration, generally, of county, franchise, and borough coroners, is dealt with under the respective heads of sections 43, 30, and 33. The further fees to which they are entitled are by this section limited to those given them by statute.

PART II.

SUPPLEMENTAL.

Procedure.

18. The following enactments shall be made with respect to procedure at coroners' inquests :

Enactments w'tl' respect to procedure at inquests.

---

[1] *Naylor* v. *Sharply*, 1 Mod. 198 ; 2 Mod. 23 ; Freem. 1, 91 ; Staund. P. C. 53 a.

J.   G

S. 18 (1).

(1.) The inquisition shall be under the hands, and in the case of murder or manslaughter also under the seals, of the jurors who concur in the verdict and of the coroner.

Inquests on persons hanged.

Where an inquest has been held upon the body of any offender upon whom judgment of death has been executed, the inquisition must be in duplicate, one of the originals being delivered to the sheriff.[1]

Seal.

It was always usual for the coroner and jurors to set their seals to the inquisition. The stamp printed upon the form opposite the signatures has been considered sufficient, the inquisition concluding with the averment that it was given under their hands and seals.[2] The practice probably originated in the provisions of the statute West. 2, c. 13, which directs that sheriffs, in their tourns, shall inquire by twelve lawful men, at the least, de furtis et aliis malefactis; qui hujusmodi inquisitionibus sigilla sua apponant.[3]

Inquisition.

An inquisition, properly so called, is the written statement of the verdict or finding of a jury[4] returned for the purpose of a particular inquiry, as distinguished from an indictment,[5] which is an accusation by the oaths of jurors returned to inquire generally of all offences within the county. Where it contains the subject-matter of accusation it is equivalent to the finding of a grand jury, and the parties may be tried and convicted upon it. An indictment is a bill presented to the grand jury for them to say whether it be a true bill or not, and is delivered by them into court, usually (but not necessarily) signed by the foreman; but, in the case of an inquisition, no

[1] 31 & 32 Vict. c. 24, s. 5.
[2] *R.* v. *Skeats*, 7 L. T. 433.
[3] 2 Inst. 388.
[4] For adding to an inquisition facts not found by the jury
a coroner has been convicted of forgery; *R.* v. *Marsh*, 3 Salk. 172.
[5] See *Reg.* v. *Ingham*, 5 B. & S. 257.

bill is presented to the grand jury, and the inquisition is
verified only by the attestation of the coroner and jurymen. If there be, as frequently is the case, a charge made
both upon an indictment and upon an inquisition for the
same offence, it is not usual to proceed to trial upon both,
and in such cases the inquisition would seem to be of
little value. It seems that if the grand jury ignore the
bill, the fact may be pleaded to an arraignment upon the
coroner's inquisition ; but cases have occurred where
magistrates have refused to commit for trial, and a conviction has nevertheless been obtained at the assizes upon
the coroner's inquisition.

S. 18 (2)

(2.) An inquisition need not, except in the case
of murder or manslaughter, be on parchment, and
may be written or printed, or partly written and
partly printed, and may be in the form contained in
the Second Schedule to this Act, or to the like effect,
or in such other form as the Lord Chancellor from
time to time prescribes, or to the like effect, and the
statements therein may be made in concise and
ordinary language.

It is not imperative that this form be followed exactly.
Nor can it for instance be material that the names of the
jury should be set out at length in the body of the inquisition, or that all the adjournments should appear on the
face of it.[1] But it has always been a rule that the name
of the county or city must either be in the margin or in
the body of the caption.[2] At common law the venue
must have been laid in the county where the offence was
committed,[3] or if the jurisdiction of the coroner extended

Form of
inquisition.

---

[1] See *R.* v. *Skeats,* 7 L. T.
433.

[2] 2 Hale, P. C. 166.
[3] *Ibid.* 163.

G 2

only to part of the county, or within a particular liberty, the venue in the margin must have been coextensive with it, and the offence described as having been committed within that jurisdiction; but now the venue should be the county or jurisdiction within which the body lies and the inquisition is held. Where the inquisition is taken by the coroner of the admiralty, no venue is inserted, but in the margin "Admiralty of England."

The form of the inquisition is now, however, of small importance, provided all material facts are found, having regard to the extensive powers of amendment conferred by section 20, sub-s. (1); but any uncertainty in the designation of the person or of the offence charged would vitiate the inquisition under that sub-section, if the party charged were to be brought up for trial upon it.

(3.) The coroner, after the termination of an inquest on any death, shall send to the registrar of deaths whose duty it is by law to register the death such certificate of the finding of the jury and within such time as is required by the Registration Acts.

Registration of death.

Under the 37 & 38 Vict. c. 88, s. 16, the time required is "within five days after the finding of the jury is given." Forms are supplied by the registrar, and these may be filled up and returned by post. The particulars required are given on page 42.

Correction of errors.

With regard to the correction of errors in the register it is provided [1] that "where an error of fact or substance (other than an error relating to the cause of death) occurs in the information given by a coroner's certificate concerning a dead body upon which he has held an inquest,

---

[1] S. 36.

the coroner, if satisfied by evidence on oath or statutory declaration that such error exists, may certify under his hand to the officer having the custody of the register in which such information is entered, the nature of the error and the true facts of the case as ascertained by him on such evidence, and the error may thereupon be corrected by such officer in the register by entering in the margin (without any alteration of the original entry) the facts as so certified by the coroner."

S. 18 (6).

(4.) The coroner shall cause recognizances taken before him from a person charged by an inquisition with manslaughter to be taken, so far as circumstances admit, in one of the forms contained in the Second Schedule to this Act or in such other forms as the Lord Chancellor from time to time prescribes, and shall give notice of the recognizance to every person bound thereby.

(5.) A person charged by an inquisition with murder or manslaughter shall be entitled to have from the person having for the time being the custody of the inquisition or of the depositions of the witnesses at the inquest, copies thereof on payment of a reasonable sum for the same, not exceeding the rate of three halfpence for every folio of ninety words.

(6.) A coroner, upon holding an inquest upon any body, may, if he thinks fit after view of the body, by order under his hand, authorise the body to be buried before verdict and before registry of the death, and shall deliver such order to the relative or other person to whom the same is required by the

Registration Acts to be delivered ; but, except upon holding an inquest, no order, warrant, or other document for the burial of a body shall be given by the coroner.

Burial
order.

By the Registration Act, 1874,[1] the person to whom the burial order is to be delivered is "the relative of the deceased, or other person who causes the body to be buried, or the undertaker or other person having charge of the funeral." And by the Burials Act, 1880,[2] the order shall be delivered to the "relative, friend, or legal representative of the deceased having charge of or being responsible for the burial," where the burial is not according to the rites of the Church of England.[3]

Attendance
of witnesses
and jurors.

19.—(**1.**) Where a person duly summoned as juror at an inquest does not, after being openly called three times, appear to such summons, or appearing, refuses without reasonable excuse to serve as a juror, the coroner may impose on such person a fine not exceeding five pounds.

(**2.**) Where a person duly summoned to give evidence at an inquest does not, after being openly called three times, appear to such summons, or appearing, refuses without lawful excuse to answer a question put to him, the coroner may impose on such person a fine not exceeding forty shillings.

(**3.**) Any power by this Act vested in a coroner of imposing a fine on a juror or witness, shall be deemed to be in addition to and not in derogation

---

[1] 37 & 38 Vict. c. 88, s. 17.   [3] 44 & 45 Vict. c. 2 s. 2.
[2] 43 & 44 Vict. c. 41, s. 11.

of any power the coroner may possess independently of this Act, for compelling any person to appear and give evidence before him on any inquest or other proceeding, or for punishing any person for contempt of court in not so appearing and giving evidence, with this qualification, that a person shall not be fined by the coroner under this Act, and also be punished under the power of a coroner independently of this Act.

The coroner has power to compel the attendance of a witness by summons,[1] and, in case of disobedience, to issue a warrant to cause him to be apprehended and brought into court ; but it does not appear that there is any means provided for executing such a warrant outside the coroner's jurisdiction. The provisions of Jervis's Acts as to backing of warrants apply only to warrants for the arrest of persons charged with offences, and in the absence of statutory provision it would seem that the coroner's warrant is, like any other warrant, available only within the jurisdiction of the person who issues it. The attendance of a witness who is without the jurisdiction may be secured by a crown office subpœna.

Warrant for apprehension of witness.

The coroner has, in common with every person who administers any public duty, a common law right to preserve general order in the place where it is administered, and to turn out any person who is in that place for improper purposes. But, further, the coroner's court is a court of record,[2] and as such has attached to its jurisdiction and inherent in it a power to punish for contempt committed in court. This power is necessary to the due

Committal for contempt.

---

[1] See p. 29.
[2] Coke, 4 Inst. 271 ; Com. Dig. Officer G. 5 ; *Garnett* v. *Farrand*, 6 B. & C. 611 ; but doubted by Lord Abinger in *Jewison* v. *Dyson*, 9 M. & W., at p. 586.

S. 19 (4). administration of justice, and to prevent the business of
the court from being interrupted. The coroner may
therefore commit any person who obstructs or impedes
him in the performance of his duty, or he may cause him
to be fined or forcibly removed. This power does not,
however, as in the superior courts, extend to cases of contempt committed out of court,[1] as by the writing or publication of articles reflecting on the conduct of the coroner.

Obstruc-
tions, how
punished.

It is a misdemeanor to obstruct the coroner or his jury
in the view or inquiry.[2] An information has been
granted against the captain of a ship of war for refusing
to permit the coroner and his jury to enter the ship in
order to take a view and inquest thereon of the body of
a person who had hanged himself in the cabin of the
ship ; and this although no imputation was laid upon the
defendant as wilfully opposing justice ; for, said the
judges, it is a matter of great public concern, and an
information will lie not only where an act is done maliciously and forcibly, but also where persons are hindered
in the execution of their lawful authority.[3] And recently
in the Court for the consideration of Crown cases reserved
it was held to be a misdemeanor to burn or otherwise
dispose of a dead body with intent thereby to prevent
the holding of an intended inquest, and so to obstruct
the coroner in the execution of his duty, in a case where
the inquest is one which the coroner has jurisdiction to
hold, that is to say, in any case in which the coroner is
bonâ fide of opinion that an inquest ought to be held.[4]

(**4**.) Where a coroner imposes a fine upon a person, he shall sign a certificate describing such person

---

[1] See *Ex parte Pater*, 33 L. J.
M. C. 142, and *Reg.* v. *Lefroy*,
L. R. 8 Q. B. 134.
[2] Umfreville, citing Calth.
MS.

[3] 2 Str. 1097 ; And. 231.
[4] *Reg.* v. *Stephenson*, 13 Q. B.
D. 331. See also 7 Mod. Rep.,
case 15 ; and *Reg.* v. *Price*, 12
Q. B. D. 247.

and stating the amount of the fine imposed and the cause of the fine, and shall send such certificate to the clerk of the peace for the county or place in which such person resides on or before the first day of the quarter sessions then next ensuing, and shall, twenty-four hours at the least before that day, cause a copy of such certificate to be served upon the person fined by leaving it at his residence, and the clerk of the peace shall copy every fine so certified on the roll on which fines and forfeitures imposed at the said quarter sessions are copied, and the same shall be estreated, levied, and applied in like manner and subject to the like powers, provisions, and penalties in all respects as if such fine had been part of the fines imposed at the said quarter sessions.

(5.) Where a recognizance is forfeited at an inquest held before a coroner, the coroner shall proceed in like manner under this section as if he had imposed a fine under this section upon the person forfeiting that recognizance, and the provisions of this section shall apply accordingly.

20.—(1.) If in the opinion of the court having cognizance of the case an inquisition finds sufficiently the matters required to be found thereby, and where it charges a person with murder or manslaughter sufficiently designates that person and the offence charged, the inquisition shall not be quashed for any defects, and the court may order the proper officer of the court to amend any defect in the inquisition, and any variance occurring between the inquisition

S. 20 (1). and the evidence offered in proof thereof, if the court are of opinion that such defect or variance is not material to the merits of the case, and that the defendant or person traversing the inquisition cannot be prejudiced by the amendment in his defence or traverse on the merits, and the court may order the amendment on such terms as to postponing the trial to be had before the same or another jury as to the court may seem reasonable, and after the amendment the trial shall proceed in like manner, and the inquisition, verdict, and judgment, shall be of the same effect, and the record shall be drawn up in the same form in all respects as if the inquisition had originally been in the form in which it stands when so amended.

Uncertainty.

Many trifling irregularities in drawing up the inquisition could formerly be taken advantage of upon the trial of the person charged as affording sufficient ground for the quashing of the inquisition. There now remain only two points in which the inquisition cannot be amended at the trial : uncertainty in the designation of the person or of the offence charged.

Person charged.

The person charged must be designated with the same precision as in an indictment. Thus an inquisition for manslaughter against "the directors of the Great Western Railway," without naming them, was quashed by a Divisional Court, who held further that the jurisdiction to amend was limited to the court before which the trial takes place.[1]

Offence charged.

And the offence charged must not be expressed as a matter of doubt or belief. Thus a finding "nos certè credimus esse causam mortis" has been held bad.[2] And

---

[1] 20 Q. B. D. 410.   [2] Anon. 12 Mod. 112.

a finding that the deceased killed himself, " but in what state of mind there was no evidence to show," would be merely equivalent to a verdict of felo de se; or again a verdict by which the jury, without accusing a person of manslaughter, desire to have a sort of vote of censure recorded against him. It is not the duty of the coroner to record a verdict of this description. In cases of accidents in mines, or in connection with explosives, where the inquest is not attended by any person on behalf of the Secretary of State, the coroner is by statute directed to send notice to the inspector of the district of any neglect contributing to the accident, or of any defect appearing to require a remedy;[1] but in ordinary cases expressions of opinion by the jury are irregular.

S. 21 (1).

(2.) For the purpose of any such amendment, the court may respite any of the recognizances taken before the coroner, and the persons bound by such recognizances shall be bound without entering into any fresh recognizances to appear and prosecute, give evidence, or be tried at the time and place to which the trial is postponed, as if they were originally bound by their recognizances to appear and prosecute, give evidence, or be tried at that time and place.

Medical Witnesses and Post-mortem Examinations.

21.—(1.) Where it appears to the coroner that the deceased was attended at his death or during his last illness by any legally qualified medical practitioner, the coroner may summon

Power of coroner to summon medical witnesses and to direct performance of post-mortem examination.

---

[1] 35 & 36 Vict. c. 77, s. 22; 38 Vict. c. 17, s. 65; and 50 & 51 Vict. c. 58, s. 48. See these sections post, p. 126.

S. 21 (3). such practitioner as a witness; but if it appears to the coroner that the deceased person was not attended at his death or during his last illness by any legally qualified medical practitioner, the coroner may summon any legally qualified medical practitioner who is at the time in actual practice in or near the place where the death happened, and any such medical witness as is summoned in pursuance of this section, may be asked to give evidence as to how, in his opinion, the deceased came to his death.

(2.) The coroner may, either in his summons for the attendance of such medical witness or at any time between the issuing of that summons and the end of the inquest, direct such medical witness to make a post-mortem examination of the body of the deceased, with or without an analysis of the contents of the stomach or intestines.

Provided that where a person states upon oath before the coroner that in his belief the death of the deceased was caused partly or entirely by the improper or negligent treatment of a medical practitioner or other person, such medical practitioner or other person shall not be allowed to perform or assist at the post-mortem examination of the deceased.

(3.) If a majority of the jury sitting at an inquest are of opinion that the cause of death has not been satisfactorily explained by the evidence of the medical practitioner or other witnesses brought before them, they may require the coroner in writing to summon as a witness some other legally qualified medical practitioner named by them, and further to direct a post-mortem examination of the deceased, with or without an analysis of the contents of the stomach or intestines, to be made by such last-mentioned practitioner, and that whether such examination has been previously made or not, and the coroner shall comply with such requisition, and in default shall be guilty of a misdemeanor.

S. 22 (2).

22. A legally qualified medical practitioner who has attended at a coroner's inquest in obedience to a summons of the coroner under this Act shall be entitled to receive such remuneration as follows; that is to say,

Fees to medical witnesses.

(*a*.) For attending to give evidence at any inquest whereat no post-mortem examination has been made by such practitioner, one guinea; and

(*b*.) For making a post-mortem examination of the body of the deceased, with or without an analysis of the contents of the stomach or intestines, and for attending to give evidence thereon, two guineas:

Provided that—

(1.) Any fee or remuneration shall not be paid to a medical practitioner for the performance of a post-mortem examination instituted without the previous direction of the coroner:

(2.) Where an inquest is held on the body of a person who has died in a county or other lunatic asylum, or in a public hospital, infirmary, or other

S. 23. medical institution, or in a building or place belonging thereto, or used for the reception of the patients thereof, whether the same be supported by endowments or by voluntary subscriptions, the medical officer, whose duty it may have been to attend the deceased person as a medical officer of such institution as aforesaid, shall not be entitled to such fee or remuneration.

Public institutions.

This section does not define very clearly the institutions to which it is intended to apply. It has been held by a County Court judge that the sick wards of a workhouse are within the terms of the enactment, but among other institutions, such as prisons, military hospitals, public schools, training colleges, almshouses and asylums for the aged, dispensaries, cottage hospitals, and nurses' homes, doubts may well arise as to whether the medical officer is entitled to claim any fee.

In the not unfrequent case of an accident happening in the street, and death resulting before the body reaches the public hospital to which it is being carried, the medical officer of the hospital may be summoned under section 21, sub-s. (1), as an expert to give his opinion as to the cause of death, and in such case he would be entitled to the usual fee.

Penalty on medical practitioner for neglecting to attend.

23. Where a medical practitioner fails to obey a summons of a coroner issued in pursuance of this Act, he shall, unless he shows a good and sufficient cause for not having obeyed the same, be liable on summary conviction on the prosecution of the coroner or of any two of the jury, to a fine not exceeding five pounds.

It does not appear whether this section (which re-enacts 6 & 7 Will. 4, c. 89, s. 6,) is intended to be in addition to, or in substitution for, the powers conferred by section 19 (which re-enacts 7 & 8 Vict. c. 92, s. 17,) for securing the attendance of witnesses generally. It is submitted that the provisions of section 19 are wide enough to cover medical practitioners ; and, if so, the trouble and inconvenience of instituting a prosecution in which the decision as to the necessity of summoning the medical practitioner would rest with the justices instead of with the coroner would practically make this section a dead letter.

S. 24.

24. Where a place has been provided by a sanitary authority or nuisance authority for the reception of dead bodies during the time required to conduct a post-mortem examination, the coroner may order the removal of a dead body to and from such place for carrying out such examination, and the cost of such removal shall be deemed to be part of the expenses incurred in and about the holding of an inquest.

Removal of body for post-mortem examination.

A difficulty is sometimes experienced in finding a place to deposit the body for examination—innkeepers not being bound to receive a dead body. It seems to be the common law duty of the parish officers to provide some place, and therefore it is suggested that if no other convenient place can be found the body may be left at the house of the churchwarden of the parish. By the Public Health Act, 1875,[1] the sanitary authority is empowered to provide and maintain a proper place (otherwise than at a workhouse or at a mortuary) for the reception of dead

Where post-mortem may be held.

---

[1] 38 & 39 Vict. c. 55, s. 143 ; and in the Metropolis, 29 & 30 Vict. c. 90, s. 28.

S. 26. bodies during the time required to conduct any post-mortem examination ordered by a coroner, and to make regulations with respect to the management of such place.

Expenses and Returns of Inquests.

Schedule of fees and disbursements payable on holding inquest.

25. The local authority for a county or borough from time to time may make, and when made may alter and vary, a schedule of fees, allowances, and disbursements which on the holding of an inquest may lawfully be paid and made by the coroner holding such inquest (other than the fees payable to medical witnesses in pursuance of this Act), and the local authority shall cause a copy of every such schedule to be deposited with the clerk of the peace of the county or with the town clerk of the borough, and one other copy thereof to be delivered to every coroner concerned.

Payment of expenses by coroner.

26. A coroner holding an inquest shall immediately after the termination of the proceedings pay the fees of every medical witness not exceeding the fees fixed by this Act, and all expenses reasonably incurred in and about the holding thereof, not exceeding the sums set forth in the schedule of fees for the time being in force under this Act, and the sums so paid shall be repaid to the coroner in manner provided by this Act.

Medical analysis.

The fees of medical witnesses are fixed by section 22. If it appears necessary that further expenses should be incurred, as for example where a more exhaustive examination or analysis is required, the coroner should obtain the permission of the local authority beforehand.

By the 7 & 8 Vict. c. 92, s. 21, the sessions are empowered to order payment to a county coroner of travelling allowances where he has "been compelled,[1] in the discharge of his office, to travel from his usual place of abode for the purpose of taking an inquisition, but which in the exercise of his discretion he deemed to be unnecessary and declined to take."

S. 2.
Travelling expenses where no inquest held.

27.—(1.) Every coroner shall, within four months after holding an inquest, cause a full and true account of all sums paid by him under this Act to be laid before the local authority of the county or borough by whom the sums are to be reimbursed to him.

Coroners to lay their accounts before the local authority.

(**2.**) Every account shall be accompanied by such vouchers as under the circumstances may to the local authority seem reasonable, and the local authority may, if they think fit, examine the said coroner on oath as to the account, and on being satisfied of the correctness thereof, the local authority shall order their treasurer to pay to the coroner the sum due to him on such account, with the addition, in the case of a coroner of a borough, of six shillings and eight pence for each inquest; and the treasurer shall pay the same out of the local rate, without any abatement or deduction whatever, and shall be allowed the same on passing his accounts.

It has been held[2] that the local authority[3] were the

---

[1] See *R.* v. *JJ. of Oxford*, 2 B. & Ald. 213 ; *R.* v. *JJ. of Warwick*, 5 B. & C. 430.
[2] *R.* v. *Justices of Gloucester-shire*, 7 E. & B. 805 ; 27 L. J., M. C. 15.
[3] Now, under the 51 & 52 Vict. c. 41, the council.

J.   H

S. 28. proper judges of whether a coroner had acted rightly in
        holding an inquest, so as to entitle him to his fee of
        twenty shillings ; but under this sub-section, actual dis-
        bursements which had been made by the coroner after the
        termination of the inquest (such as the fees of medical
        witnesses, the payment of the jurors, for the hire of rooms,
        and such like), stand on a different footing, and it has
        been held that they must be repaid to him, whether it
        was proper that such inquest should be held or not, and
        that the local authority has no power to disallow them ;
        the power of examining the coroner on oath being only as
        to the fact of the expenses having been incurred, and not
        as to the propriety of holding the inquest.[1] The principle
        of this decision applies also to the fee of six and eight-
        pence to which borough coroners are entitled under this
        section for every inquest held by them.

Coroners to   **28.** Every coroner of a borough shall on or before
make yearly
returns to   the first day of February in every year make and
Secretary of
State.   transmit to a Secretary of State a return in writing,
        in such form and containing such particulars as the
        Secretary of State from time to time directs, of all
        cases in which an inquest has been held by him, or
        by some person in lieu of him, during the year end-
        ing on the thirty-first day of December immediately
        preceding.

        It appears to be also the practice for county coroners
        to make a similar return, but this is not done in pur-
        suance of any statutory obligation.

        ---

        [1] *Reg.* v. *Justices of Carmar-*   upon the similar provisions of
        thenshire, 10 Q. B. 796 ; decided   the repealed statute.

Coroner of the Queen's Household.

29.—(1.) The coroner of Her Majesty the Queen's household shall continue to be appointed by the Lord Steward for the time being of the Queen's household.

(**2.**) The coroner of the Queen's household shall have exclusive jurisdiction in respect of inquests on persons whose bodies are lying within the limits of any of the Queen's palaces or within the limits of any other house where Her Majesty is then demurrant and abiding in her own royal person, notwithstanding the subsequent removal of Her Majesty from such palace or house.

(**3.**) The jurors on an inquest held by the coroner of the Queen's household, shall consist of officers of the Queen's household, to be returned by such officer of the Queen's household as may be directed to summon the same by the warrant of the said coroner.

(**4.**) The limits of the said palace or house shall be deemed to extend to any courts, gardens, or other places within the curtilage of such palace or house but not further, and where a body is lying dead in any place beyond those limits, the coroner of the Queen's household shall not have jurisdiction to hold an inquest on such body, and the coroner of the county or borough shall have jurisdiction to hold that inquest in the same manner as if that place were not within the verge.

(5.) Where the inquisition charges a person with murder or manslaughter, the coroner of the Queen's household shall deliver the inquisition, depositions, and recognizances to the Lord Steward of the Queen's household, or in his absence, to the treasurer and comptroller of the Queen's household, and the recognizances shall be taken for the appearance of the persons bound by them before the said Lord Steward, or in his absence before the said treasurer and comptroller.

(6.) All other inquisitions, depositions, and recognizances, shall be delivered to the Lord Steward of the Queen's household to be filed among the records of his office.

(7.) The coroner of the Queen's household shall make his declaration of office before the Lord Steward of the Queen's household, and shall reside in one of the Queen's palaces, or in such other convenient place as may from time to time be allowed by the Lord Steward of the Queen's household.

(8.) Save as is in this section specially provided, the coroner of the Queen's household shall, within the said limits, have the same jurisdiction and powers, be subject to the same obligations, liabilities, and disqualifications, and generally to the provisions of this Act and to the law relating to coroners in like manner as any other franchise coroner.

(9.) The Lord Steward of the Queen's household, or the treasurer and comptroller of the Queen's

household, shall not have any jurisdiction to inquire
of, try, hear, or determine, any offence committed
beyond the limits aforesaid, or to array, try, or give
judgment upon any person charged by any inquisition found before a coroner for any place beyond
the limits aforesaid, and every such offence shall be
inquired of, tried, heard, determined, and every such
person shall be arraigned, tried, and have judgment
according to the ordinary course of law.

Franchise Coroners.

30.—(**1.**) Where a franchise coroner is, at the
passing of this Act, paid a salary out of the local
rate, the provisions of this Act with respect to the
expenses of inquests, shall apply as if such coroner
were a coroner for a county.

(**2.**) Nothing in this Act shall affect the remuneration to which a franchise coroner who is not at the
passing of this Act paid a salary out of the local
rate is entitled at the passing of this Act, and every
such coroner shall continue to be entitled to receive
the same fees, allowances, and remuneration as he
would have been entitled to if this Act had not
passed.

(**3.**) Nothing in this Act shall affect the mode in
which a franchise coroner is appointed, or is, otherwise than is provided by this Act, removed.

(**4.**) Subject as aforesaid, the provisions of this
Act shall apply to a franchise coroner, except those

S 30.

Saving for remunera-
tion of fran-
chise coro-
ners.

S. 30. provisions in which a coroner for a county or a coroner of a borough is expressly named.

Franchise coroners are defined in section 42. They comprise all coroners other than the county coroners who are elected by the freeholders, the borough coroners who are appointed by the respective town councils, and the justices of the High Court who are coroners by virtue of their office. Their jurisdiction is confined to the particular precinct over which they are appointed, and depends upon the terms of the grant in each particular liberty. Where the lord of a franchise, or the head or chief of a corporation, personally discharges this office, whatever be the case with respect to his other duties, yet if he take an inquisition super visum corporis, he must entitle himself "coroner" upon the record, for otherwise the inquisition will be erroneous, and coram non judice; for, except as coroner, he has no authority, even though both offices be vested in the same person.[1] And depositions taken on an inquisition before a mayor quà coroner are not admissible unless by the proceedings he appear to have acted as coroner.[2]

The privilege of appointing a franchise coroner may be claimed by the Crown by prescription, but such a franchise is of so high a nature that no subject can claim it otherwise than by grant from the Crown.[3] This privilege was expressly exempted from the operation of the statute 28 Edw. 3, c. 6, which confirmed to the county the power of electing coroners, and from that of the subsequent statutes relating to the election of county coroners, and from the present act;[4] and therefore the Queen, within certain precincts, and the lords of franchises, in all

---

[1] Bro. Ab. "*Nosme*," 50; 22 E. 4, 12.
[2] 1 C. Cas. 306.
[3] Co. Lit. 114 a; 2 Hawk. P. C. c. 9, s. 11; 9 Rep. 29 b.
[4] 7 & 8 Vict. c. 92, s. 29; 23 & 24 Vict. c. 116, s. 9.

S. 30.

cases in which they were formerly empowered to nominate and appoint their own coroners, may, notwithstanding the provisions of these statutes, exercise the same authority at this day.

Thus the mayor and commonalty of London may by charter elect a coroner for London ; and the Cinque Ports, from their great antiquity, have their own coroner. The dean and chapter of Westminster have their own coroner, who, by their appointment, is coroner for the city and liberty of Westminster. In the stannaries in Cornwall the wardens are coroners. The master of the crown office, or clerk of the Crown, still retains the title of the queen's coroner, and used, before the passing of the Prison Act, 1865,[1] to have jurisdiction over matters arising within the Queen's Bench prison. He holds his office by letters patent under the great seal. By section 257 of the Municipal Corporations Act, 1882,[2] the privileges of the Universities of Oxford and Cambridge are reserved, the former of which still accordingly appoints its own two coroners.

There are also other exclusive jurisdictions and corporations for which coroners are appointed ; although by the Municipal Corporations Act, 1883,[3] many of the latter are abolished.

The two principal franchise coroners are those of the Verge. Admiralty, and of the Queen's household, both of whom were appointed by letters patent. The appointment of the latter was by statute 33 Hen. 8, c. 12, settled in perpetuity on the lord steward, and is now dealt with by section 29 of this Act.

Of the Admiralty the president of the Admiralty Admiralty. Division of the High Court is appointed coroner by letters patent, which empower him to take cognizance of and

---

[1] 28 & 29 Vict. c. 126, s. 48.   [3] 46 & 47 Vict. c. 18.
[2] 45 & 46 Vict. c. 50.

decide of wreck of the sea, great or small, and of the death, drowning, and view of dead bodies of all persons whatsoever in the sea, or public rivers, ports, fresh-waters, or creeks whatsoever, within the ebbing and flowing of the sea and high water mark, throughout the kingdom and the jurisdiction of the admiralty, together with the custody and conservation of the statutes concerning wreck of the sea, and the office of coroner made in the 3 & 4 Edw. I. He is also empowered to appoint deputies, whose appointment is usually in the same terms, and their jurisdiction therefore extends to matters within the duty of the coroner, arising upon the open sea, or between the high and low water mark when the tide is in ; but when the tide is out, the authority of the coroner of the county attaches in such places.[1]

By the common law, the coroner of the county had jurisdiction in matters arising on the arms of the sea, infra corpus comitatûs, exclusive of the coroner of the admiralty ;[2] according to some authorities, in all cases where one shore might have been seen from the other ;[3] but, by others, only where a man standing upon the one side might see what was done on the other.[4] Upon such places, the coroner of the admiralty had originally no jurisdiction, but it was conferred by the stat. 15 Rich. 2, c. 3, which enacts that " of the death of man and maihem in great ships hovering in the main streams in great rivers, below the bridges, near to the sea, the admiral shall have jurisdiction."

Concurrent jurisdiction of county or borough coroner.
But this is not exclusive of the county or borough coroner, who had a concurrent jurisdiction with the coroner of the admiralty, and may still take an inquisition in great rivers of the death of man and maihem, to

---

[1] 3 Inst. 113 ; 5 Rep. 107.   51 ; Hale, Sum. 151.
[2] 3 Hale, P. C. 15, 54.   [4] F. Cor. 399 ; 5 Inst. 140 ; 2
[3] Owen, 122 ; Moor. 892 ; 2   Roll. Abr. 169.
Hale, P. C. 54 ; Staund. P. C.

which alone the statute applies.[1] It extends only to rivers that are arms of the sea, that flow and reflow, and bear great ships; and does not apply to deaths which happen in small vessels, but to great ships only.[2] The body of A. was taken up drowned at St. Katherine's, on the river Thames, below the bridge: the coroner of the admiralty having taken an inquisition upon a view of the body, which was found to have been drowned by accident, the coroner of the county afterwards demanded the body, that he might take an inquisition, which the coroner of the admiralty refused to permit, and had the body buried. This was complained of as an abuse, the admiralty having no jurisdiction unless the death happened in a great ship; and an attachment was granted against the coroner of the admiralty.[3]

Portsmouth harbour has been decided to be infra corpus comitatûs; and the Court of King's Bench granted an information against the captain of a ship lying there, for obstructing the coroner of that place, who attempted to enter the ship for the purpose of taking a view of the body lying dead there, no inquisition having previously been taken by the coroner of the admiralty.[4]

Where the jurisdiction of the county or borough coroner and of the admiralty is concurrent, the coroner who first obtains possession of the body should take the inquisition ; and if he proceed to do so, the authority of the other is determined.

It seems to have been a matter of great doubt at common law, where the mortal stroke or poison which occasioned the death was given or administered at sea, and the party died on shore, or vice versâ, whether either jurisdiction could try the offender. The admiral

Coroner within whose jurisdiction body lies, to hold inquest.

---

[1] 2 Hale, P. C. 15, 16, 54 ; 8 E. 2, Cor. 399.
[2] Ibid.

[3] Cited Umf. Lex Cor. 63.
[4] 2 Str. 1097 ; Andrews, 231.

S. 33.   had no authority, for the death, which consummated the offence, occurred on land ; so neither had the common law, for the causa causans was not infra corpus comitatûs.[1] To prevent any failure of justice in such cases certain statutes, now repealed, were passed, and the law upon the subject is at present regulated by section 7 of the present act.

Provisions as to expenses of inquests to extend to city of London.
31. The provisions of this Act with respect to the expenses of inquests shall apply to the city of London and the borough of Southwark.[2]

Payment of travelling expenses of coroner in Cinque Ports where inquisition is not taken.
32. Where a coroner appointed and acting for the jurisdiction of the Cinque Ports who is not paid a salary out of the local rate in lieu of allowances deems it unnecessary to hold and declines to hold an inquest, and shows to the justices in general or quarter sessions assembled that he had nevertheless been compelled in the discharge of his office to travel from his usual place of abode for the purpose of taking that inquest, such justices may order the payment to that coroner of the same allowances for travelling as might be allowed in any other case.

Savings and Miscellaneous.

Saving as to borough coroners. 45 & 46 Vict. c. 50.
33. Nothing in this Act shall affect the application to coroners of a borough of the provisions of the Municipal Corporations Act, 1882, with respect to the appointment, qualification, tenure of office, and payment of a coroner of a borough, and the appointment of a deputy by such coroner.

[1] 1 Hale, P. C. 426 ; 1 East, P. C. 355.
[2] See 51 & 52 Vict. c. 41, ss. 40-45.

By section 171 of the Municipal Corporations Act, 1882,[1] it is provided that "the council of a borough having a separate court of quarter sessions[2] shall, within ten days next after the receipt of the grant thereof by the council, and thenceforward from time to time, appoint a fit person, not an alderman or councillor of the borough, to be coroner of the borough."

S. 33.

Appointment of borough coroner.

"The coroner shall hold office during good behaviour."

"A vacancy in the office shall be filled up within ten days after it occurs."

"The coroner shall have, by order of the recorder, remuneration (subject to the provisions of any other act relating to coroners[3]) for every inquisition which he duly takes in the borough, twenty shillings, and for every mile exceeding two miles which he is compelled to travel from his usual place of abode to take such inquisition, ninepence;" to which is added under section 27, sub-s. (2) of the present Act, a further sum of six-and-eightpence for each inquest.

Fees.

It may be observed that the above section does not impose any qualification by estate, residence, or otherwise, but leaves the council entire discretion. By the 7th section of the present Coroners Act the borough coroner has (except in admiralty cases), exclusive jurisdiction to hold inquests within the borough. By section 28 he must make to the Secretary of State a yearly return of inquests held.

Qualification.

Jurisdiction.

It seems that a borough coroner is not a "corporate officer" within the meaning of the Statutes of Limitation.[4]

By section 172 of the same Municipal Corporations Act, 1882, it is enacted that "in case of illness or unavoidable absence the coroner shall appoint by writing signed by him a fit person, being a barrister or solicitor,

---

[1] 45 & 46 Vict. c. 50.
[2] Now limited to the "larger boroughs;" see p. 69.
[3] See s. 25 of Coroners Act.
[4] *Reg.* v. *Grimshaw*, 10 Q. B 747.

and not an alderman or councillor of the borough, to act
for him as deputy coroner during his illness or unavoidable absence, but not longer or otherwise."

"The mayor or two justices for the borough shall on
each occasion certify by writing signed by him or them
the necessity for the appointment of a deputy coroner.
This certificate shall state the cause of absence of the
coroner, and shall be openly read to every inquest jury
summoned by the deputy coroner."

Saving
clause as to
official
coroners.
34. Nothing in this Act shall prejudice the jurisdiction of a judge exercising the jurisdiction of a
coroner by virtue of his office, and such judge may,
notwithstanding the passing of this Act, exercise
any jurisdiction, statutable or otherwise, previously
exerciseable by him, in the same manner as if this
Act had not passed.

The Lord Chief Justice of England is, by virtue of his
office, supreme coroner over all England, and the justices
of the High Court are by the' same authority sovereign
coroners. The jurisdiction of these high officers extends
over the whole realm and within the Queen's Household,
and all other exempt jurisdictions and franchises.[1] But
they have no power to delegate their authority, which
can be exercised in person only.

Saving of
jurisdiction.
as to re-
moval of
coroner, or
otherwise
in relation
to a coroner.
35. Nothing in this Act shall prejudice the jurisdiction of the Lord Chancellor or the High Court
of Justice in relation to removing a coroner otherwise than in manner provided by this Act, or in any
manner prejudice or affect the jurisdiction of the
High Court of Justice or of any judge thereof in
relation to or over a coroner or his duties.

---

[1] 4 Rep. 47.

The provisions of this Act relating to the removal of
coroners are contained in section 8, which is declaratory
of the common law, and of the power of the Chancellor to
issue writs de coronatore exonerando, which is established
by constant usage.[1] The only jurisdiction which is not
in terms preserved in section 8, appears to be the power
of the High Court to treat any misdemeanour on the
part of a coroner as a contempt of court, and to visit it
accordingly with censure or other punishment.

36. A coroner shall continue as heretofore to
have jurisdiction to inquire of treasure that is found,
who were the finders, and who suspected thereof,
and the provisions of this Act shall, so far as consis-
tent with the tenor thereof, apply to every such
inquest.

By the statute 4 Edw. 1 it was enacted that a coroner
ought to inquire of treasure that is found, who were the
finders, and likewise who is suspected thereof; and that
may be well perceived where one liveth riotously, haunting
taverns, and hath done so of long time; hereupon he
may be attached for this suspicion by four or six or more
pledges, if they may be found.[2]

Treasure trove is where any gold or silver coin, plate,
or bullion is found concealed in a house, or in the earth,
or other private place, the owner thereof being unknown,
in which case the treasure belongs to the Queen or her
grantee having the franchise of treasure trove; but if he
that laid it down be known or afterwards discovered, th
owner and not the Queen is entitled to it; this prerogative right only applying in the absence of an owner to
claim the property.[3] If the owner instead of hiding the

S. 36.

Inquest on
treasure
trove.

---

[1] See *Ex parte Parnell*, 1 J.
& W. 455.
[2] 2 Hawk. P. C. c. 9, s. 36.
See Form of Inquisition, App.,
Form 8.
[3] 3 Inst. 132 ; Dalton's
Sheriffs, c. 16 ; 1 Bl. Com. 295.

treasure has casually lost it, or parted with it in such a
manner that it is evident he intended to abandon the
property altogether, and did not purpose to resume it on
another occasion,—as if he threw it on the ground, or
other public place, or in the sea,—the first finder is
entitled to the property as against every one but the
owner, and the royal prerogative does not in this respect
obtain.[1] So that it is the hiding and not the abandon-
ment of the property that entitles the Queen to it.

It is the duty of every person who finds any treasure
or has knowledge that any treasure has been found, to
make it known to the coroner of the district. The
punishment for concealing it is fine and imprisonment.[2]

Effect of
Schedules.

37. The Schedules to this Act shall be construed
and have effect as part of this Act, and the forms
given in any of those schedules, or such other forms
as the Lord Chancellor from time to time directs,
may be used in all matters to which they apply, and
when so used shall be sufficient in law.

The first schedule relating to the election of county
coroners, is repealed by the Local Government Act of
1888. The second schedule gives the first four of the
forms as printed in the Appendix. The third schedule
contains a list of acts repealed which it is not considered
necessary to set out in this work.

Definitions.

Construc-
tion of Act
with respect
to counties.

38. In this Act the expression "county," unless
there is something inconsistent in the context, does
not include a county of a city or a county of a town,

---

[1] Brit. c. 17 ; Finch, L. 171 ;
1 Bl. Com. 295 ; Stra. 505.
[2] 3 Inst. 133 ; 1 Bla. Com.
296; *R.* v. *Thomas*, 9 Cox, C. C.

376, where also the inquisition
and indictment are set out in
full.

but includes any division or liberty of a county which has a separate court of quarter sessions for which a separate coroner has customarily been elected, but the whole of Yorkshire and the whole of Lincoln shire shall respectively be a county for the purposes of this Act.

The counties in Wales, and the counties of Durham and Chester, and the liberty of the Isle of Ely shall, save as is otherwise expressly provided by this Act, be, for the purposes of this Act and any other Act relating to coroners, subject to the same provisions as the other counties of England, and the coroners thereof shall have the same jurisdiction as other coroners in England ; and for the purpose of the provisions of any Act with respect to coroners' districts, a ward in the county of Durham shall be deemed to be a coroner's district in that county.

39. This Act and any other Act relating to coroners shall apply to the county of Lancaster in like manner as it applies to the other counties of England, subject as follows :

S. 39.

Provision for application of Act to county of Lancaster.

(1.) The provisions of this Act with respect to the Lord Chancellor shall be construed in the case of the said county to mean the Chancellor of the Duchy and county palatine of Lancaster, and all writs relating to coroners issued by that Chancellor shall be issued by such persons and in such manner as the Chancellor and the council of the Duchy of Lancaster from time to time direct :

(2.) An Order in Council with respect to coroners'

districts in the county of Lancaster shall be made on the recommendation of the Chancellor and council of the Duchy of Lancaster.

Provisions
as to de-
tached parts
of counties.
40.—(**1.**) For the purpose of holding coroners' inquests every detached part of a county shall be deemed to be within the county by which it is wholly surrounded, or where it is partly surrounded by two or more counties, within the county with which it has the longest common boundary.

(**2.**) The treasurer of every county shall keep an account of all expenses occasioned to such county by any inquest in or in respect to any such detached part of any other county, and shall twice in every year send a copy of such account to the treasurer of the other county to which such detached part belongs, and the last-mentioned treasurer shall, out of the moneys in his hand as such treasurer, pay to the treasurer sending the account the sum appearing thereby to be due, together with all reasonable charges for making and sending the account.

(**3.**) Any difference which may arise concerning the said account, if not adjusted by agreement, shall be determined by an arbitrator, who shall be a barrister-at-law nominated on the application of either party by one of the justices of assize of the last preceding circuit or of the next succeeding circuit. Such arbitrator must adjourn the hearing from time to time, and require all such information from either party as appears to him necessary, and his award shall be final. He shall also assess the

costs of the arbitration and direct by whom and out
of what fund the same shall be paid.

41. For the purposes of this Act—

(*a*.) The local authority of a county shall be the Definition of "local authority" and "local rate."
court of quarter sessions of the county ; and

(*b*.) The local authority of a borough shall be the
mayor, aldermen, and burgesses of the borough acting by the council ; and

(*c*.) The local rate shall be, in the case of a county,
the county rate, or rate in the nature of a county
rate, and, in the case of a borough, the borough fund
or borough rate ; and

(*d*.) In Lincolnshire and Yorkshire respectively the
justices in gaol sessions shall be the local authority,
and the clerk to such justices shall act as clerk of
the peace, and the rate in the nature of a county
rate levied by those sessions shall be the local rate.

These definitions must all be read subject to the pro- Definitions.
visions of the Local Government Act, 1888.

42. In this Act, if not inconsistent with the context, the following terms and expressions have the
meanings hereinafter respectively assigned to them ·

The expression " quarter sessions " includes "Quarter sessions"
general sessions.

The expression " borough " means any place for "Borough." 45 & 46 Vict. c. 50.
the time being subject to the Municipal Corporations
Act, 1882, and the Acts amending the same.

The expression " franchise coroner " means any "Franchise coroner."
of the following coroners, that is to say, the coroner of
the Queen's household, a coroner or deputy coroner

S. 43.   for the jurisdiction of the Admiralty, a coroner appointed by Her Majesty the Queen in right of her
Duchy of Lancaster, and a coroner appointed for a
town corporate, liberty, lordship, manor, university,
or other place, the coroner for which has heretofore
been appointed by any lord, or otherwise than by
election of the freeholders of a county, or of any part
of a county, or by the council of a borough, and the
expression "franchise" means the area within which
the franchise coroner exercises jurisdiction.

" Secretary   The expression " Secretary of State " means one
of State."   of Her Majesty's Principal Secretaries of State.

"Murder."   The expression "murder" includes the offence
of being an accessory before the fact to a murder.

"Parish."   The expression "parish" means a parish, township, or place for which a separate poor rate is or
can be made, or for which a separate overseer is or
can be appointed.

The expression "the Lord Chancellor" means
the Lord High Chancellor of Great Britain.

The expression " Registration Acts " means the
Acts for the time being in force relating to the re
gistration of deaths, inclusive of any enactment
amending the same.

Temporary Provisions and Repeal.

Saving as to   **43.** Nothing in this Act shall affect the law re-
coroners'
salaries and   specting the salaries of coroners for counties, or the
districts.
division of a county into coroners' districts, or the
rights and duties of coroners as respects such districts.

Anciently, this office was of so great dignity, that no coroners would condescend to be paid for serving their country;[1] and accordingly, by the statute Westm. 1, c. 10, which is in affirmance of the common law, it was enacted, that no coroner demand any thing of any man to do his office, upon pain of great forfeiture to the king.[2] Although no remuneration was in ancient times received by coroners for their labour and trouble, yet they were entitled to one penny from every visne, when they came before the justices in eyre, as appertaining to their office, for and towards their travail, attendance and charges. " This contribution," observes Sir E. Coke, " was neither against the common law, nor the statute of Westm. 1, c. 10, for they took it not for doing their office, but as a right due to their office, which might have a reasonable beginning." [3]

Subsequently, however, from time to time statutes were passed entitling coroners to certain fees. The 3 Hen. 7, c. 1, s. 4, after reciting that " forasmuch as coroners had not, nor ought to have any thing by the law for their office doing, which ofttime hath been the occasion that coroners have been remiss in doing their office," ordains " that a coroner have for his fee, upon every inquisition taken upon the view of the body slain, thirteen shillings and fourpence of the goods and chattels of him that is the slayer and murderer, if he have any goods; and if he have no goods, then the coroner have for his said fee of such amerciaments as shall fortune any township for escape of such murderer as is aforesaid ;" the policy of which enactment was condemned by Lord Coke in strong terms.[4] In later times this fee, which was originally the equivalent probably of about £8 of modern money, was found to be an inadequate remuneration, and

---

[1] 1 Bl. Com. 347.
[2] 2 Inst. 173, 176.
[3] 2 Inst. 176.
[4] 2 Inst. 176, 209.

S. 43.

the amount was fixed by the 25 Geo. 2, c. 29, at twenty shillings, with ninepence a mile for travelling expenses.

But great difficulty and inconvenience having been found to result from the payment of county coroners by fees, the system was at length put an end to as regards them by 23 & 24 Vict. c. 116, by section 4 of which it is enacted that "there shall be paid to every county coroner, in lieu of the fees, mileage and allowances which if this act had not been passed he would have been entitled to receive, such an annual salary as shall be agreed upon between him and the justices" (now the county council [1]) "for the county for which, or for some portion of which, such coroner shall act, such salary in the case of any person holding the office of county coroner at the time of the passing of this act not being less than the average amount of the fees, mileage and allowances actually received by such coroner and his predecessors, if any, for the five years immediately preceding the 31st day of December, 1859 : and such salary shall be paid quarterly to such coroner by the treasurer of the county out of the county rate ; and whenever from death, removal, or any other cause whatever, any county coroner shall not be entitled to a salary for the whole of a quarter, a proportionate part of the salary shall be paid to him, or in case of his death to his personal representatives : provided always, that in case any such [council] and any such county coroner as aforesaid shall be unable to agree as to the amount of the salary to be paid to such coroner, it shall be lawful for her Majesty's principal secretary of state for the home department, and he is required, upon the application of such coroner, to fix and determine the amount of such salary, having regard to such average as aforesaid, also the average number of inquests held by any such coroner in the preceding five years as aforesaid,

Annual
salary of
county
coroner.

---

[1] 51 & 52 Vict. c. 41, s. 3.

and also to the special circumstances of each case, and
the general scale of salaries of county coroners : provided
also, that after the lapse of every successive period of five
years it shall be lawful for any such [council] and such
coroner as aforesaid to revise, and thereby increase or
diminish any such salary, having regard to the average
number of inquests held by any such coroner in the five
years immediately preceding, and subject, in case of their
disagreement, to such appeal to the home secretary as
before mentioned."

§. 43.
Revision of
salary.

It has been held that the words of the above enactment as to the salary of the county coroner, when first
fixed, being not less than the average amount of fees
actually received for the five years preceding, are not to
be extended so as to govern the subsequent proviso relating to readjustment of the salary at the end of successive
periods of five years ; but that in such cases all the circumstances might be taken into account and the amount
fixed at less than the average of the fees, mileage, and
allowances during the five years immediately preceding.[1]

Provision is made for the payment of the expenses
and disbursements connected with coroners' inquests by
section 27 of the present Act. As to other fees, see
under section 17.

The division of counties into districts is regulated by
the 7 & 8 Vict. c. 92. Inasmuch as no specific number
of coroners is limited by law for each county, it is competent for the lord chancellor to issue a writ de coronatore
eligendo for the election of one or more additional coroners,
if the business of the county require that their number
should be increased. The writ in this case may be
obtained in the same manner as in other cases, but it is
now under such circumstances more usual to subdivide
the county under the provisions of the above statute.

Division of
counties in-
to districts.

---

[1] *Ex parte Driffield*, L. R., 7 Q. B. 207.

S. 43.

Petition.

By sect. 2 of that Act, it is provided that " when and so often as it shall seem expedient to the [council] of any county [in England, sect. 30], that such county should be divided into two or more districts for the purposes of this Act, or that any alteration should be made of any division, theretofore made under this Act, it shall be lawful for the said [council] to resolve that a petition shall be presented to her Majesty, praying that such division or alteration be made, and thereupon to adjourn the further consideration of such petition until notice thereof shall be given to the coroner or coroners of such county, as hereinafter provided."

Preparation of petition.

The third section provides " that the clerk of the peace shall give notice of any such resolution to every coroner for such county, and of the time when the petition will be taken by the said [council] into consideration, and the [council] shall confer with every such coroner, who shall attend the meeting of the [council] for that purpose, touching such petition, having due regard to the size and nature of their employments, and such other circumstances as shall appear to the justices fit to be considered in carrying into execution the provisions of this Act ; and such petition, with a description of the several proposed districts, and of the boundaries thereof, with the reasons upon which the petition is founded, shall be certified to her Majesty under the hands and seals of two or more of the [council] present when such petition shall be agreed to, and the clerk of the [council] for such county shall forthwith give or send a true copy of such petition, certified under his hand, to every coroner for such county."

Division of counties.

The 4th section then empowers her Majesty, " if she shall think fit, with the advice of her privy council, after taking into consideration any such petition, and also any petition which may be presented to her by any coroner of the same county concerning such proposed division or alteration, or whenever it shall seem fit to her Majesty to direct the issue of a writ de coronatore eligendo for the purpose of authorizing the election of an additional coroner above the number of those who have been theretofore customarily elected in such county, to order that such county shall be divided into such and so many districts, for the purposes of this Act, as to her Majesty, with the advice aforesaid, shall seem expedient, and to give a name to each of such districts, and to determine at what place within each district the court for the election of coroner for such district shall be holden as hereinafter provided, and every such order shall be published in the London Gazette."

S. 43.

By the 5th section the council must "assign one of such districts to each of the persons holding the office of coroner in such county, and upon the death, resignation, or removal of any such person, each of his successors, and also every other person thereafter elected into the office of coroner in such county, shall be elected to and shall exercise the office of coroner, according to the provisions of this Act, and shall reside within the district in and for which he shall be so elected, or in some place wholly or partly surrounded by such district, or not more than two miles beyond the outer boundary of such district."

Districts to be assigned to coroners.

The 6th section enacts "that whenever it shall appear to her Majesty, with the advice aforesaid, and shall be set forth in the said order in council, that any such county has been customarily divided into districts for the purpose of holding inquests during the space of seven years before the passing of this Act, and it shall seem expedient to her Majesty, with the advice aforesaid, that the same division of the county be made under this Act, each of such districts shall be assigned to the coroner usually acting in and for the same district before the passing of this Act, but if it shall appear expedient to her Majesty

Provision for existing districts.

S. 45.   with the advice aforesaid, that a different division of such county be made, and any such coroner shall present a petition to her Majesty, praying for compensation to him for the loss of his emoluments arising out of such change it shall be lawful for her Majesty, with the advice aforesaid, to order the lord high treasurer or commissioners of her Majesty's treasury to assess the amount of compensation which it shall appear to him or them ought to be awarded to such coroner, and the amount of such compensation shall be paid by the treasurer of the county to such coroner, his executors or administrators, out of the county rate." [1]

Abolition of certain jurisdictions of the coroner.   **44.** A coroner shall not take pleas of the Crown nor hold inquests of royal fish nor of wreck nor of felonies except felonies on inquisitions of death ; and he shall not inquire of the goods of such as by the inquest are found guilty of murder or manslaughter, nor cause them to be valued and delivered to the township.

Pleas of the Crown were taken by coroners before the statute of Magna Charta, but by c. 17 of that statute their power in proceeding to trial and judgment was taken away and has never since been exercised. The forfeiture of felon's goods was comparatively recently abolished. Until the passing of this section, however, the jurisdiction of the coroner to inquire of royal fish and of wreck has never been abolished.

Repeal of Acts in schedule.   **45.** The Acts specified in the Third Schedule to this Act are hereby repealed, from and after the

----

[1] See *Reg.* v. *Lechmere*, 16 Q. B. 284.

passing of this Act, to the extent specified in the
third column of that schedule.

Provided that—

(**1.**) A coroner elected before the passing of this
Act, shall continue to hold office in like manner as
if he had been elected under this Act ; and

(**2.**) Any schedule of fees, allowances, and dis
bursements made by a local authority for a county
or borough before the passing of this Act shall,
until a schedule is made in pursuance of this Act, be
of the same effect as if the schedule had been made
in pursuance of this Act ; and

(**3.**) This repeal shall not affect—

    (*a.*) The past operation of any enactment here-
    by repealed, nor anything duly done or
    suffered under any enactment hereby re-
    pealed ; or

    (*b*) Any right, privilege, obligation, or liability
    acquired, accrued, or incurred under any en-
    actment hereby repealed ; or

    (*c.*) Any penalty, forfeiture, or punishment in-
    curred in respect of any offence committed
    against any enactment hereby repealed ; or

    (*d.*) Any inquest on any death which occurred
    before the commencement of this Act or an
    inquisition found thereon, or any investiga-
    tion, legal proceeding, or remedy in respect
    of any such right, privilege, obligation,
    liability, penalty, forfeiture, or punishment
    as aforesaid ; and any such inquest, investi-

gation, legal proceeding, and remedy, and the trial of any such inquisition, may be carried on as if this Act had not passed.

(4.) This repeal shall not revive any jurisdiction, office, duty, fee, franchise, liberty, custom, right, title, privilege, restriction, exemption, usage, practice, procedure, or other matter or thing not in force or existing at the passing of this Act.

(5.) Save in so far as is inconsistent with this Act, any principle or rule of law, or established jurisdiction, practice, or procedure, or existing usage, franchise, liberty, or custom, shall, notwithstanding the repeal of any enactment by this Act, remain in full force.

OUTLAWRY.

No allusion is made in this Act to the duties of the coroner in cases of outlawry, which although now very rarely,[1] if ever, used, is not abolished.[2] The entry of the judgment in outlawry is, and always has been, except in London, where by custom the recorder presides, per judicium coronatorum; it being the duty of the coroner to be present at the sheriff's county court, to pronounce judgment of outlawry upon the exigent, after quinto exactus, at the fifth court, if the defendant does not appear.[3]

Outlawry is a punishment inflicted on a person who is guilty of a contempt and contumacy, by refusing to be amenable to and abide by the justice of that court which has lawful authority to call him before it. As this is a crime of the highest nature, being an act of rebellion against the state and community of which the offender is a member, it subjects him to heavy forfeitures and disabilities;[4] and therefore, the consequences being so highly penal, the greatest particularity is required in the proceedings, and the slightest irregularity will be fatal.

The execution of the process in outlawry belongs especially to the office of sheriff;[5] and it would be foreign to the present treatise to trace the practice through the

---

[1] The last reported case was in 1867, *Ex parte Stoffel*, L. R., 3 Ch. 240.

[2] See Crown Office Rules of 1886, rr. 99 121.

[3] Wood's Inst. b. 4, c. 1.

See App., Form 9.

[4] Co. Litt. 128 ; 2 Roll. Abr. 802 ; Doct. & Stu. Dial. 2, c. 3.

[5] See Crown Office Rules of 1886, rr. 99—112.

different stages up to the period at which the duty of the coroner commences.

Where the sheriff has made a return of non est inventus to an order of arrest or attachment, a writ of exigi facias may issue; and thereupon, if the party fail to appear on or before the fifth county court or day of exaction under the writ, judgment of outlawry, or, if a woman, of waiver, is given by the coroners, or one of them. For this purpose one of the coroners must be personally present at the County Court.[1] If he fail to attend, he is liable to fine and imprisonment.

The calling upon the exigent may be by one coroner, and the judgment may be pronounced by one; but the entry and return must be in the name of all.[2] It has been said that the names of the coroners must be subscribed to the judgment of outlawry;[3] but they need not so appear upon the record of the outlawry,[4] if their names are stated:[5] for it will suffice, if, by the record, the judgment appear to have been pronounced by the coroners. In order that the judgment may appear from the record to have been pronounced by the coroners, their name of office must be stated upon the record;[6] and if it be not, the judgment will be erroneous, except in London, where the judgment is given by the recorder; in which case the mayor, who is coroner, need not be named.[7]

Having pronounced the judgment, the coroners are functi officio, the exigent, with the proceedings thereon, and the judgment of outlawry, being returned by the sheriff.[8]

It would appear from some authorities,[9] that a coroner

---

[1] 1 Britt. c. 14, s. 2 (edition by Nichols).
[2] Hob. 70; 1 Hale, P. C. 417; 2 Id. 55.
[3] 2 Hale, P. C. 204; 2 R. Abr. 802
[4] 4 T. R. 542.
[5] 4 T. R. 542; Cro. Jac. 528.
[6] Bac. Abr. Outl. E. 4, 1.
[7] Co. Litt. 288; Br. Utl. 31; Dyer, 317; 8 Rep. 126; 2 H. 7, 33; Cro. Eliz. 648.
[8] 4 T. R. 529, 530.
[9] 27 Ass. 47; Br. Utl. 38.

upon an inquisition found before him, might award process of outlawry; but this is doubted by Lord Hale;[1] and we find no instance, in comparatively modern times, of such a course having been adopted by a coroner. If the offender be taken, he is committed to gaol; but if he be not found, the coroner returns his inquisition to the next gaol delivery, when, if the offender, having in the mean time been taken, be in gaol, the justices of gaol delivery proceed against him; but if he be not in custody, the inquisition is certified into the crown office, from whence process of outlawry may be awarded against him.[2]

It has been said, that such credit is given to the coroner's record of the judgment in outlawry, that if the sheriff return a quinto exactus only upon the exigent, and the coroners, upon a certiorari directed to them, certify that the defendant has been outlawed, the return of the sheriff shall be amended by the certificate, upon which the consequences of outlawry shall attach;[3] but the contrary seems to have been held in one authority,[4] and in another the extent of this proposition is made the subject of doubt.[5]

RAILWAY ACCIDENTS.

Where a coroner holds or is about to hold an inquest on the death of any person occasioned by a railway accident, of which notice is required by the Railway Regulation Amendment Act, 1871, to be sent to the Board of Trade, and makes a written request to the Board of Trade they may appoint an inspector or some person possessing

---

[1] 2 Hale, P. C. 199.
[2] 2 Hale, P. C. 64.
[3] 2 Hale, P. C. 203; Latch. 210; Palm. 480; 2 Hawk. P.
C. c. 48, s. 27.
[4] Dyer, 223.
[5] 38 Ed. 3, 14.

legal or special knowledge to assist in holding such inquest, and such appointee acts as the assessor of the coroner, and must make his report to the Board of Trade as required by that Act.[1]

ACCIDENTS IN MINES AND BY EXPLOSIVES.

Coal mines. By the Coal Mines Regulation Act, 1887,[2] provisions are made with respect to coroners' inquests on the bodies of persons whose death may have been caused by explosions or accidents in or about mines. It is enacted that where loss of life occurs in or about any mine, whether above or below ground, to any person employed there by reason of any explosion of gas, or of any explosive, or of any steam boiler, or by reason of any accident whatever, it is the duty of the owner, agent, or manager of the mine to send notice thereof to the inspector of the district; and where the coroner holds an inquest upon a body of any person whose death may have been caused by any such accident, he must adjourn the inquest unless an inspector, or some person on behalf of the Secretary of State, is present to watch the proceedings. And at least four days before holding the adjourned inquest he must send to the inspector of the district notice in writing of the time and place of holding the adjourned inquest. The coroner, before the adjournment, may take evidence to identify the body, and may order the interment thereof. If an explosion or accident has not occasioned the death of more than one person, and the coroner has sent to the inspector of the district notice of the time and place of holding the inquest at such time as to reach the

---

[1] 34 & 35 Vict. c. 78, s. 8.   [2] 50 & 51 Vict. c. 58, s. 48.

ADDENDUM to face page 126.

RAILWAY ACCIDENTS.—Every coroner in England and Ireland within seven days after holding an inquest on the body of any person who is proved to have been killed on a railway or to have died in consequence of injuries received on a railway shall make to one of Her Majesty's Principal Secretaries of State, in such form as he may require, a return of the death and the cause thereof.—36 & 37 Vict. c. 76, s. 5.

inspector not less than twenty-four hours before the time of holding the same, it is not imperative on him to adjourn such inquest if the majority of the jury think it unnecessary. An inspector is at liberty at any such inquest to examine any witness, subject nevertheless to the order of the coroner. Where evidence is given at an inquest at which an inspector is not present of any neglect as having caused or contributed to the explosion or accident, or of any defect in or about the mine appearing to the coroner or jury to require a remedy, the coroner must send to the inspector of the district notice in writing of such neglect or default. Any person having a personal interest in, or employed in, or in the management of, the mine in which the explosion or accident occurred, is not qualified to serve on the jury empannelled on the inquest; and it is the duty of the constable or other officer not to summon any person disqualified under this provision, and it is the duty of the coroner not to allow any such person to be sworn or to sit on the jury.

The provisions of the Metalliferous Mines Regulation Act, 1872,[1] are almost identical with the foregoing.

Metalliferous mines.

With respect to coroners' inquests on the bodies of persons whose death may have been caused by the explosion of any explosive, or by any accident in connection with an explosive, similar provisions are made by the Explosives Act, 1875.[2] The word explosive is (in sect. 3) defined to mean "gunpowder, nitro-glycerine, dynamite, gun-cotton, blasting powders, fulminate of mercury or of other metals, coloured fires, and every other substance, whether similar to those above mentioned or not, used or manufactured with a view to produce a practical effect by explosion or a pyrotechnic effect, and includes fog-signals, fireworks, fuzes, rockets, percussion caps, detonators, cartridges, ammunition of all descriptions, and every adapta-

Explosive substances.

---

[1] 35 & 36 Vict. c. 77, s. 22.   [2] 38 & 39 Vict. c. 17, s. 65.

tion or preparation of an explosive as above defined."
These words are wide enough to include many cases to
which it is submitted they are not intended to apply;
cases of ordinary gunshot wounds, for example, would
hardly be held to be included, unless at least where the
weapon has burst.

CRIMINAL CASES.

Man who is naturally endowed with an understanding
and liberty of will, has in respect of those faculties
capacity to obey the laws of his country, and is conse
quently implicated in guilt, and exposed to punishment,
by the violation of them.   It is the consent of the will
which renders human actions commendable and culpable;
and as, where there is no law, there can be no transgres-
sion; so, regularly, where there is no will to commit an
offence, there can be no just reason to incur the penalty
of a law instituted for the punishment of offenders.

The liberty or choice of the will pre-supposes an act
of understanding; and therefore, inasmuch as no person
can be excused from the penalties attaching upon disobedience of the laws, unless he be expressly designated
and exempted by the laws themselves, it has been the
constant practice of all states and law-givers to prescribe
limits and bounds to general notions, and to define what
persons and actions are privileged or exempted from the
severity of the general punishment of penal laws, in
respect of their incapacities or defects, whether natural,
affected, accidental, or in respect of civil subjection.

These causes of exemption or privilege, founded upon
a defect or want of will, are reducible under five heads,
viz., infancy, insanity, civil subjection to the power
of others, ignorance, and misfortune.

Infants.   Although, in common parlance, and indeed by the law of England, both men and women are termed infants if within the age of twenty-one years;[1] yet, with respect to capital punishment, the incapacity of infants ceases upon their attaining the age of fourteen years; for, by presumption of law, they are then doli capaces, capable of discerning good from evil, and subject, with respect to their criminal actions, to the same rule of construction as others of a more mature age.[2]

Within the age of seven years, no infant can be guilty of felony, or be punished for any capital offence; for, within that age, he cannot, by presumption of law, be endowed with any discretion; against which presumption no averment can be received.[3] But between that age and the age of fourteen, the presumption of law, that an infant is doli incapax, and incapable of judging inter bonum et malum, may be rebutted by strong and pregnant evidence of a mischievous discretion; for the strength of understanding and judgment, and not the age, is the true criterion of the capacity of the delinquent to do evil or contract guilt.[4] But in cases of this nature, the evidence of a mischievous discretion, to rebut the primâ facie presumption of law arising from non-age, should be strong and pregnant, and such as to satisfy the jury of the capacity of the delinquent to discern good from evil.[5] Malitia supplet ætatem, and therefore, if circumstances of malice be proved to the satisfaction of the jury, a delinquent between the age of fourteen years and seven may be convicted of and punished for a capital offence.

Accordingly, it is said that an infant eight years old may be indicted for murder, and may be hanged for it;[6] and an infant between the age of eight and nine years

---

[1] Co. Litt. ss. 104, 259.
[2] 1 Hale, P. C. 25.
[3] Reg. 309 b; 1 Hale, P. C. 27, 28; I Hawk. P. C. c. 1, s. 1; 4 Bl. Com. 23.

[4] 4 Bl. Com. 23.
[5] 1 Hale, P. C. 26, 27; 4 Bl. Com. 23.
[6] Dalt. Just. c. 147.

J.

K

was executed for arson, he appearing to have been actuated
by malice and revenge, and to have perpetrated the offence
by craft and cunning.[1] So, a girl of thirteen was burnt
for killing her mistress :[2] and where an infant, nine years
of age, killed an infant of the like age, and confessed the
felony, it appearing upon examination that he had hid
both the blood and the body, the justices were of opinion
that he ought to be hanged, but respited the execution
that he might be pardoned.[3]

Effect of
finding of
infancy.

It has been said, that though a jury find an infant,
apparently wanting discretion, guilty of a felony, the Court
ex officio must discharge him ;[4] but this can only be
understood of a reprieve before judgment, or of a case
where the jury find the prisoner under seven years of age,
or that he did the fact and was under fourteen years of age
not having discretion to discern between good and evil ;
in which cases the Court may discharge him, because
there would be no felony.[5] Without a special finding,
the Court has no authority to dismiss an infant convicted
by a jury, but can only respite the execution, and recom-
mend him for a pardon ; which is said by a learned author
to be the proper course, even where the jury return a
special finding.[6]

If an infant, under the age of seven, or between that
age and fourteen, not having discretion to discern between
good and evil, be arraigned upon an indictment found by
the grand inquest, the petit jury may find him not guilty
generally, or find the special matter and conclude non per
feloniam ;[7] but if he be arraigned upon the coroner's inquisition for murder or manslaughter, they ought regularly
to find the special matter ; for if they find the party kill-

---

[1] 1 Hale, P. C. 25 (edit. by
Emlyn).
[2] 1 Hale, P. C. 25.
[3] Fitz. Cor. 57, 118 ; see Fost.
C. L. 70 ; 4 Bl. Com. 24 ; *R.* v.
Wild, 1 Mood. C. C. 452 ; *R.* v.
Owen, 4 C. & P. 236. See also

R. v. *York,* Fost. C. L. 70.
[4] 35 H. 6, 11, 12.
[5] 1 Hale, P. C. 27 ; 1 Hawk.
P. C. c. 1, s. 8.
[6] 1 Russ. on Crimes, 5th ed.
113, note (*i*).
[7] 21 H. 7, 31 ; Bro. Ab. Cor. 61.

ing not guilty, they must inquire how the party slain came to his death.[1] If the grand jury ignore the bill, it seems the fact may be pleaded to the arraignment upon the coroner's inquisition ; but it is unusual in such cases to proceed to trial.

Every person at the age of discretion is, unless the con- Insanity. trary be proved, presumed by law to be sane, and to be accountable for his actions. But if there be an incapacity, or defect in the understanding, as there can be no consent of the will, so the act cannot be culpable. The question, whether compos mentis or not, is a question of fact for the jury upon the trial, but does not fall within the province of the coroner's jury except in cases of suicide, where the fact may be found by them and stated in the inquisition. In other cases, if they are of opinion that the acts done are such as, if they had been done by a person of sound mind, would have amounted to murder or manslaughter, it is their duty to find a verdict of murder or manslaughter, otherwise they do not afford to the public the security of the arrest of the accused person under the coroner's warrant, and his ultimate confinement if found insane by the jury at the trial.[2]

There is no necessity for producing evidence of insanity at the precise moment of the commission of the offence, provided no reason exist for suspecting the party to have been at that period a rational and accountable being.[3] Nor will he be criminally responsible if he become sane before the offence be completed, having committed the original act under the influence of a temporary delusion. If, therefore, a man non sanæ memoriæ give himself a mortal wound, and become sane before he die, he is not felo de se ; for, although the death completed the suicide, yet the law always respects the original act, and the death has relation to the stroke or wound.[4]

[1] 1 Hale, P. C. 28; 2 Id. 300 ; 195.
Co. Ent 356.   [3] 1 Collinson on Idiots, 480.
[2] R. v. Hodges, 8 C. & P.   [4] 1 Hale, P. C. 36, 412.

Drunken-
ness.

The vice of drunkenness, which deprives men of the use of reason, and throws them into a perfect, though temporary, frenzy or insanity, usually denominated dementia affectata, or acquired madness, so far from exensing the commission of any crime, aggravates the enormity of it ; and an offender under the influence of intoxication can derive no privilege from a madness voluntarily contracted, but is amenable to the justice of his country, equally as if he had been in the full possession of his senses at the time.[1] Qui peccat ebrius luat sobrius. Yet, if the primary cause of the frenzy be involuntary, or habitual and confirmed, this species of insanity with reference to crimes will excuse the offender equally as the former descriptions of this malady. Thus, for instance, if a person, through the unskilfulness of his physician, or the contrivance of his enemies, take that which may produce temporary frenzy, he will not be accountable for his actions whilst under the influence of it. So, neither will he be liable to punishment for the commission of any crime perpetrated under the influence of insanity which is habitual and fixed, though caused by frequent intoxication, and originally contracted by the vice and will of the party.[2] And the intoxication of the accused person may always be taken into consideration as a circumstance tending to show that his act was not premeditated;[3] or in cases where the question is whether what the law deems sufficient provocation has been given to extenuate an offence.[4]

Suicide.

The question of insanity is, however, as we have seen, one which can only be inquired into by the coroner's jury in cases of suicide ; and, since the abolition of forfeiture, and the doubts which have been raised as to whether the

---

[1] 1 Hale, P. C. 32 ; Co. Litt. 247 a ; 1 Hawk. c. 1, s. 6.
[2] 1 Hale, P. C. 32.
[3] R. v. Carroll, 7 C. & P. 145 ; R. v. Meakin, ib. 297 ; R. v. Cruse, 8 C. & P. 541 ; R. v. Monkhouse, 4 Cox, C. C. 55.
[4] R. v. Thomas, 7 C. & P 817.

inquisition is at all admissible as evidence of the insanity of the deceased upon an issue on that fact,[1] this question has lost much of its importance, and has become more a matter of sentiment, in which juries often incline to spare the feelings of the family of the deceased by returning a verdict of temporary insanity. Indeed, it has been the remark of very able men, judges and others, who have considered the question as it arose on an inquest, that if people were judged by the common and known standard of a sound mind, a partial insanity was the condition of a vast number of persons. There need not necessarily be any specific delusion, nor such an amount of general unsoundness, as would excuse a person from punishment if tried for a serious crime. But the effects were often seen ; and, if examined closely in their personal acts, in the course of their ordinary conduct in life, it would appear how little such persons are able to control themselves in important matters affecting themselves. There comes some sudden impulse—often no intelligible motive : but a temptation is offered of immediate change —rather than relief—from circumstances of difficulty or anxiety, and a man is unable to resist it. A woman is even still less able. They do not see the consequences and one may well doubt whether they are able to control the morbid feeling, or resist the sudden impulse.

The same sound principle which excuses those who have no mental will in the perpetration of an offence, protects from the punishment of the law those who commit crimes in subjection to the power of others, and not as the result of an uncontrolled free action proceeding from themselves.[2] The civil coercion or subjection which originates this protection is twofold, and arises out of the public and private relations of society : public, as between subject and prince, obedience to existing laws

Persons in subjection to the power of others.

---

[1] *Jones* v. *White*, 1 Str. 68.
[2] 4 Bl. Com. 27 ; 1 Hale, P. C. 43.

being a sufficient extenuation of civil guilt before a muni
cipal tribunal ; and private, proceeding from the matri
monial subjection of the wife to her husband, from which
the law presumes a coercion, which in many cases excuses
the wife from the consequences of criminal misconduct.

Married
women.

If a felony be committed by a feme coverte in the
presence of her husband, the law, out of tenderness to
the relation which subsists between them, raises a primâ
facie presumption that she, who was sub potestate viri,
acted under his immediate coercion ;[1] but this protection
is not allowed in all classes of offences. Those which are
mala in se and prohibited by the law of nature,[2] or most
heinous in their character, and dangerous in their consequences, do not range themselves within the protection
presumed from the matrimonial connection ; and therefore, if a married woman be guilty of treason, murder,
homicide, or the like, in company with or by coercion of
her husband, she is punishable equally as if she were
sole.[3] She will not, however, be answerable for the consequences of his breach of duty, however fatal, though
she may be privy to his misconduct, where she acts
merely as the servant or agent of her husband. A
passive concurrence in his neglect will not make her
amenable to justice, although in foro conscientiæ she
may be equally guilty.[4]

It would be superfluous to enter into a minute
enumeration of the offences foreign to the inquiry of
the coroner, which are and are not excused by this legal
presumption of coercion. Coverture, in all cases where
insisted on, must be proved ;[5] but evidence of cohabi-
tation and reputation will be sufficient for that purpose.

---

[1] 1 Hale, P. C. 516.
[2] 4 Bl. Com. 29.
[3] 1 Hale, P. C. 45, 47, 48,
516 ; 1 Hawk. P. C. c. 1, s. 11 ;
4 Bl. Com. 29 ; 1 St. Tr 28 ;

And. 104.
[4] *R.* v. *Squire*, 1 Russ. on Cr.,
5th ed. 653, 949.
[5] Kel. 37.

There are other relations arising out of the connection
subsisting between parent and child, and master and
servant, neither of which will excuse the commission of
any crime of whatever denomination ; for the command
is void in law, and can protect neither the commander
nor the instrument.[1] Threats of personal injury if the
command is disobeyed, may in some cases extenuate the
crime ; and may excuse it altogether if committed un-
willingly, and if the injury threatened is immediate and
cannot be resisted.[2]

Ignorance of the law will not excuse from the conse- Ignorance.
quences of guilt any person who has capacity to understand the law of this country, of which all (even foreigners
residing in England),[3] are presumed to have knowledge.[4]
Such ignorance may, however, sometimes be material in
considering the intention with which an act is done, and
mistake or ignorance of the fact may in some cases be
allowed as an excuse for the inadvertent commission of a
crime ; as, for instance, if a man, intending to kill a
thief or housebreaker in his own house, kill one of his
own family, he will be guilty of no offence.[5] In such
cases he is in general deemed to have acted under that
state of facts which he in good faith, and on reasonable
grounds, believed to exist when he did the act.

Where an unlawful act occurs by misfortune or chance, Misfortune
and not by design, the will observes a total neutrality,
and does not co-operate with the deed ; which therefore
wants one main ingredient of a crime. But this
is not so where the first act from which the unfore-
seen consequence ensued was unlawful; for, by doing

[1] 1 Hale, P. C. 44, 516.
[2] R. v. M'Growther, 18 St.
Tr. 394 ; R. v. Crutchley, 5 C.
& P. 133.
[3] R. v. Esop, 7 C. & P. 456.
[4] 1 Hale, P. C. 42 ; see R. v.
Bailey, R. & R. 1, where the

prisoner, having had no opportunity of acquiring a knowledge
of the law, was recommended by
the judges for a pardon.
[5] Cro. Car. 538 ; 1 Hale, P.
C. 42, 43 ; 4 Bl. Com. 27.

antecedently that which was in itself unlawful, the actor is criminally guilty of whatever consequence may follow his first behaviour. Thus it is, that if any accidental mischief happen to follow from the performance of a lawful act, the party stands excused from all guilt ; but if a man be doing anything unlawful, and a consequence ensue which he did not foresee or intend, as the death of a man or the like, his want of foresight is no excuse.[1]

PRINCIPALS AND ACCESSORIES.

Principals and accessories.

Where several persons are concerned in the commission of a felony, they are eithers principals in the first degree ; aiders and abettors, or principals in the second degree ; accessories before the fact ; or accessories after the fact ; and each, in construction of law, is guilty of the offence, and liable to punishment, according to the part which he takes in the perpetration of the crime. The inquiry of the coroner is, however, restricted to the cause of the death of the person upon whom the inquest is taken, and does not embrace accessories after the fact, who being guilty ex post facto only, are not instrumental to the death. It must be remembered also that in cases of manslaughter per infortunium, or se defendendo, there can be no accessories before the fact, for the offence is sudden and unpremeditated.

Principals in the first degree.

Those are of the first class, or principals in the first degree, who perpetrate the offence with their own hands, or through the instrumentality of an innocent agent. Yet it is not necessary, to render a person a principal in the first degree, that he should be actually present when the crime is consummated. Thus, if one lay poison purposely for another, who takes it and dies therefrom, the person who laid the poison, though absent when it

---

[1] 4 Bl. Com. 27.

was taken, is a principal in the first degree.[1] Or if an
instrument be excused by defect of understanding, ignorance of the fact, or other cause, from the responsibility
of his actions, the inciter, though absent when the fact
was committed, is ex necessitate liable for the act of
his agent, and a principal in the first degree.[2] But it is
otherwise if the instrument, being aware of the consequences of his act, be amenable to justice ; for in that
case the inciter is either an accessory before the fact, or
an aider and abettor, according to the circumstances of
the case.[3]

Persons who are present aiding and abetting when a
felony is committed, were formerly defined to be accessories at the fact only, and were not punishable until
the principal had been convicted or outlawed.[4] But this
rule, productive of manifest injustice, has, in the wisdom
of modern times, been relaxed, and such persons are now
considered as principals in the second degree.[5]

Aiders and abettors.

To constitute an aider and abettor, the party must be
both present and participating in the commission of the
offence, or ready to afford assistance if necessary. Those
who are barely present when a felony is committed, and
remain passive, neither encouraging nor endeavouring to
prevent it, although highly punishable by fine and imprisonment for their neglect in not endeavouring to
apprehend the offenders and prevent the felony, are not
guilty either as principals or accessories to it.[6]

Presence, in this sense, is either actual or construc-
tive. It is not necessary that the party should be

Presence of abettor.

---

[1] Fost. C. L. 349 ; 4 Rep.
44 b.
[2] R. v. *Palmer*, 1 N. R. 96 ;
R. v. *Giles*, 1 Mood. C. C. 166 ;
R. v. *Michael*, 2 Mood. C. C.
120, 301 ; 9 C. & P. 356 ; R. v.
Clifford, 2 C. & K. 202.
[3] Fost. C. L. 349 ; R. v.
Stewart, R. & R. 363 ; R. v.

Williams, 1 Den. C. C. 39 ; 1
C. & K. 589.
[4] Fost. C. L. 347.
[5] *The Coalheavers' case*, 1 L.
C. L. 66 ; Fost. C. L. 428 ; R.
v. *Towle*, R. & R. 314 ; R. v.
Kelly, ib. 421.
[6] 2 Hawk. P. C. c. 29, s. 10.

actually present, an ear or eye witness of the transaction ; he is, in construction of law, present aiding and
abetting, if, with the intention of giving assistance, he
be near enough to afford it, should occasion require.
Thus, if several persons set out together, or in small
parties, upon one common design, be it murder or other
felony, or for any other purpose unlawful in itself, and
each take the part assigned him ; some to commit the
fact, others to watch at proper distances and stations to
prevent a surprise, or to favour, if need be, the escape of
those who are more immediately engaged, they are all,
provided the fact be committed, in the eye of the law
present at it ; for it was made a common cause with
them, each man operated in his station at one and the
same instant towards the same common end, and the part
each man took tended to give encouragement, countenance and protection to the whole gang, and to insure the
success of their common enterprise.[1] So are all who are
present aiding and abetting at the immediate cause of a
felony, although it may be consummated in their absence,
in construction of law present. As, for instance, if
poison be laid for a man, who takes it and is killed, all
who aided and abetted when the poison was laid, are
principals in the second degree, although absent when
the poison was taken.[2]

Participa
tiOn in the
act.

It has been already observed, that, to constitute an
aiding and abetting, there must be a participation in the
act.[3] Where a particular intent is material to the
criminality of the act, there must also be a participation

---

[1] 1 Russ. on Cr., 157 ; Fost.
C. L. 350 ; 2 Hawk. P. C. c.
29, ss. 7, 8 ; Arch. Cr. Pl. 4,
5 ; R. v. Howell, 9 C. & P. 437;
R. v. Vanderstein, 10 Cox, C.
C. 177.

[2] Fost. C. L. 349 Kel. 52 ;
4 Rep. 44 b.

[3] Dougl. 207. See R. v. Coney,
8 Q. B. D. 534, where the full
court were divided in opinion
upon the question whether mere
voluntary presence at a fight
would justify a conviction for
an assault as aiding and abetting
in the fight.

in, or knowledge of, such intent.[1] Participation is of two kinds, proceeding either from a concerted design to commit a specific offence, or arising out of a previous combination to resist all opposers to the prosecution of some collateral unlawful purpose, of whatever denomination.[2] The latter is proved either by direct evidence of a general resolution against every opposer, or may be inferred from the arms, number, and conduct of the confederates at the time when the fact is committed.[3] But the act must be the result of the confederacy ; for, if several are out for the purpose of committing a felony, and, upon alarm and pursuit, run different ways, and one of them maim a pursuer to avoid being taken, the others are not to be considered as principals in that maiming.[4] So, the purpose must be unlawful in itself, for if the original intention be lawful, and be prosecuted by lawful means, should opposition be offered by others, and one of the opposing party be killed in the struggle, although the party killing may, according to the circumstances of the case, be guilty of murder or manslaughter, yet those engaged with him will not, unless they actually aided and abetted him in the fact, be involved in the guilt.[5]

When two persons driving carriages incited each other to drive furiously, and one of them ran over and killed a man, it was held to be manslaughter in both.[6] If one person encourage another to commit suicide, and be present abetting him while he does so, such person is guilty of murder as a principal. So, if two persons encourage each other to commit suicide, and one kills himself but the other fails in the attempt, the latter is a principal in the murder of the other.[7]

---

[1] *R.* v. *Cruse*, 8 C. & P. 546.
[2] 2 Hawk. P. C. c. 29, s. 9.
[3] Fost. C. L. 353, 354 ; 2 Hawk. P. C. c. 29, s. 8.
[4] *R.* v. *White*, R. & R. 99.
[5] Fost. C. L. 354 ; 2 Hawk. P. C. c. 29, s. 9.

[6] *R.* v. *Swindall*, 2 C. & K. 230.
[7] *R.* v. *Dyson*, R. & R. 523 ; *R.* v. *Russell*, 1 Mood. C. C. 356 ; *R.* v. *Alison*, 8 C. & P. 418.

When several are present aiding and abetting, the inquisition may lay it generally as done by all, or, according to the fact, as done by one, and abetted by the rest.[1]

It has already been stated[2] that the Coroner has authority to inquire of accessories before the fact, such being instrumental to the death, but not of accessories after the fact, who are guilty ex post facto only. An accessory before the fact has been defined to be one who, being absent at the time of the felony committed, doth yet procure, counsel, command, or abet another to commit a felony.[3] But the abetting must be by some sort of active proceeding ; a mere stakeholder who had nothing further to do with a fight upon which the stakes depended has been held not to be an accessory where manslaughter ensued.[4]

If the party be present when the felony is committed, or so near that the principal may be encouraged by the hopes of immediate assistance, we have seen that he is an aider and abettor, and not an accessory ;[5] but the same person may be both an aider and abettor, and an accessory before the fact, to the same felony, if. having counselled and procured it, he be present at the fact.[6] And, in either case, he may now be charged in the indictment, dealt with, and punished as if he alone and independently had committed the felony.[7]

The procurement is either direct, by hire, counsel, command, or conspiracy ; or indirect, by evincing an express liking, approbation, or assent to another's

---

[1] 2 Hawk. P. C. c. 23, s. 76 ; c. 25, s. 64 ; *R.* v. *Folkes*, 1 Mood. C. C. 354 ; *R.* v. *Crisham*, C. & Mar. 187 ; *R.* v. *Downing*, 1 Den. C. C. 52.

[2] Under section 42 of the Coroners Act the expression "murder" includes the offence of being accessory before the

fact to a murder.

[3] 1 Halo, P. C. 615.

[4] *R.* v. *Taylor*, L. R. 2 C. C. R. 149.

[5] *R.* v. *Gordon*, 1 L. C. L. 515, 1 East, P. C. 352.

[6] 2 Hawk. P. C. c. 29, s. 1.

[7] 24 & 25 Vict. c. 94, s. 2 ; *R.* v. *Hughes*, Bell, C. C. 242.

felonious design of committing a felony.[1] But the bare concealment of a felony to be committed, will not make the party concealing it an accessory before the fact, although he will be guilty of a misprision of felony.[2] So, neither will a tacit acquiescence, nor words which amount to a bare permission only, constitute this offence.[3]

The procurement may be either personal or through the intervention of another, for no direct connexion between the first mover and the actor is necessary, and he who procures a felony to be done is undoubtedly a felon. Thus, if one having contrived a murder, direct another to hire a third person to complete it, and the murder be committed, the first mover and contriver is an accessory before the fact, although he have no communication whatsoever with the principal felon.

An accessory will not be implicated in the guilt of the principal, unless the procurement be continuing, and the act be committed under the influence of the flagitious advice.

If the contriver of a felony repent, and, before the completion of it, countermand his agent, who following the suggestions of his own wicked heart pursues his object, and commits the felony, the original contriver will not be an accessory, for his consent continues not, and he gave timely countermand; but if the agent commit the felony before he was countermanded, the contriver, although he may have repented, is nevertheless an accessory.[5] It cannot be doubted, but that if a man advise a woman to kill her child as soon as it be born, and she kill it in pursuance of such advice, he is an accessory to the murder, though, at the time of the

Counter-mand.

---

[1] 2 Hawk. P. C. c. 29, s. 16.
[2] 2 Hawk. P. C. c. 29, s. 23.
[3] 1 Hale, P. C. 616 ; Cromp. 41 b.
[4] *R.* v. *Macdaniel*, Fost. C.

L. 125 ; 19 How. St. Tr. 746, 748, 804 ; R. v. *Cooper*, 5 C. & P. 535.
[5] 1 Hale, P. C. 618.

---

advice, the child not being born, no murder could be committed of it ; for the influence of the felonious advice continuing till the child was born, makes the adviser as much a felon as if he had given his advice after the birth.[1]

Where command not obeyed.

The act must be the result of the flagitious advice, for the contriver will not be implicated in the guilt of a principal who intentionally commits an offence substantially variant from the terms of the instigation.[2] It seems, however, to be agreed, that if the felony committed be the same in substance with that which was intended, and variant only in circumstances, as in respect of the time and place at which, or the means whereby it was effected, the abettor of the intent is altogether as much an accessory as if there had been no variance at all between the intent and the execution of it. Thus, if a man advise another to kill such an one in the night, and he kill him in the day, or to kill him in the fields, and he kill him in the town, or to poison him, and he stab or shoot him the contriver is an accessory to the guilt of the principal, who varied from the instigation not in substance, but only in the means and manner of executing it.[3] So although the principal exceed the term of the instigation, yet if the act done be, in the ordinary course of things, the natural result of the felony solicited, the contriver will be answerable for the consequences of his solicitation to their full extent. Thus, if I command another to beat a man, and he beat him in such a manner that he dies thereof, I am accessory before the fact to that felony, because it happened in the execution of a command which naturally tended to endanger the life of another.[4] A fortiori it follows, that if one command another to rob a man, and he in robbing him kill

---

[1] 2 Hawk. P. C. c. 29, s. 18 ; Dyer, 186.
[2] Fost. C. L. 369.
[3] 2 Hawk. P. C. c. 29, s. 20.
[4] 1 Hale, P. C. 617.

him, or to burn the house of J. S., and he, by burning it, burn also the house of J. H., the commander is as much an accessory to the subsequent felony as to that which was directly commanded.[1] It is said that if I command a man to rob another, and he kill him in the attempt, but do not rob him, I am guilty of the murder, because it was the direct and immediate effect of an act done in execution of my command to commit a felony.[2] But to an act which proceeds from the wicked impulse of the principal, and is totally and substantially variant from the instigation, the contriver will not be accessory; as, for instance, if a man command another to commit a felony upon a particular person or thing, and he do it intentionally upon another: to kill A., and he kill B.; to burn the house of A., and he burn the house of B.; to steal an ox, and he steal a horse; to steal a particular horse, and he steal another; in fine, to command him to commit one felony, and he commit another of a quite different nature, the commander will not be an accessory, because the act done varies in substance from that which was commanded.[3] But, if having accomplished the object of the instigation, the principal be guilty of an excess not naturally proceeding from the original act, the contriver is an accessory to the former, although not implicated in the guilt of the latter.[4]

It is doubted whether one who commands a felony is implicated in the guilt of the principal who, pursuing the object of the instigation, commits a felony unintentionally upon a different subject. In support of this doubt, Saunders's case is cited from Plowden.[5] In that case, Saunders wishing to kill his wife, in order that he might marry another woman, with whom he was in love, *Saunders's case.*

---

[1] 2 Hawk. P. C. c. 29, s. 18; Fost. C. L. 370.
[2] *R.* v. *Saunders*, Plowd. 475; Dalt. c. 108; Crompt. 42.

[3] 2 Hawk. P. C. c. 29, s. 21.
[4] 1 Hale, P. C. 617.
[5] Page 473.

communicated his design to Archer, and desired his
assistance and advice in the execution of his purpose :
Archer advised him to put an end to her life by poison,
and with that intent bought poison, which he delivered
to Saunders to give to his wife, who accordingly gave it
to her, she being sick, in a roasted apple, part of which
she ate, and gave the rest to an infant, their daughter :
Saunders blamed the wife for giving the apple to the
child, and said that apples were not good for such
infants ; to which the wife replied, that they were better
for such infants than for herself : the daughter ate the
poisoned apple, and her father saw her eat it, but did
not offer to take it from her, lest he should be suspected :
the daughter died of the poison.   Upon these facts, two
questions arose ; first, whether Saunders was guilty of
the murder, which was decided in the affirmative ; and,
secondly, whether Archer was an accessory before the
fact, which was decided in the negative, because he did
not assent that the daughter should be poisoned, but
only that the wife should be poisoned, which assent
could not be drawn further than he gave it, for the
poisoning of the daughter was a distinct thing from that
to which he was privy.   Upon the authority of this case,
Lord Hale [1] observes, that, " if A. command B. to kill C.,
and B. by mistake kill D., or else, in striking at C., kills
D., but misseth C., A. is not accessory to the murder of
D., because it differs in the person."   The case cited
does not, however, support this position, but is referable
to those cases in which the commander is not answerable
for an excess committed intentionally by the principal.
Saunders being present when the infant ate the poisoned
apple, might have prevented it, and by not doing so,
was intentionally guilty, through the innocent agency
of his wife, of murder upon a different object.   Had

---

[1] 1 Hale, P. C. 617.

Saunders been absent when the mother gave the poisoned apple to the child, the decision would have supported the position of Lord Hale; but the facts of the case reduce it merely to an authority for that which is admitted by all writers, viz., that if A. provide B. with poison to be administered to C., A. will not, if B. administer that poison intentionally to D., E., and F., and they die, be implicated in the guilt of B. The learned reporter, in a note to Saunders's case, says, "If I command one to burn the house of such an one, whom he well knows, and he burn the house of another, there I shall not be accessory to this; because it is another distinct thing, to which I gave no assent or command, but was wholly different from my command." This seems to imply that it is a necessary ingredient in such a case to excuse the commander, that the principal knew the house he was to burn; and that if he did not know it, but, intending to burn the house he was commanded to burn, by mistake burnt the other, the commander would be accessory to that burning, because it was the direct and immediate effect of an act wholly influenced by his command, which the principal intended to pursue.[1]

With reference to this decision, Foster, J., puts the following case:—"B. is an utter stranger to the person of C., A. therefore takes upon himself to describe him by his stature, dress, age, complexion, &c., and acquaints B. when and where he may be probably met with; B. is punctual at the time and place, and D., a person possibly, in the opinion of B., answering the description, unhappily comes by, and is murdered, upon a strong belief on the part of B. that this is the man marked out for destruction. Here is a lamentable mistake:—but who is answerable for it? B. undoubtedly is; the malice on his part ingreditur personam. And may not the same

---

[1] 2 Hawk. P. C. c. 29, s. 22.

be said on the part of A. ? The pit which he with murderous intention dug for C., D. through his guilt fell in, and perished ; for B. not knowing the person of C., had no other guide to lead him to his prey, than the description A. gave of him. B., in following this guide, fell into a mistake, which it is great odds any man in his circumstances might have fallen into. I therefore, as at present advised, conceive that A. was answerable for the consequence of the flagitious order he gave, since that consequence appears in the ordinary course of things to have been highly probable."[1]

Upon the whole, it appears more consonant to sound reasoning and justice, to reject the merciful opinion of Lord Hale, and to adopt the criteria of Foster, J., upon this subject :—" Did the principal commit the felony he stands charged with under the influence of the flagitious advice, and was the event, in the ordinary course of things, a probable consequence of that felony ; or did he, following the suggestions of his own wicked heart, wilfully and knowingly commit a felony of another kind, or upon a different subject."[2]

Accessories in man-slaughter.

In offences of the highest and lowest denomination, as in high treason and trespass, there can be no accessories, all being principals ;[3] but in murders and felonies in general, there may be accessories, except where the offence is sudden and unpremeditated, as in most cases of manslaughter, in which it has been said that there can be no accessories before the fact.[4] But in R. v. Gaylor,[5] where the prisoner was indicted for manslaughter, and the evidence showed that the prisoner had given his wife a drug with intent to procure abortion, from the effects of which she died, the question was reserved for the

[1] Fost. C. L. 370, 371.
[2] Fost. C. L. 372.
[3] 2 Inst. 183 ; 4 Bl. Com. 36.
[4] 1 Hale, P. C. 450, 616, re-ferring to R. v. Bibithe, 4 Rep.
43 b.
[5] Dears. & B. C. C. 288 ; see R. v. Taylor, L. R., 2 C. C. 147.

Court whether, if the husband was an accessory to the felony, an indictment for manslaughter could be supported, Erle, J., saying that, "if the manslaughter be per infortunium, or se defendendo, there is no accessory, but there are other cases in which there may be accessories." The conviction in this case was upheld, but no judgments were delivered. The cases where there may be accessories seem to be those where the act or omission by which death is caused is not such an act or omission as, but for the provocation received by the person killing, would have amounted to murder.[1]

An accessory cannot be guilty of a higher crime than his principal, for accessorius sequitur naturam sui principalis.[2] This maxim applied even in petit treason (now abolished by 9 Geo. 4, c. 31), and therefore, if one owing special obedience employed a stranger to murder his superior, he would, if absent, have been but an accessory to murder, although, if present aiding and assisting, he would have been guilty of petit treason, and the stranger of murder only.[3]

Prior to the statute 7 Geo. 4, c. 64, the practice was to Indictment include the principal and accessory before the fact in the same indictment, and in no other way could the accessory, without his own consent, have been arraigned and convicted, before the guilt of the principal had been legally ascertained by conviction or outlawry. Section 9 of that act contained provisions for the conviction of accessories either with the principal or for a substantive felony, although the principal may not have been previously convicted, or amenable to justice ; and by 11 & 12 Vict. c. 46, s. 1, accessories were made triable and punishable as principals. Both these sections are, however, repealed by the 24 & 25 Vict. c. 94; section 1 of which enacts " that whosoever shall become an accessory

---

[1] Stephen's Cr. L., art. 229.   [3] 4 Bl. Com. 36 ; Dy. 264.
[2] 3 Inst. 139.

before the fact to any felony, whether the same be a felony at common law, or by virtue of any act passed, or to be passed, may be indicted, tried and punished in all respects as if he were a principal felon." By section 2, "whosoever shall counsel, procure or command any other person to commit any felony, whether the same be a felony at common law or by virtue of any act passed, or to be passed, shall be guilty of felony, and may be indicted and convicted either as an accessory before the fact to the principal felony, together with the principal felon, or after the conviction of the principal felon, or may be indicted and convicted of a substantive felony, whether the principal felon shall or shall not have been previously convicted, or shall or shall not be amenable to justice, and may thereupon be punished in the same manner as any accessory before the fact to the same felony, if convicted as an accessory, may be punished." And under section 5, if any principal offender be convicted of any felony, accessories before and after the fact may be proceeded against in the same manner as if such principal felon had been attainted thereof, notwithstanding such principal felon should die, be pardoned or otherwise be delivered before attainder ; and every such accessory shall, upon conviction, suffer the same punishment as he would have suffered if the principal had been attainted.

SUICIDE.

A FELO DE SE is he who deliberately puts an end to his own existence, or commits any unlawful act, the consequence of which is his own death. It is not only a direct and deliberate purpose of self-destruction that will constitute this offence, but also, in some cases, he who unlawfully and maliciously attempts to kill another, and in pursuance of that design unwittingly kills himself, shall be adjudged in the eye of the law a felo de se.[1] An act done with a murderous intent makes the offender a murderer; and therefore, if one, attempting to kill another, run upon his antagonist's sword, or shooting at another, the gun burst and kill himself, he is a felo de se.

He who kills another at his own desire or command is murderer, for the assent of the party killed, being against the laws of God and man, was merely void; for which reason the party killed was not felo de se.[2] But if two persons agree to die together, and one, at the persuasion of the other, buy the poison, which both take, and he who bought it survives, and the other dies, it is the better opinion that he who dies shall be adjudged felo de se, because all that happened was originally owing to his own wicked purpose, which the other only put in his power to execute in that particular manner.[3] *Aiders and abettors.*

If the original act were innocent, although voluntary, the party will not be culpable, however fatal the consequences may be. As for instance, if A., with intent to prevent a gangrene beginning in his hand, without any advice cut off his hand, by which he dies, he is not thereby felo de se, for though it was a voluntary act, it was not done with intent to kill himself.[4] *Innoce acts.*

A person could not formerly be tried as an accessory before the fact for inciting another to commit suicide, if that person committed suicide, because the conviction of the principal was impossible. But the 24 & 25 Vict. c. 94, s. 1, has removed this difficulty. So, if the party persuading another to destroy himself be present when the felony is committed, he who dies is felo de se, and he who aided and abetted is a principal in the murder.[5] *Accessories*

---

[1] 1 Hawk. P. C. c. 9, s. 4.
[2] 1 Hawk. P. C. c. 9, s. 6.
[3] Moor, 754; 1 Hawk. P. C. c. 9, s. 6.
[4] 1 Hale, P. C. 412.
[5] *R.* v. *Dyson,* R. & R. 523; *ante,* p. 139.

Insanity.

In this, as in other offences, the consent of the will is necessary, and therefore the offender ought to be of the age of discretion, and compos mentis ; for if an infant under the age of discretion, or a lunatic during his frenzy, destroy himself, he cannot be felo de se.[1] But this excuse ought not to be strained to that length to which coroners' juries have sometimes been too apt to carry it. A notion too generally prevails that he who destroys himself must be non compos, that the very act of suicide is evidence of insanity, and that no one in his senses would commit that which is so contrary both to reason and nature. This very argument urged in extenuation, is in fact the aggravation of the offence. If tenable, it would excuse every criminal equally with the suicide, and would apply more forcibly in proportion to the enormity of the crime. To murder a parent, or a child, is as much repugnant to nature as self-murder, but if none but mad-men could commit such crimes, no one would be culpable in the eye of the law. The law very rationally judges that every melancholy and hypochondriac fit does not deprive a man of the capacity of discerning good from evil, which is necessary to form a legal excuse. And therefore, if a real lunatic kills himself in a lucid interval, he is felo de se as much as another man.[2]

To constitute the offence of felo de se, the party must die within a year and a day of the stroke received or the cause of the death administered, in the computation of which the whole day upon which the hurt was done is to be reckoned as the first. The party cannot, however, in the interval purge the offence by repentance.[3]

Conse-
quences of
self-murder.

Before the passing of the 33 & 34 Vict. c. 23, all the goods and chattels of a felo de se were, upon the finding of the inquisition, forfeited to the Crown. By that Act the forfeiture was abolished ; the offence, however, still

[1] 1 Hawk. P. C. c. 9, s. 1.   and 3.
[2] 1 Hawk. P. C. c. 9, ss. 2   [3] 1 Hale, P. C. 412

incurs an ecclesiastical forfeiture of the Christian rites
of the church of England, as the rubric directs that the
office for the burial of the dead " is not to be used for any
that have laid violent hands upon themselves."

It was formerly usual for the coroners to grant a warrant,
directing the constables and churchwardens of the parish
where the inquest was held, to cause the body of a felo de
se to be buried in some public street or highway, which was
usually complied with by burying the party in a public
cross road, and by driving a stake through his body.[1]

The unseemliness of this practice long called for Burial.
amendment, and accordingly it was put an end to by
the 4 Geo. 4, c. 52, which, however, directed that the
interment should take place at night, and did not
authorize the performing of any of the rites of Christian
burial. The burial is now regulated by the Interments
(felo de se) Act, 1882,[2] which provides that " it shall
not be lawful for any coroner or other officer having
authority to hold inquests to issue any warrant or other
process directing the interment of the remains of persons
against whom a finding of felo de se shall be had in any
public highway or with any stake being driven through
the body of such person, but such coroner or other
officer shall give directions for the interment of the
remains of such person felo de se in the churchyard or
other burial ground of the parish or place in which the
remains of such person might by the laws or custom of
England be interred if the verdict of felo de se had not
been found against such person."

The interment may be in any of the ways prescribed
or authorized, by the Burial Laws Amendment Act,
1880,[3] but the rites of Christian burial are still not
authorized nor are any of the other laws or usages
relating to the burial of such persons altered by the Act.

[1] 4 Bl. Com. 190.   [2] 45 & 46 Vict. c. 19.
[3] 43 & 44 Vict. c. 41.

MURDER.

MURDER[1] is defined to be when a person, of sound memory and discretion, unlawfully kills any reasonable creature in being, and under the queen's peace, by any means, with malice aforethought, either express or implied.[2] This general definition presents several branches for consideration :—1. Of the person killing ; 2. Of the person killed ; 3. Of the means of killing ; 4. Of the malice, which is the grand distinction between this and the other species of homicide.

But, before entering upon these inquiries, it may be premised as a rule applicable to all classes of this offence, that to make the killing murder, it is requisite that the party die within a year and a day after the stroke received, or the cause of death administered ; in the computation of which, the whole day upon which the hurt was done is to be reckoned the first.[3]

The person killing.

The person killing must be of sound memory and discretion ; for lunatics and infants are incapable of committing any crime, unless in cases where they show a consciousness of doing wrong, and a discretion or discernment between good and evil ; although, as we have seen, it is not within the province of the coroner's jury to inquire into the state of mind of any person other than the deceased.

So he must be a free agent, not under actual force when the act is committed ; for if A. by force take the arm of B., in which is a weapon, and therewith kill C., A. is guilty of murder, but B. is excused.[4] A moral force, however, as threats, duress, or impri-

---

[1] By the statute 9 Geo. 4, c. 31, s. 2, the distinction between petit treason and murder was abolished. See 24 & 25 Vict. c. 100, s. 8.

[2] 3 Inst. 47.

[3] 4 Bl. Com. 197 ; 3 Inst. 47.

[4] 1 Hale, P. C. 434 ; 1 East, P. C. 225.

sonment, will not amount to a legal excuse.[1] And hence it is that coverture is no exemption from punishment in cases of murder. But although a defect of will, proceeding from imbecility of understanding or actual constraint, excuses the instrument, the inciter or principal is guilty of the murder; for if it were otherwise, the instrument being excused, the offence would go unpunished.

The distinction between principals in the first degree, aiders and abettors, and accessories before the fact, has already been adverted to ;[2] but several may be actually present at the death of a man, and be guilty of different degrees of homicide ; for, as malice is an essential requisite in murder, if there be malice in the abettor, and none in the party striking, the former will be guilty of murder, and the latter of manslaughter only.[3] Thus, if A. assault B., of malice, and they fight, and A.'s servant come to his assistance, if B. be killed, it is murder in A., but manslaughter only in his servant.[4]

The person killed must be a reasonable being, and under the queen's peace. All persons, therefore, of whatever denomination, whether outlaw, alien, or Jew, being under the queen's peace and protection, may be the subject of this offence.[5] The killing of a foreigner on land out of the queen's dominions is murder, for which the person killing, if a British subject, is liable in England, under the stat. 24 & 25 Vict. c. 100, s. 9.[6] And if a man kill an alien enemy within this kingdom, yet it is felony, unless it be in the heat of war and in the actual exercise thereof.[7]

The person killed.

The party must also be in rerum naturâ ; and therefore a child in ventre sa mère cannot be the

Infants.

[1] 1 Hale, P. C. 51, 434.
[2] Ante, p. 136 et seq.
[3] 1 East, P. C. 350.
[4] 1 Hale, P. C. 446 ; Plowd. 97.
[5] 3 Inst. 50.
[6] See R. v. Azzopardi, 2 Mood. C. C. 288 ; 1 C. & K. 203.
[7] 1 Hale, P. C. 433.

subject of murder; although the contrary was formerly held. But if the child be born alive, and die in consequence of any potions or bruises received when in the womb, it seems always to have been the better opinion that it was murder in such as administered or gave them.[1]

Thus, if a person, intending to procure abortion, do an act which causes a child to be born so much before the natural time that it is born in a state much less capable of living, and dies in consequence of its exposure to the external world, such person is guilty of murder.[2] So, if a mortal wound be given to a child during the act of parturition, for instance, upon the head as soon as the head appears and before the child has breathed, and the child is afterwards born alive and dies of such wound, it may be murder.[3] But the child must have been actually born into the world in a living state, and before it can be accounted alive there must be in it an independent circulation ;[4] the mere fact, therefore, of its having breathed is not a conclusive proof of its having been born alive ;[5] nor conversely, is the fact that it has not breathed necessarily inconsistent with its having been born alive.[6] On the other hand, if a child be wholly produced and then destroyed, it is murder, although the umbilical cord be not severed.[7]

The means of killing. Any unlawful means, employed without warrant or excuse, are sufficient to constitute murder. In fact, the killing may be either by poisoning, striking, starving, drowning, or any of the thousand other forms of death

[1] 3 Inst. 50 ; 1 Hawk. P. C. c. 31, s. 16 ; 4 Bl. Com. 198 ; 1 East, P. C. c. 5, s. 14 ; contra, 1 Hale, 432 ; and Staund. 21. See also 1 Russ. on Cr., 646.
[2] R. v. West, 2 C. & K. 784.
[3] R. v. Senior, 1 Mood. C. C. 346.
[4] R. v. Poulton, 5 C. & P. 329 ; R. v. Pulley, ib. 539 ; R. v. Wright, 9 C. & P. 754 ; R. v. Handley, 13 Cox, C. C. 79.
[5] R. v. Sellis, 7 C. & P. 850.
[6] R. v. Brain, 6 C. & P. 349.
[7] R. v. Reeves, 9 C. & P. 25 ; R. v. Trilloes, 2 Mood. C. C. 260 ; C. & Mar. 650.

by which human nature may be overcome;[1] for the means and manner of the death are immaterial; with this reservation, however, that there must be a corporal damage to the party.[2] And this, although by care and skilful treatment the party might have recovered from the stroke received, or cause of death administered,[3] or was, at the time, afflicted with a disease which at a more remote period might, in the course of nature, have terminated his existence, if the hurt received, by provoking and irritating the disease, hastened his death; for then the death cannot be said to be ex visitatione Dei, and the offender cannot apportion his own wrong.[4] A man is not bound to have his body always in such a condition as to withstand any unwarrantable attack that may be made upon him.

It is not only such acts as obviously tend to cause death that constitute murder, but also all such as may apparently endanger the life of another, and ultimately occasion his death, if wilfully and deliberately committed.[5] Such was the case of him who carried his sick father against his will, in a severe season, from one town to another, by reason whereof he died;[6] of the harlot, who, being delivered of a child, left it in an orchard, covered only with leaves, in which condition it was killed by a kite;[7] of another, who hid her child in a hog-sty where it was devoured;[8] of another, who threw it on a heap of ashes, and left it there in the open air exposed to the cold, whereby it died;[9] of the parish officers, who shifted a child from parish to parish, till it died for want of care and sustenance;[10] and of the master, who by pre-

---

[1] 4 Bl. Com. 196.
[2] 1 East, P. C. 225.
[3] 1 Hale, P. C. 428.
[4] 1 Hale, P. C. 428; R. v. Holland, 2 M. & Rob. 351.
[5] 1 East, P. C. 225.
[6] Ibid.

[7] Ibid.; 1 Hawk. P. C. c. 13, s. 6.
[8] 1 East, P. C. 226.
[9] 1 Den. C. C. 356; 2 C. & K. 864; R. v. Handley, 13 Cox, C. C. 79.
[10] 1 East, P. C. 226.

meditated negligence and hard usage, caused the death
of his apprentice.[1] And such, also, was the case of the
gaoler, who by duress and rigorous imprisonment caused
the death of a prisoner in his custody ;[2] for in such cases
the law will infer malice.

Corporal
damage.

So, although to put a person into such passion of grief
or fear, by working on his feelings, that he suddenly die,
is not generally such a killing as the law can notice, because there is, in such a case, no corporal damage or
external violence ;[3] yet in a case where an assault had
been committed upon a woman carrying an infant, which
so frightened the infant that it died in about six weeks,
it was left to the jury to say whether the assault was the
direct cause of the death.[4] Again, threats may constitute
such a force as will render the party threatening answerable for the consequences of an act done under their influence ; as where a husband, by beating his wife, and
threatening to throw her out of the window and murder
her, so terrified her that she jumped out of the window
and was killed ; it was held, that if she jumped out of the
window under the constraint of a well-grounded apprehension of such further violence as would endanger her
life, he was answerable for the consequences of the act as
much as if he had thrown her out of the window himself.[5]

Death by
poison.

Of all the forms in which human nature may be subdued, that by poison is the most detestable, and the
least to be guarded against by foresight and manhood ;
in such cases, therefore, the law implies malice, even if
the poison be not taken by the party marked out for

---

[1] 1 Russ. on Cr., 652 ; see *R.*
v. *Saunders*, 7 C. & P. 277 ; *R.*
v. *Cheeseman*, *ib.* 455 ; *R.* v.
Smith, 8 C. & P. 153 ; *R.* v.
Marriott, ib. 425.

[2] Ld. Raym. 1574.

[3] 1 Hale, P. C. 429 ; 1 East,
P. C. 225.

[4] *R.* v. *Towers*, 12 Cox, C.
C. 53.

[5] *R.* v. *Evans*, 1 Russ. on Cr.,
651 ; *R.* v. *Pitts*, C. & Mar.
284 ; *R.* v. *Hickman*, 5 C. & P.
151.

destruction, and no particular enmity be shown to exist.[1]
But if the poison be administered by mistake, or laid
with an innocent intent, as to destroy vermin, it will
amount to homicide per infortunium merely.[2] So, if a
medical practitioner gives his patient a potion or plaster,
to cure him, which, contrary to expectation, kills him,[3]
or if he administer an anæsthetic for the relief of pain
in a case, for instance, of a surgical operation, and the
patient do not recover, this, in the absence of gross
negligence, is neither murder nor manslaughter, but misadventure. A distinction has indeed been taken, in this
case, between a regular surgeon or physician and one
that is not so, and, in the latter, the death is said to
amount to manslaughter at the least ;[4] but the sound-
ness of this distinction is doubted by Lord Hale, upon
the ground that physic and salves were in use before
licensed physicians and surgeons existed ;[5] and has been
altogether repudiated in recent cases.[6]

The rule of law is thus laid down by Lord Lynd- Medical
hurst, in Rex *v.* Webb :[7]—" In these cases there is no treatment.
difference between a licensed physician or surgeon, and a
person acting as physician or surgeon without a licence.
In either case, if a party, having a competent degree of
skill and knowledge, makes an accidental mistake in his
treatment of a patient, through which mistake death ensues, he is not thereby guilty of manslaughter ; but if,
where proper medical assistance can be had, a person
totally ignorant of the science of medicine takes upon
himself to administer a violent and dangerous remedy to

---

[1] 1 Hale, P. C. 455; 4 Bl.
Com. 200 ; 3 Inst. 48.
[2] 1 Hawk. P. C. c. 13, s. 43.
[3] 4 Inst. 251 ; *R.* v. *McLeod,*
12 Cox, C. C. 534.
[4] 1 Britt. c. vi. (edition by
Nichols).
[5] 1 Hale, P. C. 430.
[6] *R.* v. *Van Butchell,* 3 C. &

P. 629 ; *R.* v. *Williamson, ib.*
635; *R.* v. *Long,* 4 C. & P. 398,
423 ; *R.* v. *Spiller,* 5 C. & P.
33 ; *R.* v. *Senior,* 1 Mood.
C. C. 346 ; *R.* v. *Ellis,* 2 C. &
K. 470 ; *R.* v. *Spilling,* 2 M. &
Rob. 107 ; *R.* v. *Finney,* 12
Cox, C. C. 625.
[7] 1 M. & Rob. 405.

one labouring under disease, and death ensues in consequence of that dangerous remedy having been so administered, he is guilty of manslaughter. . . . . I shall
leave it to the jury to say, first, whether death was occa
sioned or accelerated by the medicines administered ; and
if they think it was, then I shall tell them, secondly,
that the prisoner is guilty of manslaughter, if they think
that in so administering the medicine he acted with a
criminal intention or from very gross negligence." And
in the case of Rex v. Long,[1] Park, J., addressed the jury
in these terms :—" On the one hand we must be careful,
and most anxious to prevent people from tampering with
physic, so as to trifle with the life of man ; and on the
other hand we must take care not to charge criminally a
person who is of general skill because he has been unfor-
tunate in a particular case. It is God that gives, man
only administers, medicine ; and the medicine that the
most skilful may administer may not be productive of the
expected effect ; but it would be a dreadful thing if a
man were to be called in question criminally whenever he
happened to miscarry in his practice. I call it acting
wickedly when a man is grossly ignorant and yet affects
to cure people ; or when he is grossly inattentive to their
safety. If you think there was gross ignorance, or scan-
dalous inattention, you will find him guilty." Unless
some guard is thrown around the practitioner, his judgment may be clouded, or his confidence shaken by the
dread of responsibility at the critical moment when it is
all important that he should retain the free and undis-
turbed enjoyment of his faculties in order to use them for
the benefit of his patient.

Killing by
neglect.

Death ensuing as the direct consequence of the omission of a duty, imposed by contract or otherwise, will be
murder or manslaughter, according as the omission is

[1] 4 C. & P. 410, approving R. v. Williamson, 3 C. & P. 635.

wilful or negligent. Thus, where the death of an apprentice has been caused by negligence or harsh usage,[1] the master may be criminally responsible; and so may a person who, having the custody of another who is helpless, leaves that other with insufficient food, and so causes his death.[2] It is the bounden duty of all persons having children, when they themselves cannot support them, to endeavour to obtain the means of getting them support, and if they wilfully abstain from going to the union, where by law they have a right to support, and the children die in consequence, they are criminally responsible.[3] And the statute 31 & 32 Vict. c. 122, s. 37, has imposed on parents a positive and absolute duty, whatever their conscientious or superstitious opinions may be, to provide medical aid for their children if in their custody, and under the age of fourteen years.[4] But where no duty is imposed, it is no criminal offence to cause death, even intentionally, by omitting to do any act which might have prevented the death. If, therefore, A. sees B. drowning, and is able to save him by holding out his hand, but abstains from doing so in order that he may be drowned, and B. is drowned, A. is not guilty of manslaughter.[5] So, where a mother had purposely neglected to procure proper attendance for her daughter in her confinement, by reason of which she died in childbirth, being about eighteen years old, and unmarried, it was held that although the deceased was living with her mother at the time, there was no such omission of duty as to render the mother liable to be convicted of man-

[1] R. v. Self, 1 East, P. C. c. 5, s. 13; R. v. Squire, 1 Russ. on Cr. (by Prentice) 653; R. v. Smith, 8 C. & P. 135.
[2] R. v. Smith, 34 L. J., M. C. 53; R. v. Bubb, 4 Cox, C. C. 455; R. v. Conde, 10 Cox, C. C. 547; R. v. Nicholls, 13 Cox, C. C., 75.
[3] R. v. Mabett, 5 Cox, C. C. 339.
[4] R. v. Downes, 45 L. J., M. C. 8; 13 Cox, C. C. 111; R. v. Morby, 7 Q. B. D. 571.
[5] Stephen's Cr. L., art. 212; see R. v. Smith, 11 Cox, C. C. 210.

slaughter.[1] Again, the wilful neglect to take the necessary precautions before the birth of a child for the preservation of its life afterwards, was held to be no such
omission of duty on the part of the mother;[2] but it
would be otherwise if a mother, being able to suckle her
child, were to cause its death by neglecting to do so.[3]
Where a person undertakes to provide necessaries for
another who is so helpless or infirm that he is incapable
of doing so for himself, or where a party confines another,
if death occurs through neglect to provide necessaries,
the former becomes criminally responsible,[4] and if he
delegates such a duty to his wife or to a servant, and
supplies them with the means of discharging the duty so
delegated, it becomes the legal duty of the wife or
servant to discharge it, and of the person who delegates to use ordinary care to see that it is properly discharged.[5]

Negligence. Other cases of death caused by negligence are more
properly referred to under the head of manslaughter;
indeed, it has been observed that the word "negligence"
excludes intention, and that if there were the very
slightest omission of caution in order to cause death, this
would constitute malice aforethought, if death were caused
thereby.[6]

Innocent Murder may also be committed through the instru-
Agents. mentality of an innocent agent; as by persuading a
lunatic to kill another person, or by turning loose a
furious animal, with a knowledge of its disposition,
even though it be merely for the purpose of frightening

---

[1] *R.* v. *Shepherd*, 1 L. & C.
147.
[2] *R.* v. *Knights*, 1 F. & F.
46.
[3] *R.* v. *Edwards*, 8 C. & P.
611; *R.* v. *Handley*, 13 Cox,
C. C. 79.
[4] *R.* v. *Marriott*, 8 C. & P.
25; *R. v. Nicholls*, 13 Cox.

C. C. 75. As to the duty of a
husband to provide shelter for
his wife, see *R.* v. *Plummer,*
1 C. & K. 600.
[5] *R.* v. *Bubb*, and *R.* v. *Hook*,
4 Cox, C. C. 455.
[6] Stephen's Cr. L., note to
art. 211.

others.[1] In the case of R. v. Dant[2] the prisoner had turned out a horse, known to him to be vicious, upon a common where he had right to pasture his horses, but where, to his knowledge, there were open paths on which the public had a right to pass; the horse kicked and killed a child who was very near one of the paths, and a conviction for manslaughter was affirmed by the Court.

It is observable, that the consent of the party killed Consent. will not purge the offence, for the consent is merely void. He, therefore, who kills another by his desire and command, is a murderer;[3] and he who persuades another to destroy himself, which he does, is, though he be absent when the act is committed, a principal in the murder. But it seems to be uncertain to what extent any person has a right to consent to his being put in danger of death by the act of another,[4] provided it do not amount to a consent to the actual infliction of bodily harm in such a manner as to amount to a breach of the peace, as in a prize fight, or other exhibition calculated to collect together disorderly persons.[5]

The difficulty of proving that the child was born alive, Conceal- in the case of the murder of bastard children by the ment of birth. unnatural mother, produced a legislative enactment,[6] which required the mother endeavouring to conceal its death to prove, by one witness at least, that the child was actually born dead, and in default of such proof, inflicted upon her punishment as in the case of murder. The effect of this enactment was, that the bare concealment was almost conclusive evidence of the murder; and, accordingly, this species of offence was

---

[1] 1 Hawk. P. C. c. 13, s. 7; 1 Hale, P. C. 431; R. v. Michael, 2 Mood. C. C. 120; 9 C. & P. 356.

[2] 10 Cox, C. C. 102; 34 L. J. M. C. 119.

[3] 1 Hawk. P. C. c. 9, s. 6.

[4] Stephen's Cr. L., arts. 203–209.

[5] R. v. Billingham, 2 C. & P. 234; R. v. Perkins, 4 C. & P. 537; Stephen's Cr. L., art. 208.

[6] 21 Jac. 1, c. 27.

J.

M

formerly within the province of the coroner. But the
duty of the coroner in this respect was abrogated by the
43 Geo. 3, c. 58, which repealed that statute, and
enacted (sects. 4 and 5), that such cases should proceed
and be governed by the like rules of evidence and of
presumption as were by law used and allowed in other
cases of murder ; with a provision, however, that, under
an indictment for murder, the mother might be found
guilty of the concealment, and punished accordingly.
The 43 Geo. 3, c. 58, was repealed by the 9 Geo. 4, c. 31,
sect. 14 of which, however, re-enacted in substance the
provisions of sects. 4 and 5 of the former statute, with
this new provision, that the mother might be indicted for
the concealment, as a specific misdemeanor. The 9
Geo. 4, c. 31, is in its turn wholly repealed by the 24 &
25 Vict. c. 95 (Criminal Statutes Repeal Act), and the
concealment of the birth of children is now provided for
by the 24 & 25 Vict. c. 100, s. 60, by which the secret
disposition of the dead body of a child, whether such
child died before, at, or after birth, is constituted a
misdemeanor, with a proviso, that if any person tried
for the murder of a child be acquitted it shall be lawful
for the jury to find, in case it shall so appear in evidence,
that the child had recently been born, and that such
person, by some secret disposition of the body of the
child, endeavoured to conceal the birth thereof, and
thereupon the court may pass such sentence as if such
person had been convicted upon an indictment for the
concealment of birth.

Were it not that cases have occurred in which coroners
have assumed jurisdiction in cases of concealment, it
would seem almost superfluous to observe that they have
no power in this respect. Formerly, the bare concealment was evidence of the murder, and the onus of
proving the contrary lay upon the party accused. The
inquest of the coroner is an inquest of office to ascertain

the cause of the death, with which the concealment, since the repeal of that statute, has no connection. An inquisition finding a concealment will neither put the party upon her trial, nor justify the coroner, as such, in committing her, which can only be done by a magistrate's warrant for the misdemeanor.

Some few observations upon the subject of infanticide Infanticide. may not be misplaced here. The first question which naturally presents itself is, whether the child was born alive. As a test of this, it was formerly usual to immerse the lungs in water, it being supposed that, if they floated, the child must have respired. But this test is now exploded; for it is obvious, that if the child make but one gasp, and instantly die, the lungs will swim in water, in many cases, as readily as if the child had breathed longer; and it is not uncommon for an infant to breathe and make some kind of cry as soon as its mouth is protruded from the mother, although it may die before its body be born.[1] Air may also be passed into the lungs by inflation, or be generated by putre-faction, and both will produce the same effect.

The question is, however, less difficult in cases of immature birth. Under the fifth month, it is scarcely possible that a foetus can be born alive; from the fifth to the seventh, it may come into the world alive, but cannot generally maintain existence; but at the seventh it may be reared. As the period of gestation may be pretty accurately ascertained from the appearance of the foetus, in these cases the doubt is more easily resolved.[2]

The next question is the cause of the death. Now, the child may die in the womb,—during the labour, by pressure,—or by strangulation from the umbilical cord;[3] in which latter cases, the body presents appearances,

---

[1] Hunt. 17. See also the cases cited *ante*, p. 154.
[2] See For. Med. 312; Prac.
Mid. 112; 3 Par. 100.
[3] Elem. of Mid. 180.

M 2

which, to a common observer, would seem to be the marks of a violent death. Upon this subject Dr. Hunter says,—" When a child's head or face looks swollen, and is very red or black, the vulgar, because hanged people look so, conclude that it must have been strangled :—nothing more common in natural births "[1]

But the child, though safely delivered, may still die without any criminal act of the mother. Children may be born so weak, that, if left to themselves, after breathing or sobbing, they would die ; or even a strong child may be suffocated by being left upon its face, either in the pool made by the natural discharges, or upon wet clothes.[2] These and a variety of other causes may contribute to the death of new-born infants, particularly where the mother is delivered in secret by herself, and, being exhausted, frequently faints and becomes insensible.

The preceding observations are made rather with a view of pointing the attention to these questions, than as infallible rules upon which to proceed. The reader may find abundant information upon this subject in the books referred to.

Malice.   Malice is the grand criterion which distinguishes murder from other homicides. In its common acceptation it is a settled anger in one person against another, and a desire only of revenge ; but in its legal sense, malice prepense, malitia præcogitata, is not so properly spite and malevolence to the deceased in particular, as an evil design in general ; the dictate of a wicked, depraved, and malignant heart : une disposition à faire un mal chose.[3] Hence it is that the act done follows the nature of the act intended to be done, and that if the latter were founded in malice, and the stroke, from whence death ensued, fell by accident upon a person for whom it

---

[1] Elem. of Med. p. 13.   [3] 4 Bl. Com. 198.
[2] Hunt. 18.

was not intended, the motive being malicious, the act amounts to murder.[1] As if A., having malice against B., strike at him, but kill C, this is murder in A. ;[2] so, it is murder if A., having malice against B., assault him, and kill C., the servant of B., who comes to his assistance, for C. was justified in attacking A. in defence of his master.[3] Or if one give poison to another, who innocently adminis ters it to a third person, he who provides it is guilty of murder. For the same reason it is, that, if one, attempting to kill another, run upon his antagonist's sword, or, shooting at another, the gun burst and kill himself, he is felo de se; for the original intent was, in its nature, malicious and deliberate, and the act follows the nature of the intent. So, although the act may originally have been committed for another and different object, as to procure abortion, if death ensue, the party killing is guilty of murder.[4] But wherever the act would, if operating upon the object intended, have admitted of extenuation or excuse, the same rule will hold, though it unhappily fall upon a different person.[5]

Malice is either express or implied in law. Express malice is where one with a sedate deliberate mind, and formed design, kills another ; which formed design is evidenced by external circumstances discovering that inward intention, as lying in wait, antecedent menaces, former grudges, and concerted schemes to do him some bodily harm.[6] But where no malice is expressed or openly indicated, the law will imply it where any person wilfully does an act injurious to another without lawful excuse ;[7] and all homicide is presumed to be malicious until circumstances of alleviation, excuse, or justification, are satisfac-

Implied malice.

---

[1] 1 East, P. C. 230.
[2] Ibid.
[3] 1 East, P. C. 230.
[4] 1 East, P. C. 230.
[5] Fost. C. L. 262 ; 1 East,

P. C. 245.
[6] 4 Bl. Com. 199.
[7] *R.* v. *Pembliton,* L. R. 2, C. C. R. 122.

torily proved by the accused, or arise out of the evidence adduced against him.[1]

The grosser cases of murder, where the malice is apparent in itself, need no observation ; the circumstances of every such case are peculiar to itself. But there are many nice distinctions upon the subject of malice, which will be considered more fully under the following heads.

Killing upon provocation.

The law regards with an indulgent eye the frailties of human nature, and makes allowances, in many cases, for acts committed during the first paroxysm of passion, which, while the frenzy lasts, stills the voice of reason, and renders the victim of it reckless of the consequences of his acts. When therefore death ensues from the sudden transport of passion, or heat of blood, upon a reasonable provocation and without malice, it is considered as solely imputable to human infirmity, and the offence will be manslaughter. But it should be remembered that the person sheltering himself under this plea of provocation must make out the circumstances of alleviation to the satisfaction of the court and jury, unless they arise out of the evidence produced against him ; as the presumption of law deems all homicide to be malicious until the contrary is proved.[2]

It is not every trivial provocation, assault or even blows, that will extenuate the act of homicide. No breach of a man's word or promise, no trespass to either lands or goods, no affront by bare words or gestures, however false or malicious it may be, or aggravated with the most provoking circumstances, will excuse him from being guilty of murder, who is so far transported thereby as immediately to attack the person who offends him, in such a manner as manifestly endangers his life, without giving him time to put himself upon his guard, if he kill

---

[1] 1 East, P. C. 224 ; 4 Bl. Com. 200.   [2] 1 Russ. on Cr. 676.

him in pursuance of such assault, whether the party de-
fended himself or not.[1] And this rule governs all cases
where the party killing made use of a deadly weapon, or
otherwise manifested an intention to kill or to do some
bodily harm.[2]

Words of menace and bodily harm have been said to
amount to such a provocation as would reduce the offence
of killing to manslaughter ;[3] but the better opinion seems
to be the other way,[4] unless at least under very special
circumstances,[5] or where the words are accompanied by
some act indicative of actual violence. An assault, committed with circumstances of violence and indignity upon
a man's person, if it be resented immediately by the death
of the aggressor, and it appear that the party acted in the
heat of blood upon that provocation, will reduce the crime
to manslaughter.[6] So if, as the result of a violent and
unlawful restraint of personal liberty,[7] or of that most
grievous of all provocations, insupportable in the first
transport of passion, the detection of the adulterer in the
act, death ensue, the law will extenuate the offence.[8] But
if the act be deliberate and upon revenge, or the restraint
and coercion be such as one may reasonably and lawfully
use towards another, it will be murder.[9]

This rule cannot be better elucidated than by extract-
ing at length the following case reported by Foster[10] :—
" There being an affray in the street, one Stedman, a foot
soldier, ran hastily towards the combatants. A woman
seeing him run in that manner, cried out, 'You will not

Words of menace.

Stedman's case.

[1] 1 Hawk. P. C. c. 13, s. 33.
[2] Cro. Car. 131; 1 East, P. C. 233.
[3] R. v. Lord Morley, 1 Hale, P. C. 456 ; see Kel. 55.
[4] 1 East, P. C. 233.
[5] R. v. Rothwell, 12 Cox, C. C. 145.
[6] 1 East, P. C. 233.
[7] R. v. Longden, R. & R.
228 ; 1 East, P. C. 233 ; R. v. Thompson, 1 Mood. C. C. 80 ; R. v. Curvan, ib. 132.
[8] Fost. C. L. 296 ; 1 Hale, P. C. 486 ; 7 Raym. 212 ; 1 Ventr. 159 ; R. v. Kelly, 2 C. & K. 814 ; R. v. Fisher, 8 C. & P. 182.
[9] 1 East, P. C. 288.
[10] Fost. C. L. 292.

murder the man, will you?' Stedman replied, 'What is
that to you, you bitch?' The woman thereupon gave
him a box on the ear, and Stedman struck her on the
breast with the pommel of his sword. The woman then
fled; and Stedman, pursuing her, stabbed her in the
back. Holt was first of opinion that this was murder;
the single box on the ear from a woman not being a sufficient provocation to kill in such a manner, after he had
given her a blow in return for the box on the ear; and it
was proposed to have the matter found specially. But it
afterwards appearing, in the progress of the trial, that the
woman struck the soldier in the face with an iron patten,
and drew a great deal of blood, it was holden clearly to
be no more than manslaughter." The smart of the
wound, says Foster, J., and the effusion of blood, might
possibly keep his indignation boiling to the moment of
the fact.[1]

In the opinion of the same learned judge, the officers
who went for the purpose of arresting Mr. Luttrel, and
killed him in the brutal manner reported,[2] were guilty of
murder; for a slight stroke of a cane would not justify
furious acts of revenge, which, if inflicted upon trivial
provocations, are true symptoms of that malice which con-
stitutes the crime of murder.[3]

It may be added, however, that where the provocation
is by blows not sufficiently violent in themselves to reduce the killing below the crime of murder, if they be
accompanied by very aggravated words or gestures, they
may make it manslaughter only.[4]

Intention of killing.

Referable to this head are those cases of trivial provocation, in which the party killing intended an injury of a
less serious nature. With respect to these, it is observ-

---

[1] Fost. C. L. 292.
[2] 1 Str. 499.
[3] Fost. C. L. 293.

[4] *R.* v. *Sherwood,* 1 C. & K.
556; and see *R.* v. *Smith,* 4
F. & F. 1066.

able that the punishment must not be greatly disproportionate to the offence, and that much depends upon the nature of the instrument used, and the manner in which the injury is inflicted. If the chastisement be outrageous, and the instrument such as was in its nature likely to endanger life, the party killing will be guilty of murder ; but if, on the contrary, the circumstances show an intention to correct, rather than the gratification of a cruel and implacable malice, it will amount to manslaughter only.

Thus, he who, seeing his son's nose bloody, and being told by him that he had been beaten by such a boy, ran three-quarters of a mile, and, having found the boy, struck him a single blow with a small cudgel, of which he afterwards died, was adjudged to be guilty of manslaughter only ; [1] for the stroke was given with a weapon not likely to kill and without any of the circumstances which import malice. Nor was he deemed more criminal, who, being encouraged by a concourse of people, threw a pickpocket into a pond adjoining the road, in order to avenge the theft by ducking him, but without any apparent intention to take away his life, and the pickpocket was drowned.[2] So, where one found a trespasser on his land, and in the first transport of passion beat him so that he unfortunately died, this was holden to be manslaughter, for his intention was only to chastise him for the trespass, in doing which he used no dangerous or deadly weapon, and committed no violent excess.[3]

Where the instrument used under the influence of provocation is not such as will be likely to cause death, the party will not, if death ensue, be guilty of murder. Upon this ground it was, as it seems, that the judges doubted whether it amounted to murder, where, on words of provocation, a man threw a broomstick at a woman

Instrument used.

---

[1] Fost. C. L. 294.
[2] 1 East, P. C. 236.

[3] Fost. C. L. 291 ; 1 Hale, P. C. 473.

from a distance, which unfortunately killed her;[1] and, upon the same doubt, a woman was pardoned, who, upon provocation, had killed a child by throwing a four-legged stool at her, which was of size and weight to give a mortal wound, but was not thrown with an intention to kill the child.[2]

On the contrary, should the punishment be inflicted in such a manner as shows a cruel and deliberate intent to do mischief, and death ensue, the party killing will be guilty of murder. As, where the keeper of a park, finding a boy stealing wood, tied him to a horse's tail, and beat him, whereupon the horse ran away, and killed him, this was held to be murder, for the act was illegal, deliberate, and dangerous, and the chastisement was excessive, and savoured of cruelty.[3] And, generally, in all cases of slight provocation, if it may be reasonably collected from the weapon made use of, or from other circumstances, that the party intended to kill, or to do some great bodily harm, the offence will be murder.[4]

Where provocation sought for.

Secondly. The provocation must be unsought for. Whenever express malice exists, the plea of provocation is of no avail. Even blows previously received will not extenuate homicide upon malice, especially when it is to be collected from the circumstances of the case, that the provocation was sought for and induced by the party's own act in order to afford him a pretence for wreaking his vengeance. As where A. and B. having fallen out, A. says he will not strike, but will give B. a pot of ale to touch him, on which B. strikes, and A. kills him: this is murder,[5] for he shall not elude the justice of the law by such pretence to cover his malice. In such cases the act is not the immediate result of the provocation, but of a

---

[1] 1 Hale, P. C. 455.
[2] *R.* v. *Hazel*, 1 Leach, C. L. 368 ; 1 Hale, P. C. 236.
[3] 1 East, P. C. 237 ; 1 Hawk.
P. C. c. 13, s. 42.
[4] 1 Russ. on Cr. 688.
[5] 1 East, P. C. 239 ; 1 Hawk. P. C. c. 13, s. 24.

deliberate resolution to take deadly revenge, which cannot be purged by a provocation sought for, and which could not have operated upon the passions of the slayer.

Thirdly. The act must be committed under the influence of the provocation; and therefore, if there be any time intervening, sufficient for the passion to subside, and for reason to interpose; or if there be circumstances to show deliberation and reflection, which rebut the presumption of passion, the plea of provocation will be of no avail.[1] It is difficult to define any precise rules upon this subject. It must be remembered that, in these cases, the immediate object of inquiry is, whether the suspension of reason arising from sudden passion continued from the time of the provocation received to the very instant of the mortal stroke given; for if, from any circumstances whatsoever, it appear that the party reflected, deliberated, or cooled, any time before the fatal stroke given; or if, in legal presumption, there was time or opportunity for cooling; the killing will amount to murder, it being in that case attributable to malice and revenge, rather than to human infirmity.[2]

Where time for reflection.

Where death is the consequence of mutual combat, the important consideration is, whether the occasion was altogether sudden and unpremeditated, or the result of a preconceived malice. In the former case, the killing will admit of extenuation; but, in the latter, it will amount to murder.[3]

Killing in mutual combat.

Provided the parties be on an equal footing in point of defence, at least at the onset, particularly where it is made with deadly and dangerous weapons, it matters not

Where premeditated.

---

[1] Ld. Raym. 1485; 1 Lev. 180; 1 Sid. 277; Fost. C. L. 296; *R.* v. *Lynch*, 5 C. & P. 324; *R.* v. *Hayward*, 6 C. & P. 157; *R.* v. *Thomas*, 7 C. & P. 817.

[2] 1 East, P. C. 252; R. & R. 43.

[3] 1 East, P. C. 421.

whether the cause be real or imaginary, or who commences the attack, if it be sudden, and not urged as a cloak for pre-existing malice.[1] If, even upon a sudden quarrel, a man be so far provoked by any bare words or gesture of another, as to make a push at him with a sword, or to strike at him with any other such weapon as manifestly endangers his life, before the other's sword is drawn, and thereupon a fight ensues, and he who made such assault kill the other, he is guilty of murder ; because, by assaulting the other in so outrageous a manner, without giving him an opportunity to defend himself, he showed that he intended not to fight with him, but to kill him.[2] But if he had first drawn, and forborne until his adversary had also drawn, the case would have been different, and have amounted to manslaughter only.[3]

Where deadly weapon used.

It will not, however, vary the case, where the combat is sudden and unpremeditated, and both parties are on equal terms at the onset, if, in the heat of blood, one kill the other with a deadly weapon,[4] or commit a violent and outrageous excess, the consequence of which is fatal. Thus, where, after mutual blows between the prisoner and the deceased, the prisoner knocked the deceased down, and, after he was on the ground, stamped upon his stomach and belly with great force, this was held to be only manslaughter.[5] But if the quarrel be used as a cloak, and for the purpose of gratifying a concerted malicious design, to be executed under that colour, the killing will amount to murder.[6]

Persons assisting

If there be an affray and actual fighting between two parties, and another run in and take part with one of the combatants, and kill the other, it will be manslaughter.

[1] 1 East, P. C. 241.
[2] 1 Hawk. P. C. c. 13, s. 27 ; Kel. 61, 131.
[3] 1 Hawk. P. C. c. 13, s. 28.
[4] 1 East, P. C. 243 ; 5 Bur.

2793 ; 1 Russ. on Cr. 695 ; *R*. v. *Kessall*, 1 C. & P. 437.
[5] *R*. v. *Ayes*, R. & R. 166.
[6] 1 Russ. on Cr. 700.

But if the party assisting knew that the combat was malicious, the killing will be murder.[1]

This doctrine, as in the former case, is founded on the frailties of human nature, for which the law makes great allowances. It therefore cannot apply where, between the provocation and the act, there has been time for the passions to subside, or where the conduct of the party, or the expressions used, manifest a deliberation.[2] But even though there may have been malice originally between the parties, it will not be murder, if, after a bonâ fide reconciliation, they fight upon a sudden and fresh quarrel, and one is killed.[3]

The second description of mutual combat is the case of cool and deliberate duelling, where both parties meet avowedly with the intent to murder; upon which the law has justly affixed that crime, and the punishment attaching to it, not only upon the principals, but upon the seconds also.[4] Yet to implicate in the guilt the second of the party killed, has been said to be a severe construction of the law.[5] No provocation, however grievous, can excuse or extenuate this deliberate act.[6]

The topics urged in extenuation of this offence—the vindication of character from the imputation of cowardice, the dread of even an undeserved contempt, are as unfounded in the principles of true valour, as they are unsupported by laws, either human or divine. Yet so prevalent has been this false notion of honour, and so strong a degree of passive valour is requisite to combat existing prejudices, that the strongest prohibitions and penalties of the law were entirely ineffectual to eradicate

Duelling.

[1] 1 Hawk. P. C. c. 13, ss. 35, 36; 1 East, P. C. 291.
[2] R. v. Oneby, Ld. Raym. 1485; 2 Str. 766.
[3] 1 Hawk. P. C. c. 13, s. 30; 1 Hale, P. C. 452.
[4] 4 Bl. Com. 199.
[5] 1 Hale, P. C. 443. But see Reg. v. Cuddy, 1 C. & K. 210.
[6] 3 East, 581; 1 Hale, P. C. 452; 2 Str. 766; R. v. Young, 8 C. & P. 644; R. v. Cuddy, 1 C. & K. 210.

altogether this unhappy custom, and it is only as one of the consequences of a higher civilization and an altered tone of society, that it has become possible for a person insulted to be content with reparation other than that which was formerly given at the hazard as well of his own life as of the life of him who had been the aggressor.

He who deliberately engages in an act highly unlawful, in defiance of the laws, must, at his peril, abide the consequences of his act. Hence it follows, that if two persons quarrel over night, and appoint to fight the next day, or at such a considerable time after, that, in common intendment, it must be presumed that the blood was cooled, the person killing will be guilty of murder.[1] And the same rule will hold, wherever circumstances concur to show that the parties did not engage in the heat of passion.[2] Thus, if B. challenge A., who refuses to meet him, but, in order to avoid the law, tells B. that he shall go the next day to such a town about his business, and B. meets him on the road going there, and assaults him, whereupon they fight, and A. kills B. : A. will be guilty of murder, unless it appear that he gave B. the information undesignedly, and not to afford him an opportunity of fighting.[3]

Killing by correction.

Parents, masters and other persons having authority in foro domestico, may give reasonable correction to those under their care ; and if death ensue from such correction, it will be no more than accidental death.[4] But they are not justified in correcting those who are too young to be capable of appreciating it,[5] nor may the correction exceed the bounds of moderation, either in the manner, the instrument, or the quality of the punishment ; in such cases, if death ensue, it is murder or

---

[1] 1 Hawk. P. C. c. 13, s. 22.
[2] 1 Lev. 180 ; 1 Hawk. P. C. c. 31, ss. 23, 24.
[3] 1 Hawk. P. C. c. 13, s. 25.
[4] 1 East, P. C. 261.
[5] R. v. Griffin, 11 Cox, C. C. 402.

manslaughter, according to the circumstances of the case.[1] Where a woman stamped upon her child's belly, and a blacksmith corrected his servant with an iron bar, and in each case the party died, these were holden to be murder; because the correction being excessive, and such as could not proceed but from a bad heart, it was equivalent to a deliberate act of killing.[2] Where a master struck his servant with a clog, because he had not cleaned it, and death ensued, this was holden to be manslaughter only, because the clog being very unlikely to cause death, the use of such an instrument negatived any malicious intention.[3] So where a mother, being angry with her child, took up a poker, and running to the door of the room, threw it out after him, and killed another child who was entering the room at the time; this was holden to be manslaughter, though she did not intend to hit the child she threw the poker at, but only to frighten him; it being an improper mode of correction.[4]

The distinction which arises under this head is between acts which ensue from a collateral unlawful purpose, and those which are the consequence of a lawful purpose, criminally and improperly performed. The former class may be subdivided into cases where the act intended or attempted was felonious or malicious, and those in which it was unlawful only, but not amounting to felony, that is to say, constituting an actionable wrong, or being contrary to public policy or morality, or being injurious to the public.

Killing without intention, whilst doing another act.

Should death ensue from an act done with a felonious intent, it will be murder. As, if A. shoot or strike at B., miss him, but kill C.;[5] or lay poison for B., which C. (against whom A. had no malicious intent) takes and is

Felonious intent.

[1] 1 East, P. C. 461.
[2] Ibid.; Fost. C. L. 262; 1 Hale, P. C. 473.
[3] Comb. 407, 408; 1 L. C. L. 378; 1 East, P. C. 261.
[4] R. v. Conner, 7 C. & P.

438.
[5] Fost. C. L. 261; 1 Hawk. P. C. c. 13, s. 44. See R. v. Smith, 25 L. J., M. C. 29; Dears. C. C. 559.

killed ;[1] this is murder. If a man shoot at another's
poultry with intent to steal them, and by accident kill a
man, this is murder ; but if that intention were wanting,
it would be manslaughter only, for the shooting at the
poultry is not per se felonious.[2] But it is not essential to
render the killing murder that the unlawful act intended
would, had it been effected, have amounted to felony.
For example, if whilst two are fighting of malice prepense,
another go between them to part them, and be killed by
one of them, this is murder, whether he be killed
designedly or accidentally ; for although it was not his
primary intention to commit a felony, yet inasmuch as
he persisted in the offence to the hazard of the lives of
those who only do their duty, he is in that respect
equally criminal as if his intention had been to commit
felony.[3] Again, if medicine be given to a woman to
procure an abortion, or if an instrument be put into her
womb for the same purpose, and she die, this is murder ;
for though her death be not intended, the act is
deliberate and malicious, and attended with manifest
danger to the person upon whom it is practised.[4]

If a man, breaking an unruly or vicious horse, ride him
amongst a crowd, and the horse kick a man and kill him,
this is murder if the rider brought the horse into the crowd
with an intent to do mischief, or even to divert himself
by frightening the crowd ;[5] or, if he drive a cart or carriage
furiously and purposely among a crowd ;[6] or purposely
discharge a loaded gun amongst a multitude of people,
and one is killed ;[7] or if, knowing that people are passing
along the street, he throw a stone likely to do injury, or

---

[1] 1 Hawk. P. C. c. 13, s. 45 ;
Plowd. 474 ; 9 Rep. 81.
[2] Fost. C. L. 258 ; but see
per Bramwell, B., in *R.* v.
Horsey, 3 F. & F. 287.
[3] 1 Hale, P. C. 441 ; 1 Hawk.

P. C. c. 81, s. 54.
[4] 1 Hale, P. C. 429 ; 1 East,
P. C. 230.
[5] 1 Hawk. P. C. c. 11, s. 12.
[6] 1 East, P. C. 263.
[7] 1 Hale, P. C. 475.

shoot over a house or wall with intent to do hurt to people, and one is thereby slain;[1] in each of these cases the killing amounts to murder; for although the mischief is not directed against any individual in particular, there is a general and depraved inclination, from which the law will imply malice. In all these cases the nature of the instrument and the manner of using it, as calculated to produce great bodily harm or not, will vary the offence. Thus if a man fires at another with a rifle, knowing it to be loaded, and therefore intending to kill or do grievous bodily harm, the killing would amount to murder; but if he did not know the weapon was loaded, no such presumption of intent arises.[2]

Where death is occasioned by the prosecution of a purpose not malicious or felonious but unlawful, it amounts to manslaughter only. This consideration, therefore, is properly referable to that general head. But if death ensue from a general combination to resist all opposers in the commission of any breach of the peace, or other object not felonious, executed in such a way as naturally tends to raise tumults and affrays, this will be murder;[3] for those who engage in such bold attempts must, at their peril, abide the consequences. To constitute murder, however, in such cases, the act must happen during the actual strife or endeavour, or at least within such a reasonable time afterwards as may leave it probable that no fresh provocation intervened.[4]

Unlawful intent.

When death ensues from a collateral act lawful in itself, it is in general homicide by misadventure. But if, in pursuit of their lawful and common occupations, persons see danger probably arising to others from their acts, and yet persist, without warning them of their

Lawful intent.

---

[1] 1 Hale, P.C. 475; 3 Inst. 57.   [3] 1 Hawk. P. C. c. 13, s. 51.
[2] *R.* v. *Campbell*, 11 Cox, C.   [4] 1 East, P. C. 259.
C. 323.

danger, if death ensue it will be murder. Thus, if
workmen throwing stones, rubbish, or other things from a
house in the ordinary course of their business, happen to
kill a person underneath, the question will be, whether
they deliberately saw the danger, or betrayed any consciousness of it. If they did, and yet gave no warning,
a general malignity of heart may be inferred, and the act
will amount to murder, from its gross impropriety.[1] So,
if a man driving a cart or carriage, drive over another,
and kill him, having had timely notice of the probable
danger, it will be murder.[2] For, from a wilful and
deliberate act which manifests a malignity of heart, the
law will infer malice.

Killing
officers of
justice
    All ministers of justice, and persons acting in their
aid, whether they be specially summoned thereunto or
not,[3] and all private persons endeavouring to suppress an
affray, or to apprehend a felon, are under the peculiar
protection of the law; and therefore the killing of one
so employed has been adjudged to be murder of malice
prepense, being an outrage wilfully committed in defiance
of public justice : and this, although the murderer knew
not the party that was killed.[4] This would seem to
apply only where the killing is with the intention of
inflicting bodily harm, or of resisting arrest, not where it
is caused accidentally in the course of a scuffle, in which
case it would amount to manslaughter only.[5] The
officers and persons acting in their aid, enjoy this
privilege and protection eundo, morando, et redeundo ;
and, therefore, if an officer on his way to his duty be
opposed and killed, it is murder ; so it is murder if he
arrive at the place, and, in consequence of opposition,

---

[1] 1 East, P. C. 262 ; 4 Bl.
Com. 194.

[2] 1 Hale, P. C. 476 ; Fost. C.
L. 263.

[3] 1 Hale, P. C. 462.

[4] 1 Hale, P. C. 457, 460 ;
Fost. C. L. 308.

[5] *R.* v. *Porter*, 12 Cox, C. C.
444.

retreat, and on his retreat be killed.[1] This doctrine is founded upon the necessity of protecting officers, and others acting under the like authority, in order to maintain the public tranquillity, and to secure private individual property ; and such being the source of this protection, it follows (1) that the authority must be legal ; (2) that it must be executed legally ; and (3) that it must be known to the party who resists it ; for unless all these requisites concur, the killing will not amount to murder, but only to manslaughter.

In the case of officers, it matters not, if the authority be legal, whether the party killing be guilty or innocent of the felony charged against him ; for, if an officer have a warrant from a magistrate to apprehend B. for felony, or if B. be indicted for felony, or if hue and cry be levied against him, and he or any of his accomplices kill the officer, it is murder.[2]   But, if a private person, without warrant, be killed in the attempt to arrest an innocent person, it will not be murder, but manslaughter only ; for an officer of justice has authority to arrest in such cases, but a private person has not.[3]   If a man actually commit a felony, and another, in whose presence he committed it, attempt to arrest him for it, and be resisted and killed ;[4] or, if a person present at an affray interfere for the purpose of restraining the offenders and keeping the peace, and be killed ;[5] or if a person present, when another attempts to commit a treason or felony, lay hold of him, in order to prevent him, and be killed ;[6] the killing, in each of these cases, will be murder, even though the person arresting or interfering be not an officer of justice ; for, in such cases, all persons are bound to arrest and interfere.

Authority ot private persons.

---

[1] Post. C. L. 308, 309 ; 9 Rep. 67 b ; 1 Hale, P. C. 462 ; *R.* v. *Phelps,* C. & Mar. 180.
[2] Fost. C. L. 318.
[3] 2 Hale, P. C. 84, 87, 91.
[4] 2 Hawk. P. C. c. 12, s. 1.
[5] 3 Inst. 52 ; 1 Hawk. P. C. c. 13, s. 48 ; Fost. C. L. 310.
[6] 2 Hawk. P. C. c. 12, s. 19.

180 CRIMINAL CASES.

Legality of warrant.

Many nice distinctions arise upon the legality of the warrant, and the manner in which it is executed; which, in most cases, extenuate the homicide, and reduce it to manslaughter; these will more properly be considered under that general head.

Notice.

It is essential, to constitute the offence of murder, that the slayer knew the officer's business, either expressly, or impliedly from circumstances; for, if it appear that he was ignorant in this respect, it is manslaughter only.[1] If an officer exhibit his warrant,[2] command the peace,[2] or show his staff,[3] or appear from the circumstances of the case to have been known to be an officer,[4] (even though, having a charge of felony against the party, he have no warrant, and do not tell him of the charge, and the party has in fact done nothing for which he is liable to be arrested,[5]) it will be sufficient, and the killing will amount to murder. If he be killed by one who knows him, it will be murder in the slayer, but only manslaughter in those assisting, who did not know him, unless the affray or breach of the peace which the officer endeavoured to suppress were the result of a preconcerted design, and a general determination to resist all opposition by force.[6] It will not be necessary to prove the appointment of the deceased as constable; for evidence of his having acted as such will be sufficient.[7] But unless a private person in all such cases expressly intimate his intention, the killing will amount to manslaughter only.[8]

Rescue.

It should be observed, however, that if the party who is arrested yield himself, and make no resistance, he will

---

[1] 1 Hawk. P. C. c. 13, s. 49, 50; Post. C. L. 310; 1 Hale, P. C. 458.
[2] 1 Hale, P. C. 461.
[3] Post. 311.
[4] Cro. Car. 183.

[5] *R.* v. *Woolmer*, 1 Mood. C. C. 334.
[6] 1 Hale, P. C. 438.
[7] 1 East, P. C. 315.
[8] 1 Fost. C. L. 310, 311; 1 Hawk. P. C. c. 13, s. 49.

not, unless he do some act to countenance them, be implicated in the guilt of those who attempt his rescue.[1] So, it would seem that, if, during the affray, one interfere to preserve the peace, and kill the constable unwittingly, he will not be guilty of murder; but if he interfere for the express purpose of aiding one party against the other, it will be murder.[2]

A special constable, duly appointed under the stat. 1 & 2 Will. 4, c. 41, is appointed for an indefinite time, and retains all the authority of a constable at common law, until his services are suspended or determined under the 9th section of that statute.[3] The police constables, also, who, under several statutes, general and local, are appointed to preserve the peace in the metropolis and other large towns, and in various counties, have in general by those statutes the authority and protection of a constable at common law.

Special constables.

By stat. 9 Geo. 4, c. 69, gamekeepers are empowered to apprehend poachers committing any offence either against the 1st or the 9th section of that act.[4] And if a keeper attempting lawfully to apprehend a poacher be met with violence, and in opposition to such violence, and in self defence, strike the poacher, and then be killed by him, it will be murder.[4] And though the gamekeeper cannot, without express authority, apprehend the poacher on the land of another person than his master;[5] yet an interference by a gamekeeper with persons found armed in the pursuit of game on the lands of an adjoining proprietor, without any attempt forcibly to apprehend, is not a sufficient provocation to reduce a malicious wounding and killing to manslaughter.[6] To authorize an apprehension

Game-keepers.

---

[1] Kel. 37 ; 1 Hale, P. C. 464.
[2] 1 East, P. C. 318.
[3] *R.* v. *Porter,* 9 C. & P. 778.
[4] *R.* v. *Ball,* 1 Mood. C. C. 330.

[5] *R.* v. *Price,* 7 C. & P. 178 ; *R.* v. *Davis,* Ib. 785 ; *R.* v. *Fielding,* 2 C. & K. 621.
[6] *R.* v. *Warner,* 1 Mood. C. C. 380.

under this statute, it is not necessary that the game-keeper should give notice of his purpose.[1]

Killing by officers and others

As officers of justice, and others acting under authority, are protected in the legitimate execution of their office, so it behoves them to act within the limits of their authority ; for if they wilfully exceed it without just cause, and death ensue, the law will imply malice, and they will be guilty of murder.

If resisted in the legal execution of his duty, an officer of justice or other person may repel force by force ; but if he kill where no resistance is made, or after the resistance be over, and time has elapsed for the blood to cool, it will be murder.[2] So, although he may be justified in killing a felon who cannot otherwise be overtaken, yet for a misdemeanor he must not kill the accused, though there be a warrant to apprehend him, and he cannot otherwise be overtaken.[3] So neither in civil suits will the officer be justified in using a deadly weapon, if the party against whom the process has issued fly, even after the arrest has been made, or from execution ; and if he do, and death ensue, he will be guilty of murder.[4] One shot at another, who was out at night as a ghost, dressed in white, for the purpose of alarming the neighbourhood, and it was holden to amount to murder ; for he who appeared as a ghost was only guilty of a misdemeanor.[5]

Absence of authority.

Officers, who, making an arrest out of their proper district, or without any warrant or authority, purposely kill the party for not submitting to such illegal arrest, will, in general, be guilty of murder, unless it be done

[1] *R.* v. *Payne,* 1 Mood. C. C. 378.
[2] 1 East, P. C. 297.
[3] Post. C. L. 271 ; 1 Hale, P. C. 481.
[4] Ibid.
[5] *Rex* v. *Smith,* Old Bailey, Jan. 1804, MS., Bayley, J., 1 Russ. on Cr. 770 ; 4 Bl. Com. 201, n.

under circumstances which would justify a private individual in so doing.

Gaolers and their officers are under the same special Gaolers. protection as other ministers of justice; but the law watches with great jealousy the conduct of such persons. If death be occasioned by duress of imprisonment, the law will imply malice, and the gaoler will be guilty of murder.[1] To constitute this duress, blows are not necessary; any cruel or oppressive treatment will be sufficient; and where a gaoler wilfully confined with a prisoner infected with the small pox one not having had that distemper, who caught it and died, this was holden to be murder.[2] The trust and charge which the law imposes on gaolers is the safe custody, and not the punishment of offenders; Carcer ad continendum, non ad puniendum haberi debeat. He only who does the act is criminally punishable for the consequences; and a principal will not, without participation in the act, be liable for the criminal misconduct of his under officer.[3]

Where a criminal is executed by the proper officer in Executions. pursuance of his sentence, this is justifiable homicide.[4] But if it be done by any other person, or not in strict conformity to the sentence, as by beheading where the sentence is hanging, it is murder.[5]

MANSLAUGHTER.

MANSLAUGHTER is the unlawful killing of another, without malice, either express or implied; and is either voluntary, from sudden transport of passion; or involun-

---

[1] Fost. C. L. 321; 1 Hale, P. C. 465.
[2] 2 Str. 856; Fost. C. L. 322.
[3] 2 Str. 854; Ld. Raym. 1574; Fost. C. L. 322; 1 E. P. C. 331.
[4] 4 Bl. Com. 178; 1 Hale, P. C. 501.
[5] 3 Inst. 52; 1 Hale, P. C. 433—501.

tary, ensuing from the commission of some unlawful act, or from the pursuit of some lawful act criminally or improperly performed,[1] or from the negligent omission of some duty. The absence of malice is, as has been already observed, the main distinction between this species of homicide and murder; and though manslaughter is in its degree felonious, and in the eye of the law criminal, yet it is imputed, by the benignity of the law, to the infirmity of human nature.[2]

The parties by and upon whom, and the means by which homicide may be committed, have already been discussed; it has also been observed, that all homicide is presumed to be malicious, until the contrary be proved; and it remains only under this title to enumerate the different grounds of extenuation.

Killing upon provocation. No provocation, however grievous, can render homicide justifiable, or even excusable; the least that it can amount to in contemplation of law is manslaughter.[3]

No insult, however grievous, whether by words of reproach or contemptuous actions or gestures, even though menacing bodily harm, unless accompanied by some act indicative of actual and immediate violence, will extenuate the guilt of murder, where a malicious intention is manifested by the use of deadly weapons, or other circumstances in the case. In the absence of such intention, however, if death unfortunately ensue from a blow, as a box on the ear, or stroke with a cane, it will be manslaughter only.[4] So if, upon insulting language, one strike another, and the blow be returned, upon which a scuffle ensue and the party insulting be killed, this is manslaughter only; for the blow is a new provocation, and the conflict sudden and unpremeditated.[5]

---

[1] 4 Bl. Com. 191.
[2] Fost. C. L. 290; 1 Hale, P. C. 466.
[3] 1 Russ. on Cr. 676.
[4] 1 East. P. C. 233; Fost. C. L. 291.
[5] 1 Hale, P. C. 456.

So, likewise, an assault made with violence and circumstances of indignity will, unless the punishment be disproportionate to the provocation, reduce the killing to
manslaughter. But it should be remembered, that the
act can merit no lenient consideration, nor be extenuated
as proceeding from the transport of passion, where the
revenge is disproportioned to the injury, and outrageous
and barbarous in its nature.

The unlawful restraint of personal liberty will also be
admitted in extenuation of the offence. A creditor placed
at the door of his debtor a man with a drawn sword to prevent his escape, while a bailiff was sent for to arrest him ;
the debtor stabbed the creditor, and this was holden to
be manslaughter only.[1] In considerations of this sort, the
question is, whether the restraint was or was not lawful ;
in the former case, the killing will be murder ; in the
latter, it will be manslaughter only.[2]

If a husband find another man in the act of adultery
with his wife, or a father find a man in the act of committing an unnatural crime with his son, and, in the transport of passion, kill him, it will be manslaughter of the
mildest character ;[3] but if the killing be deliberate, after
the offence committed, it will be murder.

There are other provocations of a more trivial description, which are allowed in extenuation of the killing,
where the circumstances show that the punishment was
inflicted with a view to correct, rather than to inflict
serious bodily harm. These have already been enumerated :[4] but it should be observed, generally, that in such
cases much depends upon the nature of the instrument
used, and the mode in which the punishment is inflicted ;
for, if the one be calculated to cause death, or the other
be outrageous and violent, an intention to kill will be im-

[1] Sty. 467 ; 1 East, P. C. 233.
[2] 1 East, P. C. 233.
[3] *R.* v. *Fisher*, 8 C. & P. 182.
[4] *Ante*, p. 175.

plied from either of these circumstances, and the offender will be guilty of murder.[1]　Where the provocation is sought for with a malicious intent, where time has elapsed for the passion to subside, or where express malice exists, no provocation, however grievous, can be admitted in extenuation.

Killing in mutual combat.

Killing by fighting is either murder, manslaughter, or homicide se defendendo, according to the circumstances of the case.　The first has already been discussed; the second will form the subject of the present head; and the third will be reserved for future consideration.

Where no circumstances of undue advantage at the onset, none to indicate express malice, and no deliberation appear, if a party be killed in mutual combat, it will be manslaughter only.　Thus, if parties quarrel and fight immediately, or even if, immediately upon the quarrel, they go out and fight in a field, the killing will be manslaughter only; for the whole is deemed one continued act of passion; and when such encounters are once begun, the blood kindles at every blow, and the voice of reason is subdued.[2]

If the parties at the commencement attack each other upon equal terms, and afterwards, in the course of the fight, one of them in his passion snatch up a deadly weapon and kill the other with it, this is manslaughter only.[3]　So where one, having received a mortal wound in a mutual combat, fell to the ground, upon which his antagonist took him by the nape of the neck, dashed his head upon the ground, and said, "damn you, you are dead," this was holden to be manslaughter only, there being no evidence of any unfair advantage.[4]　So where,

---

[1] 1 Hawk. P. C. c. 11, s. 5; 1 Russ. on Cr. 681.
[2] 3 Inst. 51; 1 Hale, P. C. 453; 1 Hawk. P. C. c. 31, s. 29; Ecst. C. L. 295.
[3] 1 East, P. C. 243; 5 Bur. 2793.
[4] 12 St. Tr. 114.

after mutual blows between the prisoner and the deceased, the prisoner knocked the deceased down, and, after he was upon the ground, stamped upon his belly with great violence, this was holden to be only manslaughter.[1]

If, after mutual blows, the combatants separate and one take a deadly weapon, not with the malicious design of provoking his antagonist, and, under that colour, of revenging his former quarrel, and, upon a fresh provocation and assault by his former opponent, use the weapon fatally, it will not be murder, but manslaughter only.[2]

Where sports are unlawful in themselves, or tend to disturb the peace, or to produce danger, riot or disorder, if, in the pursuit of them, death ensue, the party killing will be guilty of manslaughter. Such were, in former times, a tilt or tournament—the martial diversion of our ancestors; and such are boxing, prize-fighting, sword-playing, and the like—the succeeding amusements of their posterity.[3] It is said, indeed, that if such diversion be commanded or permitted by the sovereign, the act being in that case lawful, the killing would be misadventure only.[4] Generally it may be stated that all struggles in anger, whether by fighting, wrestling, or otherwise, are unlawful, and death occasioned by them is manslaughter at least.[5] *Dangerous sports.*

If, when two persons are fighting, a third come up, and take the part of one of them, and kill the other ; this will be manslaughter only in the third party.[6] This rule comprehends not only the natural and civil relations of parent and child, husband and wife, master and servant, but is applicable also to strangers : and this, even though the combatants are fighting upon malice, if that circumstance be unknown to the party interfering ; but if he *Persons assisting.*

---

[1] *R.* v. *Ayes,* R. & R. 166.
[2] *R.* v. *Snow,* L. C. L. 151.
[3] 4 Bl. Com. 183.
[4] 1 Hale, P. C. 473.

[5] *R.* v. *Canniff,* 9 C. & P. 359.
[6] 1 Hawk. P. C. c. 31, ss. 35, 36.

knew it when he interfered, the killing will be murder, both in the party who interfered and in him whom he assisted.[1] If, on the other hand, the party who interferes be killed, it is manslaughter only.[2]

Again, whenever the act would, if operating upon the object intended, have admitted of extenuation or excuse, the same rule will hold, though it unhappily fall upon another. Hence it is, that if a blow be aimed at A. in the heat of passion, which accidentally kills B., the killing will amount to manslaughter only.[3]

Killing by correction.

The circumstances which aggravate or extenuate the offence of killing by correction have been already enumerated.[4] If it be done with a dangerous weapon, likely to endanger life or cause bodily harm, due regard being had to the strength and age of the party, it will be murder; but if with an instrument not likely to cause death, though improper for correction, it will amount to manslaughter only. And where the act is manifestly intended for a good purpose, and the instrument used is not such as in all probability must occasion death, due weight should be given to the nature of the provocation, even though the party be hurried to great excess.[5] Where a father, whose son had been frequently guilty of stealing and, complaints having been made, had often been corrected by him for it, beat his son, in the heat of passion with a rope, by way of chastisement for another theft with which he was charged, but resolutely denied, although it was proved against him, and the son died, upon which the father expressed the greatest horror, and was in the deepest affliction for what he had done, intending only to have punished him with such severity as

---

[1] 1 East, P. C. 291, 292.
[2] Ibid., 12 Rep. 87 ; Kel. 59.
[3] Fost. C. L. 262 ; L. C. L.
148 ; 1 East, P. C. 245, 246.
[4] *Ante*, p. 174.
[5] 1 East, P. C. 261.

to have cured him of his wickedness ; this was holden to be manslaughter only.[1]

Correction by privation and ill-treatment will, if death ensue, be sufficient to constitute this offence ; for active and personal violence is not necessary. A master, upon his apprentice being sent to him from Bridewell in a lousy and distempered condition, did not take that care of him which his situation required, and which he might have done, but compelled him to lie on the boards for some time without covering, on account of the vermin, and without common medical care : the apprentice died, and, upon the trial of the master, the medical persons who were examined deposed that the boy's death was most probably occasioned by the ill-treatment in Bridewell and neglect when he went home, and they inclined to the opinion, that he might have recovered, if, when he went home, he had been properly treated. The apprentice had had sufficient sustenance, and there was no evidence of any personal violence having been used by the master, although some harsh expressions were proved to have been spoken by him to the boy ; on the contrary, the master's general treatment of his apprentices was humane, and he had made application to get this boy into the hospital. Upon this evidence, it was left by the recorder to the jury to consider whether the death of the apprentice was occasioned by the ill-treatment of the master ; telling them, that if they were of opinion that the ill-treatment amounted to malice, the offence was murder ; but if, on the other hand, there was no malice, (and this was said with the concurrence of Gould, J., and Hotham, B.,) they might, as the conduct of the master towards his apprentice was highly blameable and improper, under all the

Correction by privation.

---

[1] 1 East, P. C. 261. See also *Rex* v. *Hopley*, 2 F. & F. 202, and note (*b*) ; 1 Russ. on Cr. 775.

circumstances, find him guilty of manslaughter : which they accordingly did.[1]

Killing in
defence of
property. The killing of a party who attempts to commit a felony by force, or forcibly to dispossess another of the possession of his house, is properly referable to justifiable homicide, and under that head will be considered ; but it should be here observed, that it must be proved that the intent to commit such forcible and atrocious crime was clearly manifested by the felon ;[2] for, if that intent be not es- tablished, the homicide will be manslaughter at the least, if not murder, according to the circumstances of the case.

The attempt to commit a felony without force, or a misdemeanor of any kind, will not justify or excuse the killing of one so engaged. And, therefore, in the case of felonies without force, as picking pockets ;[3] or forcible misdemeanors, as trespass in taking goods ; although a beating may be justified, a killing will amount to manslaughter.[4]

Killing
without
intention,
whilst doing
another
act. We have seen, that where death ensues collaterally from an act done with a felonious or deliberately mis- chievous intent, the killing will be murder ;[5] it remains in this place to consider of the cases in which the mis- chievous intention and deliberation do not appear, and which will at least amount to manslaughter.

If death ensue from the commission of any unlawful act, contrary to public policy or morality, which does not amount to felony ; as, if one kill a man by shooting at the poultry of another wantonly, without intending to steal them ;[6] or by throwing a stone at another's horse, though not intending bodily harm to anyone, it is man-

---

1 1 East, P. C. 226.

2 1 Hale, P. C 484.

3 1 Hale, P. C. 488.

4 1 Hale, P. C. 485, 486.

5 *Ante*, p. 175.

6 Fost. C. L. 258, 259 ; 1 Hale, P. C. 475.

slaughter:[1] which rule extends to all acts which are unlawful in themselves, and includes prize-fighting, public boxing-matches, and such like sports,[2] cock-throwing,[3] and every act done without lawful authority.

So, acts may be unlawful from the manner in which they are done, even though there be no express intention to do mischief; as, if a man heedlessly and incautiously ride an unruly and vicious horse amongst a crowd, and the horse kick a man and kill him;[4] or throw a stone, or shoot an arrow over a house into a place where people are known by him to be passing, and kill a man; the killing in these cases will be manslaughter : for, although there was no intent to do hurt to anyone, the act was unlawful.[5] For the same reason, where a gentleman came to town in a chaise, and before he got out of it fired his pistols in the street, which by accident killed a woman, it was ruled to be manslaughter; for the act was likely to breed danger, and was manifestly improper.[6]

Again, acts may be civilly unlawful, but it is now held that the fact of a civil wrong having been committed is immaterial to the question of manslaughter, as where a man unlawfully removed a box from a refreshment room on a pier, and wantonly threw it into the sea, where it unfortunately fell upon and killed the deceased, it was held that the question of the degree of negligence was the sole test of whether the homicide was culpable or not.[7]

If death ensue from the performance of a lawful act, the killing will in general be homicide by misadventure merely. But there are exceptions to this rule; for, if the act be dangerous, in order to render an unintentional homicide from it excusable it must appear that the

Dangerous acts.

---

[1] 1 Hale, P. C. 39.
[2] Fost. C. L. 260.
[3] Fost. C. L. 261.
[4] 1 East, P. C. 231.
[5] 1 Hale, P. C. 475.

[6] 1 Str. 481 ; see 8 C. & P. 163.
[7] *R.* v. *Franklin*, 15 Cox, C. C. 164, commenting on *R.* v. *Fenton*, 1 Lewin, C. C. 179.

parties, whilst doing the act, used such a degree of caution as to make it improbable that any danger or injury
should arise from it to others ; if not, the homicide will be
manslaughter at the least.   Under this rule would fall the
cases of persons having charge of dangerous things, such
as vicious animals, unfenced machinery, and the like, and
neglecting to take due care of them.   Also cases of overt
acts of carelessness, such as, for instance, if a workman
throw stones or rubbish from a house, and thereby kill a
person passing underneath, it is murder, manslaughter, or
homicide by misadventure, according to the degree of
caution taken, or the necessity for such caution.   If it
be done without looking out, and giving timely warning
to such as may be below, and there was even a small
probability of persons passing by, it will be manslaughter.[1]
And it has been said, that even after warning given, it
will be manslaughter if the act be done in London or any
other populous town :[2] but this must be taken with limitation ; for if it be done early in the morning, when few
persons are stirring, or in a place which may be unfrequented, the act will, if ordinary caution be used, be excusable.[3]   So, if a man drive a cart furiously in a street
where persons are in the habit of passing, and kill another,
it will be manslaughter ; for the furious driving savours
of negligence and impropriety ; and in such a case it
would be no defence to show that he had called repeatedly
to clear the way.[4]   So, if the driver of a carriage race
with another carriage, and urge his horses to so rapid a
pace that he cannot control them, and in consequence
the carriage upset and a passenger be killed, it is manslaughter in both drivers.[5]   The amount of caution re-

---

[1] 1 Hale, P. C. 475 ; Fost. C
L. 262.
[2] Kel. 40.
[3] Post. C. L. 263.
[4] 1 East, P. C. 263 ; R v.
Walker, 1 C. & P. 320 ; R. v.
Mastin, 6 C. & P. 396 ; R. v.
Grout, lb. 629.
[5] R. v. Swindall, 2 C. & K.
230 ; R. v. Timmins, 7 C. & P.
499.

quired would be commensurate to the liability to danger; thus, the driver of a carriage is not bound to keep on the proper side of the road, but, if he do not do so, he is bound to use more care and keep a better look out.[1] Navigation of a vessel at undue speed, or negligently conducted, imposes similar liability to an indictment for manslaughter.[2]

And, generally, if any person upon whom the law imposes any duty, or who has by contract or by any wrongful act taken upon himself any duty tending to the preservation of life, and who neglects to perform that duty and thereby·causes the death of another, is guilty at least of manslaughter.[3]   What amount of negligence is necessary to complete the offence must depend on the circumstances of each particular case, and is best summed up and illustrated by the converse definition of what does not amount to culpable negligence.   An effect is defined by Stephen, J.,[4] to be accidental " when the act by which it is caused is not done with the intention of causing it, and when its occurrence as a consequence of such act is not so probable that a person of ordinary prudence ought, under the circumstances in which it is done, to take reasonable precautions against it."

Negligence.

But it is to be observed that it is no defence in such cases that the deceased was guilty of contributory negligence.   Practically, no doubt, the same facts which go to prove contributory negligence would be taken into consideration in arriving at a conclusion upon the question whether the death was caused by the negligence or improper conduct of the person accused;[5] but this is really the only question for the jury, and if they find

Contributory negligence.

---

[1] *Pluckwell* v. *Wilson*, 5 C. & P. 375.
[2] *R.* v. *Taylor*, 9 C. & P. 672.
[3] Stephen's Cr. L. art. 211.

See *R.* v. *Curtis*, 15 Cox, C. C. 746, and cases *ante.* p. 159.
[4] Stephen's Cr. L. art. 210.
[5] See *R.* v. *Jones*, 11 Cox, C. C. 544.

J.   O

this in the affirmative it matters not whether the deceased was deaf or drunk, or negligent, or in part contributed to his own death ; and in this consists a great distinction between civil and criminal proceedings.[1] And, if a person's death be occasioned by the neglect of several, they are all guilty of manslaughter; it is no defence for one who was negligent, to say that another was negligent also, and thus as it were to try to divide the negligence between them.[2]

Where death caused indirectly. In all these cases a verdict of manslaughter is only justified where the death is the direct consequence of the act or omission. Thus, the negligence of a servant or subordinate will not generally render his employer or superior guilty of manslaughter if death ensue,[3] unless the employer be proved to have known that the servant was incapable of the duty entrusted to him.[4] Trustees, appointed under a local act for the purpose of repairing roads in a district, with power to contract for executing such repairs, have been held not chargeable with manslaughter where a person, using one of their roads, was accidentally killed in consequence of the road being out of repair through neglect of the trustees to contract for repairing it.[5]

Killing in port. Sports not unlawful in themselves must yet be exercised with a proper precaution, to prevent accidents;[6] and, therefore, although it will be homicide by misadventure only, if a man, shooting at a butt or a target,

---

[1] *Per* Pollock, C. B., in *R.* v. *Swindall,* 2 C. & K. 230 ; see also *R.* v. *Walker,* 1 C. & P. 320 ; *R.* v. *Hutchinson,* 9 Cox, C. C. 555 ; *R.* v. *Jones,* 11 Ib. 544 ; *R.* v. *Kew,* 12 Ib. 355. In *R.* v. *Birchall,* 4 F. & F. 1087, Willes, J., is reported to have taken a different view.

[2] *R.* v. *Haines,* 2 C. & K. 368 ; *R.* v. *Salmon,* 6 Q. B. D.

79.

[3] *R.* v. *Bennett,* 1 Bell, C. C. 1 ; 28 L. J., M. C. 27. See also *R.* v. *Ledger,* 2 F. & F. 858.

[4] *R.* v. *Lowe,* 3 C. & K. 123 ; *R.* v. *Haines,* 2 C. & K. 268 ; *R.* v. *Barrett,* Ib. 343.

[5] *R.* v. *Pollock,* 17 Q. B. 34.

[6] Football, see *R.* v. *Bradshaw,* 14 Cox, C. C. 83.

accidentally kill a bystander,[1] yet, if the target be placed near a highway or path where persons are in the habit of passing, the killing would probably be deemed manslaughter.[2] If death is caused by injuries received in a friendly sparring match, which is a thing not likely to cause death, it is not manslaughter unless the parties fight on until the sport becomes dangerous,[3] or unless any undue advantage has been taken.[4] A., playing with his servant, made a pass at him with a sword in a scabbard, which the servant parried with a bed-staff, and, in doing so, struck off the chape of the scabbard and exposed the end of the sword ; the thrust not being effectually broken, the servant was killed by the point of the sword ; and this was adjudged manslaughter : for the use of such a weapon in such an exercise was evidently a want of common caution, and manifestly exposed the servant to bodily harm.[5] Where a lad out of a frolic took the trapstick out of the front of a cart, in consequence of which it upset, and a carman who was loading sacks in it was killed, this was holden to be manslaughter.[6] If, heedlessly and out of brutal sport, an improper quantity of spirituous liquors be given to a child of tender years, and death ensue, it will be manslaughter.[7]

It has already been observed, that if an officer of justice, or person legally authorized, be killed while in the legal execution of that authority, by one to whom the authority is known, the killing may amount to murder ; but that, unless all these circumstances concur, the protection of the law will not be extended to such

Killing officers and others.

---

[1] 1 Hale, P. C. 38, 472, 475.
[2] Arch. C. P. 550 ; *R.* v. *Salmon*, 6 Q. B. D. 79.
[3] *R.* v. *Young*, 10 Cox, C. C. 371. See p. 187.
[4] 1 East, P. C. 269.
[5] 1 Hale, P. C. 472, 473 ;

Aleyn, 12 ; Kel. 188.
[6] *R.* v. *Sullivan*, 7 C. & P. 641.
[7] *R.* v. *Martin*, 3 C. & P. 211. See also *R.* v. *Packard*, C. & M. 236.

persons, and the killing will be manslaughter only. It becomes necessary in this place, therefore, to consider,— 1. What is a legal authority ; 2. What is a legal execution of that authority ; and, 3. What is sufficient notice of that authority to the party by whom the outrage is committed.

Authority to arrest and imprison.

Authority to arrest and imprison is of three sorts :— 1, in cases of felony ; 2, in cases of misdemeanor ; and 3, upon civil process ; to which may be added a fourth kind, which arises out of the exigency of the state, and justifies the restraint of personal liberty, viz., a press-warrant, which extends, in terms, to " seamen, seafaring men, and others, whose occupations and calling are to work in vessels and boats upon rivers." [1]

Felony.

If a felony be committed, and the felon fly from justice, or if a dangerous wound be given, or if, having been arrested, the felon break away as he is being carried to gaol, it is the duty of every one, whether he be an officer of justice or a private individual, to use his best endeavour to prevent an escape ; and not only those who are eye-witnesses of the transaction, but, if the pursuit be fresh, and à fortiori, if hue and cry be levied, all others who join in it are under the protection of the law,[2] even though there be no warrant of a justice of the peace to raise the hue and cry, and the pursuit be made without the assistance of a constable.[3]

Upon suspicion of felony.

It is the duty of all, whether peace officers or private individuals, to arrest, without warrant, those who are detected in the commission of, or in the attempt to commit, a felony ;[4] but there is a great distinction between the authority of officers and private persons to arrest upon suspicion, however well founded. In the case of the

---

[1] 1 East, 466 ; Fost. C. L. 156.
[2] 1 East, P. C. 298.
[3] 1 Hale, P. C. 464.
[4] R. v. Hunt, 1 Mood. C. C. 93.

latter, it must be clearly ascertained that a felony has been actually committed [1] by the person whom it is intended to pursue or arrest; for, if no felony have been committed, or, if committed, the party pursued or arrested be innocent, no suspicion, however well founded, will bring him who is pursuing or endeavouring to arrest within the protection of the law.[2] Upon this principle, it has been said, that a private individual is not bound to arrest, without warrant, one against whom an indictment for felony has been found; [3] but it seems agreed, that he may arrest upon that ground, although, if in so doing he be killed, the quality of the offence, whether murder or manslaughter, will depend upon the guilt or innocence of the party upon whom the attempt is made.[4] But officers of justice are bound, ex officio, to arrest, as well on a well-founded suspicion of felony, as in the case of a felony actually committed, and may therefore arrest one who stands indicted for felony; [5] for, this is suspicion grounded upon high authority. So, an officer may justify an arrest on a charge of felony, without a warrant, upon a well-grounded suspicion,[6] even though no felony have been actually committed; but the party suspecting should be present at the arrest, and should detail to the constable the circumstances, that he may judge of the probability of the suspicion; [7] although a formal and accurate charge is not necessary.[8]

In general it is necessary to justify an arrest for a misdemeanor that the officer have the warrant with him, eady to be produced if required; [9] but all officers of

Misdemeanor.

---

[1] 2 Inst. 52. 172 ; Fost. C. L. 318 ; Dougl. 359 ; Cro. Jac. 194.
[2] 1 Hale, P. C. 490 ; Fost. C. L. 318.
[3] 2 Hale, P. C. 84, 85, 87, 91, 93.
[4] Dalt. c. 176, s. 5 ; 1 East, P. C. 301.
[5] 1 Hawk. P. C. c. 10, s. 12.
[6] Dougl. 359 ; R. v. Ford, R. & R. 329.
[7] 1 Hale, P. C. 79—93 ; 3 Inst. 221 ; 1 East, P. C. 301.
[8] R. v. Ford, R. & R. 329.
[9] R. v. Chapman, 12 Cox, C. C. 4.

justice have authority to interpose, upon their own view, for the purpose of preventing a breach of the peace, or quelling an affray ; in which case, both the officers and all who assist, whether specially summoned thereto or not, are within the protection of the law.[1] It seems, however, that they have not, without warrant, any authority to arrest upon a charge of a mere breach of the peace, after the affray is ended ;[2] although, where the life of another is menaced or while there is danger of a renewal of the affray,[3] a constable may, to avoid present danger, arrest the party menacing, and detain him until he can conveniently bring him before a justice of the peace, if the complaint be made to the constable forthwith.[4] But the bare circumstance of officers having authority will not, unless they act within the scope of that authority, bring them within the protection of the law. As, if two officers take different sides in an affray, and one be killed, it will be manslaughter only ; for, by becoming partisans, they lose their character of officers, and act without any authority whatsoever.[5] So, says Lord Hale, if the sheriff have a writ of possession against the house of A., and A. pretend it to be a riot upon him, and gain the constable of the vill to assist him, and to suppress the sheriff or his bailiff, and, in the conflict, the constable be killed ; this is not so much as manslaughter : but if any of the sheriff's officers be killed, it is murder, because the constable had no authority to encounter the sheriff proceeding and acting by virtue of the king's writ.[6]

Private persons.

Private persons have authority, if they give express notice of their friendly intent, to interpose, in the case of

---

[1] 1 East, P. C. 303.
[2] 1 Russ. on Cr. 721.
[3] *R.* v. *Light,* 27 L. J., M. C. 1.
[4] 2 Hale, P. C. 88 ; 1 East,

P. C. 306.
[5] 1 East, P. C. 304 ; 1 Hale, P. C. 460.
[6] 1 Hale, P. C. 460 ; 1 East, P. C. 305.

sudden affrays, to part the combatants and prevent mischief;[1] but, unless they express that intention, they are not within the protection of the law ; for, the combatants cannot know but that they interfere as partisans.

No private person has any authority to arrest in civil suits : such power can alone be conferred by writ or order, and must be limited and regulated, as well by that delegation, as by the extent of the district within which the officer is entitled to act. [2]

Civil process.

Press-warrants are always directed to commissioned officers, and if executed by any other person, he will not be within the protection which the law affords to its officers ;[3] for it is a power of an extraordinary nature, which none should assume who are not duly qualified for that purpose.

Press-warrants.

The foregoing observations upon the authority to arrest and imprison, in cases of felony and misdemeanor, have been made without reference to process ; which may here, properly, be discussed, as applicable to every kind of authority before enumerated. If an officer be resisted and killed in the endeavour to execute process, it will be murder if the process be legal—if it be illegal, the crime will amount to manslaughter only.

To constitute legal process, two things must concur ; (1) it must take its source from a Court or person having competent jurisdiction and authority ; and (2) it must be so far legal, that it be not defective in its frame.[4]

If the process issue from a Court or person having competent jurisdiction, it will confer an authority, even though there be error or irregularity in the previous proceedings,[5] or the charge contained in it be utterly

Process lawfully issued.

---

[1] 1 Hawk. P. C. c. 13, ss. 48, 49.
[2] 1 Hawk. P. C. c. 10, s. 19.
[3] Eost. C. L. 154 ; 1 East, P. C. 312, 313 ; *R.* v. *Borthwick,* 1 Dougl. 207.
[4] 1 East, P. C. 309.
[5] 1 Hale, P. C. 457.

unfounded.[1] The officer to whom the writ is directed
must, at his peril, pay obedience to the writ;[2] and it is
the duty of every man to submit himself to the regular
process of the law, even though it be obtained by gross
imposition, or be founded upon falsehood.[3] So, though
the cause be not expressed with sufficient particularity,
the process will justify the officer, if enough appear to
show that the magistrate has jurisdiction over the
subject-matter,[4] and it be not defective in the essential
requisites. It is the process which confers the authority;
and if an officer be killed in the execution of process, the
production of the writ and warrant is sufficient evidence
of his authority, without resorting to the previous proceedings.[5]

Defective
process.

If the process be defective upon the face of it, as if
there be a mistake in the name or addition of the party
to be arrested; or if the name of the officer, or of the
party to be arrested, be inserted without authority, and
after the issuing of the process; or if the officer be not
the one to whom the warrant is addressed;[6] it will
amount to manslaughter only, if the officer be killed by
him whose liberty is invaded.[7] Warrants issued in
blank, and filled up after they are sealed, are illegal, and
confer no authority:[8] but the name of the officer may be
inserted before the warrant is issued from the sheriff's
office, or before it is delivered to the officer by the
magistrate, if it be filled up by him, although it be
signed before the name is inserted.[9]

Execution
of autho-
rity.

Much depends upon the manner in which a legal

[1] 1 East, P. C. 310.
[2] 1 Hale, P. C. 459, 460.
[3] Eost. C. L. 135.
[4] 1 East, P. C. 310.
[5] Eost. C. L. 311 ; 2 Stark.
205.
[6] R v. Saunders, L. R., 1
C. 75.

[7] 1 East, P. C. 310 ; and see
the American case, Rafferty v.
The People, 12 Cox, C. C. 617.
[8] Housin v. Barrow, 6 T. R.
122 ; 19 St. Tr. 846.
[9] Per Lord Kenyon in Rex v.
Winwick, 8 T. R. 454.

authority is executed ; for the law gives no protection to
those who proceed irregularly, and exceed the limits of
their authority.[1] For example, a peace officer, making an
arrest under a justice's warrant, is bound to have the
warrant in his possession at the time, in order that it
may be produced if required.[2] And this rule applies as
well to public officers of justice as to private individuals ;
for, by exceeding their authority, they in both characters
forfeit the special protection of the law, and, if they be
killed, the killing will amount to manslaughter only.

None can execute process but a legal officer for that
purpose, or his assistant. If he make an arrest out of
the jurisdiction of the Court from whence the process
issues, or without warrant or authority ; or upon A., the
warrant being against B. ; or on a Sunday, except in
cases of treason, felony, or a breach of the peace :[3] he
will not be within the protection of the law, and if he be
killed, the killing will amount to manslaughter only.[4]
So, if an arrest be made within an exclusive jurisdiction,
under a writ not containing a non omittas clause, if the
officer be killed, it will not amount to murder.[5] But if
the process be directed to a particular constable by
name, or even by his name of office, and he execute it
within the jurisdiction from whence it issues, that is
sufficient, although it be out of the vill of the constable.[6]

Outside the jurisdiction of the person issuing the
warrant, the constable has generally no power to execute
it unless backed.[7] By the statutes 11 & 12 Vict. c. 42,
s. 10, and c. 43, ss. 2, 7, a warrant for an indictable
offence, or an offence punishable upon summary con-

Backed warrants.

---

[1] Fost. C. L. 312.
[2] *Galliard* v. *Laxton*, 2 B. &
S. 363 ; S. C. 8 Jur., N. S. 642 ;
R. v. *Chapman*, 12 Cox, C. C.
4 ; *R.* v. *Carey*, 14 Cox, C. C.
214.
[3] 29 Car. 2, c. 7, s. 6.

[4] 1 Russ. on Cr. 707 ; 1 East,
P. C. 312.
[5] 2 Stark. 205.
[6] 2 Hawk. P. C. c. 13, ss.
27, 30 ; 1 Hale, P. C. 459.
[7] See *R.* v. *Cumpton*, 5 Q. B.
D. 341 ; and 35 & 36 Vict. c. 92.

viction, may be executed by apprehending the offender
at any place within the county, riding, division, liberty,
city, borough, or place within which the justice or
justices issuing the same shall have jurisdiction, or in
case of fresh pursuit at any place in the next adjoining
county, &c., without having the warrant backed as
therein mentioned;[1] "and in all cases where such
warrant shall be directed to all constables or other peace
officers within the county or other district within which
the justice or justices issuing the same shall have jurisdiction, it shall be lawful for any constable, headborough,
tithingman, borsholder, or other peace officer for any
parish, township, hamlet, or place within such county or
district to execute the said warrant within any parish,
township, hamlet, or place situate within the jurisdiction
for which such justice or justices shall have acted when
he or they granted such warrant, in like manner as if
such warrant were directed specially to such constable by
name, and notwithstanding the place in which such
warrant shall be executed shall not be within the parish,
township, hamlet, or place for which he shall be such
constable, headborough, tithingman, borsholder, or other
peace officer : provided always, that no objection shall be
taken or allowed to any such warrant for any defect
therein in substance or in form, or for any variance
between it and the evidence adduced on the part of the
prosecution before the justice or justices who shall take the
examinations of the witnesses in that behalf, as hereinafter
mentioned ; but if any such variance shall appear to such
justice or justices to be such that the party charged has
been thereby deceived or misled, it shall be lawful for such
justice or justices, at the request of the party so charged,

---

[1] See 11 & 12 Vict. c. 42, ss. 11   101, and 19 & 20 Vict. c. 69,
—15 ; c. 43, ss. 2, 19. See also   s. 6.
5 & 6 Will. 4, c. 76, ss. 76,

to adjourn the hearing of the case to some future day, and in the meantime to remand the party so charged, or to admit him to bail in manner hereinafter mentioned." Without a warrant, a constable has at common law no authority to act out of his vill.[1] A warrant directed to several, may be executed by any one or more of the persons to whom it is directed.[2] And in no case is a constable bound to take a prisoner before a particular magistrate desired by the prisoner himself, but the constable is at liberty to use his own discretion, unless the warrant be special and direct otherwise.[3] The arrest may be as well at night as by day.

Persons found committing any indictable offence in the night may be apprehended and delivered over to a constable or other peace officer by any person whatsoever.[4]

Offences at night.

It is a maxim of law, that every man's house is his castle, for the safety and repose of himself and his family. For this reason it is, that an officer cannot justify the breaking open an outer door or window to execute civil process. By doing so, he becomes a trespasser, and cannot, therefore, be considered as acting within the scope of his authority : and consequently, if in such cases the occupier of the house resist the officer, and kill him, it will not be murder, but manslaughter only.[5] This privilege is allowed only in cases where the outer doors or windows are closed ; for, if the outer door be open, or part open,[6] the officer may enter, and break an inner door, or window if that be necessary, for the purpose of executing his process. So, having obtained peaceable entrance into a house, he may break open the door or window of a room in which a lodger resides, after notice of his purpose, and a demand and refusal to open

Breaking doors in civil process.

---

[1] 1 Hale, P. C. 459.
[2] 1 East, P. C. 320 ; 1 Hale, P. C. 459.
  5 Rep. 59.
  14 & 15 Vict c. 19, s. 11.

[5] 1 East, P. C. 321 ; Fost. C. L. 319 ; Cro. Car. 537.
[6] *Semayne's case*, 1 Smith, L. C. 85.

the door , ⸱ and this, it would seem, even though the
lodger be not within the house at the time. But in such
case the officer must first demand admittance.[2] But, if
the person or goods of the party against whom the
process issued be within the house, no demand is
necessary.[3] This privilege is confined to the occupier of
the house and his family, and to such as have their
ordinary domicile there ;[4] and is allowed only in cases
of arrests in the first instance ; for if, having been legally
arrested, one escape, and take shelter even in his own
house, it will afford him no sanctuary ; and, upon fresh
pursuit, the officer may break open the outer door in
order to retake him, after due notice of his purpose, and
a demand of admission and refusal.[5] But if it be not
upon fresh pursuit, a warrant from a magistrate is
necessary.[6] And in entering the house of a stranger the
officer will not be justified, unless the defendant or his
goods be actually therein.[7]

Breaking doors in criminal cases.

The interests of private individuals cannot be permitted to obstruct the course of justice, in which the
public are interested ; and this privilege, therefore, is
confined to arrests upon process in civil suits. Where a
felony has been committed, or a dangerous wound given,[8]
where officers of justice are armed with process founded
on a breach of the peace,[9] with process of attachment
founded upon a contempt of the courts of justice,[10] with a
writ of capias utlagatum,[11] or habere facias possessionem,[12]

[1] *Lee* v. *Gansel,* Cowp. 1 ; *Lloyd* v. *Sandilands,* 2 Moore, 207.
[2] *Ratcliffe* v. *Burton,* 3 Bos. & Pul. 223.
[3] *Hutchinson* v. *Birch,* 4 Taunt. 619.
[4] Fost. C. L. 320 ; 5 Rep. 93.
[5] 1 East, P. C. 324 ; 2 Hawk. P. C. c. 14, s. 9.
[6] 1 East, P. C. 324.
[7] *Johnson* v. *Leigh,* 6 Taunt. 246 ; *Cooke* v. *Birt,* 5 Taunt 765.
[8] 1 Hale, P. C. 459 ; Fost. C. L. 320 ; 1 East, P. C. 322.
[9] 2 Hawk. P. C. c. 14, s. 3.
[10] *Burdett* v. *Abbott,* 14 East, 157.
[11] 1 Hale, P. C. 459 ; 2 Hawk. P. C. c. 14, s. 4.
[12] *Semayne's case,* 1 Smith, L. C. 85.

the party's own house is no sanctuary for him, but the outer doors may be broken, after a notification of the business of the officer, and a demand of admittance and refusal.[1] Officers are invested with the same authority in the execution of a warrant from a magistrate for levying a penalty on a conviction upon any statute, the whole or part of which goes to the crown.[2]

A bare suspicion of guilt will not, however, even though a felony have been actually committed, justify an officer in proceeding to this extremity, unless he be armed with a warrant from a magistrate founded upon such suspicion.[3] If, without that authority, he break open the doors, he will do so at the peril of proving that the party taken was actually guilty.[3] But, according to Lord Hale,[4] if a felony be actually committed, and the charge be laid before a constable, and there be reasonable ground of suspicion ; or if there be an affray in a house, and the doors be shut, whereby there is likely to be manslaughter or bloodshed committed; or, if there be any disorderly drinking or noise at an unseasonable time of the night, especially in inns, taverns or alehouses, the constable on his watch, demanding entrance, and being refused, may break open the doors to see and suppress the disorder.[5] So, if an affray be made in the view of the constable, and he pursue the affrayers, who fly to a house into which he is not permitted to enter, he may, in the immediate pursuit, break open the doors to apprehend the affrayers.[6]

Breaking doors on suspicion.

It is essentially necessary that due notice of the authority should be given to the parties whose liberty is interfered with ; for otherwise the killing will amount to manslaughter only.[7] In the case of private individuals who interfere to suppress an affray, or part the comba-

Notice of authority.

[1] Fost. C. L. 136, 137.
[2] 2 Hawk. P. C. c. 14, s. 5.
[3] 1 East, P. C. 322.
[4] 2 Hale, P. C. 92.
[5] 2 Hale, P. C. 95.
[6] 2 Hawk. P. C. c. 14, s. 8.
[7] 1 Hale, P. C. 458 ; Fost. C. L. 310 ; 1 Hawk. P. C. c. 13, ss. 49, 50.

tants, express notice of their intention is necessary ;
for otherwise, the parties concerned may justly, in the
irritation of the moment, imagine that they engage as
parties in the affray.[1] So, for the same reason, must
constables and other officers of justice, who as conservators
of the peace, and by that authority, interfere to suppress
riots and affrays, intimate their intention to the parties
engaged.[2] In the latter case, however, an express notice
is not necessary ; for if the peace be commanded, or if, acting within their own district, or by authority of law out
of it, they be known or acknowledged to bear the office
they assume ; or if, it being day, they produce their staff
or other known ensign of office ; or, in the night, command
the peace, or make use of words indicative of their office,
the law will presume that the party killing had due
notice of the authority ; and the killing will amount to
murder.[3]

The same notification is necessary where the act is done
by virtue of a delegated authority, in the execution of
process. A bailiff pushed abruptly and violently into a
gentleman's room, early in the morning, in order to
arrest him, not telling his business, or using words of
arrest ; the party not knowing that the other was an
officer, on the first surprise snatched down a sword which
hung in his room, and killed the bailiff, this was held to
be manslaughter only.[4] There is, in this respect, a distinction between the execution of process by a known and
sworn officer, and a private or special bailiff ; in the case
of the former, the law will imply notice in the instances
before enumerated,[5] and he need not show the warrant
constituting him bailiff or constable ; in that of the latter,
he must declare his business and authority, as by using

---

[1] Fost. C. L. 310, 311.
[2] Fost. C. L. 310, 311 ; Kel.
66, 115.
[3] Fost. C. L. 310, 311 ; 1
East, P. C. 314, 315 ; *R.* v.

Woolmer, 1 Mood. C. C. 334.
[4] 1 Hale, P. C. 470 ; Fost. C.
L. 298.
[5] 1 East, P. C. 319.

words of arrest or the like ; and must, if it be demanded produce the warrant under which he acts.[1] But in neither case is notice necessary where the conduct of the party shows that he knew the business of the officer ; as where one said to a bailiff who came to arrest him, "Stand off, I know you well enough, come at your peril," and afterwards killed the bailiff; this was holden to be murder.[2] Both the public and private bailiff are, if the party submit to the arrest, bound, upon demand, to show at whose suit, and for what cause, and out of what court the process issues, and when and where it is returnable ;[3] but neither can be compelled to part with the possession of the warrant, which is their justification,[4]

If an affray be sudden and unpremeditated, and a constable, who comes to suppress it, be killed in the attempt by one who knows him, it is murder in the party killing, and in all such as know the constable, and abet in the fact; manslaughter only in those who know not the constable,[5] and yet abet in the fact ; but not even manslaughter in those who continue the affray, without a knowledge of the constable, or a participation in the killing.[6] But if the affray be deliberate, and the result of a preconcerted illegal design, if the constable be known to one only of the party, that will be sufficient, and all will be implicated in murder, if the constable be killed.[7] The rule is different, however, if an officer be killed gratuitously, in the execution of process, by a third party who knows him not, provided the business of the officer be known to the party to whom the assistance is afforded ; for he who deliberately engages in cool blood in an affray,

---

[1] East, P. C. 319.
[2] 1 Hale, P. C. 458 ; 9 Rep. 69 ; Cro. Car. 193 ; Kel. 67.
[3] 6 Rep. 54 ; 9 Rep. 68 a.
[4] 1 East, P. C. 319.
[5] 1 Hale, P. C. 438, 446,

461 ; Kel. 115, 116.
[6] 1 East, P. C. 316 ; 1 Ha P. C. 446. See 4 Rep. 40 b ; Inst. 52.
[7] Kel. 115 ; 4 Rep. 40 b.

not intending to preserve the peace, must, at his peril, satisfy himself of the justice of the cause which he espouses.[1] But if the interference were with the intent to preserve the peace only, and to prevent mischief, it would seem that the killing would amount to manslaughter only.[2]

Interference by third persons. How far the illegality of the arrest will extenuate the guilt of third persons, especially of strangers who interpose on behalf of the party illegally arrested, is a question upon which much difference of opinion exists.[3] Upon this subject, a learned author,[4] after a careful examination of the authorities, observes :—"It may be worthy of consideration, whether the illegality of the arrest does not place the officer attempting it exactly on the same footing as any other wrongdoer ; and, whether in the case of interference by a stranger or any other person, the question of provocation ought not to be governed by the same rules as regulate ordinary cases of the like sort." If this principle be correct, (and it has the sanction of Mr. Justice Foster,) nothing but an open striving or affray can be a sufficient provocation to any person to meddle with an injury done to another, so as to reduce the offence of killing to manslaughter, even in the case of an unlawful arrest ;[5] if, therefore, the party arrested submit quietly, and a mere stranger gratuitously assault and kill him whom he supposed to have done the injury, this will be murder, even though the arrest were illegal.

Killing by officers and others. Officers of justice and others having authority may repel force by force, if resisted while in the legal execution of their duty.[6] The degree of force, however, must be

---

[1] 1 Hawk. P. C. c. 31, ss. 57, 59 ; Keb. 87 ; 4 Rep. 40 b ; 1 East, P. C. 316, 317.

[2] Sid. 159 ; 1 Kel. 584.

[3] 2 Ld. Raym. 1296 ; Kel. 59 ; 1 Hale, P. C. 465 ; Cro. Car. 371 ; *R.* v. *Adey*, 1 L. C.

L. 206 ; Fost. C. L. 138.

[4] 1 East, P. C. 328.

[5] 1 Hale, P. C. 465.

[6] Fost. C. L. 270, 271 : 1 Hale, P. C. 494 ; 2 Ibid. 117, 111 ; 3 Inst. 56.

apportioned to the resistance offered ; for if upon a slight provocation they proceed to extremities,[1] or, after the resistance has ceased, but before the blood has cooled, they kill the party, the crime will amount to manslaughter at the least.[2] So, although felons may be killed if they cannot be otherwise taken, yet, if they be killed where they may be taken without resorting to such severity, it will be manslaughter.[3] If, in the attempt to arrest for a misdemeanor or breach of the peace, or in civil process, the party be killed, it will, in general, be murder, for the occasion will not justify such severity ; but even in such cases the quality of the offence depends much upon the degree of force used ; for, if death be manifestly not intended, but unfortunately ensue from an act not calculated to produce it, the killing will amount to manslaughter only.[4] Where private persons endeavour to arrest and imprison those suspected of a felony, two things must be attended to : first, that a felony has actually been committed? and secondly, that it was committed by the party arrested or pursued upon suspicion ; for, unless the party pursued or arrested be actually guilty, if he be killed, the killing will amount to manslaughter.[5]

The conduct of gaolers and their officers is also subject to the same rule of construction ; for, if death ensue from a punishment disproportionate to the provocation, they will be guilty of manslaughter. An assault upon a gaoler, which would warrant him (independently of personal danger) in killing a prisoner, must be such from whence he might reasonably apprehend that an escape was intended, which he could not otherwise prevent.[6] If, in the execution of a sentence, whipping for instance, the

Gaolers.

---

[1] 1 Vent. 216.
[2] 1 East, P. C. 297.
[3] Ibid. 298.
[4] Fost. C. L. 271 ; 1 East,

P. C. 302 ; 1 Hale, P. C. 481.
[5] Fost. C. L. 318.
[6] 1 East, P. C. 331.

J.   P

officer cruelly exceed all bounds of moderation, and death
ensue, he will at least be guilty of manslaughter.[1]

Resistance to officers. If resistance be offered to the proper officer who has a
legal warrant to impress, he may repel force by force ;
and if the party resisting be killed in the struggle, it
seems justifiable, provided the resistance cannot otherwise be overcome.[2] But, if the party fly, and be killed,
it will be manslaughter at the least, and in some cases
murder, according to the circumstances and the general
rules which govern arrests in cases of misdemeanor. If
done with a weapon likely to cause death, it will be
murder ; if with a collateral intent, it will amount to
manslaughter only.[3]

EXCUSABLE HOMICIDE.

Excusable homicide is of two sorts : either per infortunium, by misadventure ; or se et sua defendendo, upon a
principle of self-preservation.[4] In this species of homicide, as the term imports, some fault attaches upon the
party by whom it is committed, but it does not amount
to felony : and although formerly the forfeiture of goods
was inflicted as a punishment upon the delinquent, that
is now abolished, and the party is entitled to his discharge.[5]

By misad-venture Homicide per infortunium, or misadventure, is where
a man, doing an act, without any intention to inflict an
injury, unfortunately kills another, where the act is
lawful, and is performed with due caution and in a proper
manner, and without any intention of bodily harm, and
the effect is merely accidental.[6]

---

[1] 1 Hawk, P. C. c. 11, s. 5. c. 36, ss. 169 *et seq.*
[2] 1 East, P. C. 308.   [4] 4 Bl. Com. 182.
[3] Cowp. 832. In cases of [5] 24 & 25 Vict. c. 100, s. 7.
smuggling, see 39 & 40 Vict. [6] 4 Bl. Com. 182.

Parents, masters, and others having authority in foro domestico, may give reasonable correction to those under their care, and, if death ensue, it is only misadventure; for the act of correction was lawful;[1] but if the correction exceeds the bounds of moderation, either in the manner, the instrument, or the quantity of punishment, and death ensue, it is, as we have seen, manslaughter at the least, and in some cases murder, for the act is unlawful.

If in the pursuit of common and ordinary occupations death unfortunately ensue, from an act done with due caution and regard to the safety of others, the killing will be misadventure only; as where a man is at work with a hatchet, the head of which flies off and kills a by-stander; for the act is lawful, and the effect is merely accidental.[2] So, if workmen throw stones or rubbish in their ordinary occupation over a wall, or from a house in a retired situation, or where persons are occasionally passing, if it be not in a populous town or place much frequented, and timely notice be given;[3] or if one drive a cart or waggon with proper care and caution, and unfortunately kill a man;[4] in each of these cases the killing will be excusable, and be misadventure only. Where a third person whips a horse on which a man is riding, whereupon the horse springs out, and runs over a child and kills him, the rider is guilty only of homicide by misadventure; but he who gave the blow is guilty of manslaughter.[5]

In order to excuse a party from guilt where death ensues from the pursuit of ordinary occupations, due caution must be used, and be proportionate to the danger of the instrument employed or pursuit engaged in. Where a man lays poison to kill rats, and another takes it, and

Killing by correction.

Killing in pursuit of common occupations.

---

[1] 1 East, P. C. 261; 4 Bl. Com. 182.

[2] 1 Hawk. P. C. c. 11, s. 2. Fost. C. L. 262; 1 Hale,

P. C. 472, 475.

[4] 1 East, P. C. 263.

[5] 2 Hawk. P. C. c. 11, s. 3.

is killed ; if the poison were laid in such a manner or place as to be mistaken for food, it is, perhaps, manslaughter; if otherwise, misadventure only.[1] Where a man gave a loaded gun to his servant to protect a cornfield from deer during the night, with instructions to fire when he heard any bustle in the corn by the deer ; and the master himself unfortunately rushed into the corn during the night, and the servant, imagining it to be the deer, fired, and shot his master; this was holden to be misadventure.[2] A man finding a pistol in the street, brought it home, and imagining (from having tried it with the ramrod) that it was not loaded, presented it in sport at his wife, drew the trigger, and unfortunately killed her; this was ruled to be manslaughter :[3] but Mr. Justice Foster doubts the propriety of this decision, as the defendant took the usual precaution to ascertain that the pistol was not loaded ;[4] and this doubt seems well warranted, for the utmost caution is not necessary, reasonable precaution being sufficient, such as is usual in similar cases, and has been ordinarily found by experience to answer the end.[4]

Killing in support of lawful sports.

We have seen, that if death ensue from sports unlawful in themselves, or productive of danger, riot, or disorder, the party killing will be guilty of manslaughter ; but if it ensue from such sports as are innocent and allowable, the case will fall within excusable homicide.[5] Of the latter class are manly sports and exercises which tend to give strength, activity, and skill in the use of arms, as cudgel-playing, wrestling, and fencing, when entered into as private recreations merely.[5] If a man shooting at a butt, or a target, by accident kill a bystander, it is misadventure,[6] but this must be understood

---

[1] 1 Hale, P. C. 431.
[2] 1 Hale, P. C. 476.
[3] Kel. 41.
[4] Fost. 264, 265.

[5] 1 East, P. C. 268 ; ante, p. 195.
[6] 1 Hale, P. C. 472, 475, 38.

of cases where a proper precaution to prevent accidents has been taken; for, if the target or butt be placed near a highway or path, where persons are in the habit of passing, the killing would probably be deemed man-slaughter.[1] So, formerly, when a qualification as well as a licence was necessary to entitle a person to shoot game, if a man shooting at game by accident killed another, it was homicide by misadventure only, even although the party were unqualified;[2] for the use of fire-arms by one who is unqualified or unlicensed was not malum in se, out merely prohibited.

Homicide in self-defence, or se et sua defendendo, upon a sudden affray, is also excusable, rather than justifiable, by the English law. The self-defence of which we are now treating, proceeds from the allowance which is conceded to the universal principle of self-preservation, and is of three sorts : homicide, in defence of person ; homicide, in defence of property : and homicide, from unavoidable necessity, founded upon the principle of self-preservation.

Killing in defence of person.

Where a man is assaulted in the course of a sudden brawl or quarrel, he may, unless he have some other possible, or, at least, probable, means of escape, protect himself from the assault by killing the aggressor.[3] This is what the law expresses by chance medley, or chaud-medley, the former signifying a casual affray, and the latter an affray in the heat of blood and passion, both being the same in import, and applying, in strictness, to such killing as happens in self-defence upon a sudden encounter.[4] This right of natural defence does not imply a right of attacking ; for, instead of attacking one another for injuries past or impending, men need only have recourse to the proper tribunals of justice. Nor does it justify counter blows struck with a desire to fight.[5] Men

---

[1] *R.* v. *Salmon,* 6 Q. B. D. 79.
[2] Fost. C. L. 259.
[3] 4 Bl. Com. 184.
[4] 4 Bl. Com. 184.
[5] *R.* v. *Knock,* 14 Cox, C. C. 1.

cannot, therefore, exercise this right of preventive defence but in sudden and violent cases, where certain and immediate suffering would be the consequence of waiting for the assistance of the law. Wherefore it is, that to excuse homicide by the plea of self-defence, it must appear that the slayer had no other possible, or, at least, probable, means of escaping from his assailant.

Provoca-
tion. The true criterion between homicide by chance medley in self-defence, and manslaughter, which border very nearly upon each other, seems to be this :—when both parties are actually combating at the same time when the mortal stroke is given, the slayer is then guilty of manslaughter ; but if the slayer have not begun to fight, or, having begun, endeavour to decline any further struggle, and afterwards, being closely pressed by his antagonist, kills him, to avoid his own destruction, this is homicide excusable by self-defence.[1]

It matters not who gave the first blow, or from whom the provocation proceeded, if the slayer, before the act be committed, really and bonâ fide endeavour to decline any further struggle, and escape from his antagonist.[2] But, as the act can only be excused upon the principle of unavoidable necessity, the law requires that the person who kills another in his own defence, should have retreated as far as he conveniently or safely can, to avoid the violence of the assault, before he turns upon his assailant ; and that not fictitiously, or in order to watch his opportunity, but from a real anxiety to avoid bloodshed. The party assaulted must, therefore, flee as far as he conveniently can, either until his further retreat is prevented by reason of some wall, ditch, or other impediment ; or, until the fierceness of the assault renders forbearance dangerous to himself ; for, it may be so fierce as not to allow him to

[1] 4 Bl. Com. 184 ; Fost. C. L. 277.   [2] Fost. C. L. 277 ; 1 Hale, P. C. 482.

yield a step without manifest danger of his life or enormous bodily harm ; and then, in his defence, he may kill his assailant instantly.[1]

Not only the manner of the defence, but the time, also, is to be considered ; for, if the person assaulted do not fall upon the aggressor until the affray is over, or when he is running away, this is revenge, and not defence. Neither will the law permit a man to screen himself from the guilt of deliberate murder under the colour of self-defence ; for, if two persons agree deliberately to fight, one of whom makes the first onset, and the other retreats as far as he safely can, and then kills his opponent, this is murder, because of the previous malice and concerted design.[2]

Under this excuse of self-defence, the principal civil and natural relations are comprehended ; therefore, master and servant, parent and child, husband and wife, killing an assailant in the necessary defence of each other respectively, are excused ; the act of the relation assisting being construed the same as the act of the party himself.[3] Thus, under circumstances which might have induced the belief that a man was cutting the throat of his wife, their son shot and killed his father. It was held that if the son had reasonable grounds for believing and honestly believed that his act was necessary for the defence of his mother, the homicide was excusable.[4] Defence of relations.

We have seen, that in the case of forcible misdemeanors, such as trespass in taking goods, although the owner may justify beating the trespasser in order to make him desist, yet, if he kill him, it will be manslaughter, or, perhaps, murder, if he attack him with a deadly weapon after the party had desisted from the trespass. But, Killing in defence of property.

---

[1] 4 Bl. Com. 185 ; 1 Hale, P. C. 483.

[2] 1 Hale, P. C. 482

[3] 4 Bl. Com. 186 ; 1 Hale, P. C. 484.

[4] *R. v. Rose,* 15 Cox, C C. 540.

in defence of a man's house, the owner or his family may kill a trespasser who would forcibly dispossess him of it, in the same manner as he might by law kill, in self-defence, a man who attacked him personally ;[1] with this distinction, however, that, in defending his house, he need not retreat, as in other cases of se defendendo, for that would be giving up his house to his adversary.[2]

Killing from un- avoidable necessity.

There is one species of homicide, in which the party slain is equally innocent as he who occasions his death ; and yet this homicide was formerly considered to be ex- ensable, from the great universal principle of self-preser- vation, which prompts every man to save his own life in preference to that of another, where one must inevitably perish : such, amongst others, was the case mentioned by Lord Bacon,[3] where two persons, being shipwrecked, got on the same plank, but finding it not able to save them both, one of them thrust the other from it, whereby he was drowned, he who thus preserved his own life at the expense of that of another was excused through unavoid- able necessity and the principle of self-defence, since both remaining on the same weak plank is a mutual, though innocent, attempt upon and endangering by each of the life of the other.[4]   This subject was thoroughly discussed in the recent case of Reg. v. Dudley and Stephens,[5] where the facts as stated in the special verdict of the jury were that the prisoners, able-bodied seamen, and the deceased, a boy between seventeen and eighteen years of age, were cast away in a storm in an open boat 1600 miles from land.   The food they took with them had all been con- sumed in 12 days, and they had been for 8 days without food and for 6 days without water.   The prisoners then killed and eat the boy, who when killed was too weak to

---

[1] 1 Hale, P. C 486 ; Fitz.
Cor. 35 ; Crompt. 27 b.
[2] 1 Hale, P. C. 485, 486.
[3] Elem. c. 5 ; 1 Hawk. P. C.

c. 28, s. 26.
[4] 4 Bl. Com. 186.
[5] 15 Cox, C. C. 624 ; 14 Q.
B. D., 273, 560.

offer resistance, but did not assent to being killed. The jury found that " if the men had not fed upon the body of the boy, they would probably not have survived to be picked up and rescued, but would have died of famine ; that the boy being in a much weaker condition was likely to have died before them ; that at the time of the act in question there was no sail in sight nor any reasonable prospect of relief ; that under the circumstances there appeared to the prisoners every probability that unless they then fed, or very soon fed, upon the boy or one of themselves they would die of starvation ; that there was no appreciable chance of saving life except by killing someone for the others to eat; that, assuming any necessity to kill anybody, there was no greater necessity for killing the boy than any of the others." It was held that the above facts afforded no justification for killing the boy, and Lord Bacon's view that a man may save his own life by killing if necessary an innocent and unoffending neighbour, was overruled.

JUSTIFIABLE HOMICIDE.

This species of homicide is of three kinds : the first arising from unavoidable necessity, without any will, intention or desire, and without any inadvertence or negligence in the party killing, and without any shadow of blame, which is homicide in the execution of the law ; the second, which is justifiable rather by the permission than by the absolute command of the law, is homicide for the advancement of public justice, which without such indemnity would never be carried on with proper vigour ; and the third, which is of a private nature, is homicide in the just defence of person or property, or for the prevention of some atrocious crime, which cannot otherwise be avoided. In neither of these cases is the slayer in any even the minutest fault, but is entitled to his acquittal and discharge, with commendation rather than with censure.

Killing in execution of law.

Of the first class are those cases in which one is obliged by virtue of an office, in the execution of public justice, to put a malefactor to death who has forfeited his life by the laws and verdict of his country. This is an act of necessity, and even of civil duty, and therefore not only justifiable, but commendable, where the law requires it. But the law must require it, otherwise it is not justifiable; for, wantonly to kill the greatest of malefactors, a felon or a traitor, attainted or outlawed, deliberately, uncompelled, and extrajudicially, is murder.[1] If, therefore, judgment of death be given by a judge not authorized by lawful commission, and execution be done accordingly, the judge is guilty of murder.[2] So also the judgment must be executed by the proper officer or his appointed deputy, and that it must be done servato juris ordine; for, if another execute it, or the sentence be varied, it will be murder.

Killing in advancement of law.

Homicides committed for the advancement of public justice are,—1. Where an officer, or one acting in his aid, in the execution of his office, either in a civil or a criminal case, kills a person that assaults and resists him: 2. Where an officer or any private person attempts to take a man charged with felony, and, in the endeavour to take him, kills him: 3. Where an officer kills a man in the endeavour to disperse a mob: and, 4. Where prisoners in gaol, or going to gaol, assault the gaoler or officer, and he, in his defence, kills any of them for the sake of preventing an escape. To these were formerly added two further cases, in which the homicide was justifiable, viz. the killing in trial by battle (now abrogated by 59 Geo. 3, c. 46);—and the homicide of

----

[1] Hale, P. C. 497.   [2] 4 Bl. Com. 178.

trespassers in forests, parks, closes, or warrens, by virtue of several statutes now repealed, and to which further reference is therefore unnecessary. In all cases of homicide there must however be an apparent necessity for the act; for, without such absolute necessity, it will not be justifiable.[1]

Where an officer of justice is resisted in the legal execution of his duty, he may repel force by force; and if, in so doing, he kill the party resisting him, it is justifiable homicide, as well in civil as criminal cases.[2] The same rule applies to persons acting in his aid. Thus, if a peace-officer have a legal warrant against B. for felony, or if B. stand indicted for felony, or if hue and cry be levied against him, and he resist, and, in the struggle, be killed by the officer, or any person acting in his aid, or joining in the hue and cry, the killing is justifiable.[3] So, if a private person attempt to arrest and imprison one who commits a felony in his presence, or interfere to suppress an affray, and, being resisted, kill the person resisting; this is justifiable homicide.[4] And, in such cases, the party arresting is not bound to withdraw, as where the homicide is excusable se defendendo, but may stand his ground and attack the party; for, few men would submit quietly to an arrest, if, where resistance was offered, the party empowered to arrest were bound to retire and leave his business unfinished. There must, however, be an apparent necessity for resorting to this extremity; for if the officer kill after the resistance has ceased,[5] or where there is no reasonable cause for the violence,[6] the killing will be manslaughter at the least. Also, in order to justify an officer or private person in these cases, it is necessary that they should, at the time

Resistance to officers.

---

[1] 4 Bl. Com. 180.
[2] 1 Hale, P. C. 494; 2 Ibid. 118.
[3] Fost. C. L. 318.

[4] 1 Hale, P. C. 484; Fost. C. L. 275; 1 East, P. C. 297.
[5] 1 East, P. C. 297.
[6] 1 Vent. 216.

be in the legal execution of their duty, so as to entitle them to the protection of the law; for, if they act illegally so as to reduce the killing by the party resisting to manslaughter, they also will, if they kill the party resisting, be guilty of manslaughter at the least.[1]

Pursuit by officers.

Where an officer or private person, having legal authority to apprehend a man, attempts to do so, and the man, instead of resisting, flies, or resists and then flies, and is killed in the pursuit, it is murder, manslaughter, or justifiable homicide, according to the circumstances of the case.—Justifiable if the offence with which the man was charged be treason or felony, or a dangerous wound be given;[2] murder, if the arrest be intended in a civil suit, or the party be charged with a breach of the peace or misdemeanor merely, or if a pressgang kill a seaman or person flying from them;[3] but manslaughter only, if the homicide be occasioned by means not likely to cause death.

Riots.

In the case of a riot, or rebellious assembly, the officers endeavouring to disperse the mob are justified at common law in killing them :[4] and by the common law also every private person may lawfully endeavour of his own authority, and without any warrant or sanction of the magistrate, to suppress a riot by every means in his power. He may disperse or assist in dispersing those who are assembled; he may stay those who are engaged in it from executing their purpose; he may stop and prevent others whom he may see coming up from joining the rest; and not only has he authority, but it is his bounden duty as a good subject of the king, to perform

---

[1] Post. C. L. 318. 1 Hale, P. C. 490. As to the arrest of offenders against the revenue laws, see 39 & 40 Vict. c. 36, ss. 169 et seq.

[2] 1 Hale, P. C. 481; 2 Ibid. 118, 119, 79; 1 Hawk. P. C. c. 10, ss. 11, 12; Fost. C. L. 271.

[3] 1 East, P. C. 212, 308; R. v. Borthwick, 1 Dougl. 207; R. v. Dadson, 2 Den. C. C. 35.

[4] 1 Hale, P. C. 495; 1 East P. C. 304.

this to the utmost of his ability. If the riot be general and dangerous, he may arm himself against the evil-doers to keep the peace.[1] Whatever a private person may do, soldiers under arms may unquestionably do also.

If prisoners in gaol, or going to gaol, assault the gaoler, or his officer, and he in his defence kill any of them, this is justifiable, for the sake of preventing an escape.[2] Being under the special protection of the law, they are not bound to draw back, if they meet with resistance from the prisoners, either in civil or criminal suits, or from those who come to their assistance, but may repel force by force.[3] — Prisoners in gaol.

Homicide committed for the prevention of any forcible or atrocious crime is justifiable at common law.[4] If, however, any person attempt to rob or murder another, or attempt burglariously to break into any dwelling-house, or break open any dwelling-house in the daytime, with a felonious intent,[5] or attempt to burn a house, or to commit a rape,[6] or to commit any other forcible and atrocious crime, and be killed, the homicide is justifiable. Not only the party whose person or property is thus attacked, but his servants and other members of his family, and even strangers who are present at the time, are equally justified in killing the assailant.[7] And it is not necessary in such cases that the party whose person or property is attacked should retreat, as in other cases of self-defence ; he may pursue the assailant until he find himself and his property out of danger.[8] But this rule — Killing in defence of person or property.

---

[1] 1 Hawk. P. C. c. 28, s. 14 ; 5 Burn's J. 20 ; *Case of arms*, Popham, 121 ; per Tindal C. J., in charging grand jury at Bristol, reported 5 C. & P. at p. 262, and quoted in *Phillips* v. *Eyre*, L. R., 6 Q. B. 15.

[2] 1 Hale, P. C. 496.

[3] Post. C. L. 321.

[4] Bract. 155.

[5] 1 Hale. P. C. 445.

[6] Bac. Elem. 34 ; 1 Hawk. P. C. c. 28, s. 22.

[7] 1 Hale, P. C. 481, 484 ; Fost. 274.

[8] Fost. C. L. 273.

does not extend to cases of felony without force, nor to misdemeanors of any kind.

In all cases, even within the rule, it must be proved that the intent to commit the forcible and atrocious crime was manifested by the felon ;[1] for, if it be not so proved, the homicide will be manslaughter at the least, if not murder. It does not, however, seem to be necessary for the justification of the slayer, that a felony should have been actually intended, provided due circumspection be used, and there be reasonable ground for supposing that to be the case ;[2] but it should be remembered, that the manifestation of a felonious intent is absolutely necessary ; and that in no case can a party be justified, who, by his own conduct, provokes the assault.[3]

---

[1] 1 Hale, P. C. 484.
[2] Cro. Car. 538 ; 1 Hale, P. C. 42, 474.
[3] 1 East, P. C. 277 ; 1 Hawk. P. C. c. 10, s. 22 ; 1 Hale, P. C. 440, 441.

APPENDIX.

FORMS.[1]

1. *Form of Declaration of Office of Coroner.*

I solemnly, sincerely, and truly declare and affirm that I will well and truly serve our Sovereign Lady the Queen and her liege people in the office of coroner for this county [*or, borough, or as the case may be*] of   , and that I will diligently and truly do everything appertaining to my office after the best of my power for the doing of right, and for the good of the inhabitants within the said county [*or, borough, or as the case may be*].

2. *Form of Oath of Jury.*

You shall diligently inquire and a true presentment make of all such matters and things as are here given you in charge on behalf of our Sovereign Lady the Queen, touching the death of C. D., now lying dead, of whose body you shall have the view, and shall without fear or favour, affection, or ill-will, a true verdict give according to the evidence and to the best of your skill and knowledge. So help you God.

3. *Form of Inquisition.*[2]

Middlesex, to wit. An Inquisition taken for our Sovereign Lady the Queen at   , in the parish of   , in the county [*or as the case may be*] of   , on the   day of   , 18

---

[1] The first four of these forms are prescribed by the schedule to the Coroners Act.

[2] In cases of murder or manslaughter, to be written on parchment 14 inches wide.

[and by adjournment on the   day of   , *or as the case may require*] before A. B., one of the coroners of our Lady the Queen for the said [county, *or as the case may be*] upon the oath [*or*, and affirmation] of [*in the case of murder or manslaughter here insert the names of the jurors*, L. M., N. O., &c. *being*] good and lawful men of the said [county, *or as the case may be*] duly sworn to inquire for our Lady the Queen, on view of the body of C. D. [*or*, of a person to the jurors unknown] as to his death ; and those of the said jurors whose names are hereunto subscribed upon their oaths do say :—

Here set out the circumstances of the death, as, for example :

(*a.*) That the said C. D. was found dead on the   day of   in the year aforesaid at   in the county of   , [*or set out other place of death*] and

(*b.*) That the cause of his death was that he was thrown by E. F. against the ground, whereby the said C. D. had a violent concussion of the brain and instantly died [*or set out other cause of death*].

Here set out the counclsion of the jury as to the death, as for example

(*c.*) and so do further say, that the said E. F. did feloniously kill [*or*, feloniously, wilfully, and of malice aforethought murder] the said C. D.

Or, do further say that the said E. F. by misfortune and against his will did kill the said C. D.

Or, do further say that E. F. in the defence of himself [and property] did kill the said C. D.

In case of there being an accessory before the fact add :

And do further say that K. L., before the said murder was committed, did feloniously incite [*or*, procure, aid, counsel, and command, *or as the case may be*] the said E. F. to commit the said murder.

At end add .

In witness whereof as well the said coroner as the jurors have hereunto subscribed their hands and seals the day and year first above written.

Another example is :

That the said C. D. did on the   day of   fall into a pond of water situate at   , by means whereof he died.

Here set out the conclusion of the jury as to the death, as for example :

And so do further say that the said C. D., not being of sound mind, did kill himself.

Or, do further say that the said C. D. did feloniously kill himself.

Or, do further say that by the neglect of E. F. to fence the

said pond C. D. fell therein, and that therefore E. F. did
feloniously kill the said C. D.

Or, do further say that the said C. D. by misadventure fell
into the said pond and was killed.

---

4. *Form of Recognizance.*

—— *to wit.* BE it remembered that   on the   day
of   , 18 , each of the following persons, namely, J. K.
of   and R. S. of   [*insert the names of all bound over*]
personally came before me, A. B., one of the coroners of
our Lady the Queen for the county [*or as the case may be*]
of   , and acknowledged to owe to our Sovereign Lady the
Queen the sum of   pounds to be levied on his goods and
lands by way of recognizance to her majesty's use if default
is made on his part [*or,* on the part of I. K.] in the conditions following :—

*In case of recognizance to appear and give evidence before the
coroner, add :*

He shall appear personally at the court of the said coroner
to be held on the   day of   next, at   in the
said county [*or as the case may be*], for holding an inquest on
the view of the body of C. D., there to give evidence of anything he knows touching the death of C. D., and shall not
depart the said court without leave.

*In case of recognizance to prosecute and give evidence at assizes,
add :*

He shall appear personally at the next sessions of oyer and
terminer or gaol delivery to be holden at   , in and for
the county of   , there to prosecute and give evidence to
the jury that try E. F. [now in custody for the wilful murder
of C. D.], upon the inquisition taken before me, the above
named coroner, on view of the body of C. D., and shall not
depart the court without leave.

In case of recognizance to appear for trial :

He shall appear at the next sessions of oyer and terminer
or gaol delivery to be holden in and for the county of   ,
and there surrender himself into the custody of the keeper of
a gaol in which prisoners committed for trial at those sessions
are detained, and plead to the inquisition taken before me,
the above-named coroner, on view of the body of C. D.,
whereby a verdict of manslaughter has been found against
him, and shall take his trial upon that inquisition, and shall
not depart the court without leave.

In every case add at the end :

Then if the above conditions are fulfilled, this recognizance
shall be void, but otherwise shall remain in full force.

J.   Q

5. *Petition for the Election of a Coroner.*

To the Right Honorable Baron Halsbury, Lord High Chancellor of Great Britain.

The humble petition of us whose names are hereunto sub scribed, on behalf of ourselves and others, freeholders of the county of

Showeth,

That C. D., esquire, late one of the coroners for the said county of   , departed this life on or about the   day of   , and was buried on the   day of   , as appears by the annexed certificate. And that it will be for her majesty's service, and the general good of the said county, to have a proper and fit person elected coroner in the room and stead of the said C. D. deceased.

> Your petitioners, therefore, most humbly pray your lordship's order, that the clerk of the Petty Bag do make out a writ de Coronatore eligendo, for the election of a new coroner for the said county of in the room and stead of the said C. D., deceased. And your petitioners shall ever pray, &c.

6. *Writ de Coronatore eligendo.*

In case of Death.

VICTORIA, &c. To the council of   , greeting : For-asmuch as   , esquire, late one of the coroners of your county, is deceased :—We command you that, if it be so, you cause another coroner to be chosen in the place of the said   , who, having made the declaration as the manner is, may thereupon do and keep those things which concern the office of a coroner in the said county : And you shall cause to be chosen such a person as best may know and be most able to discharge that office ; and certify unto us his name. Witness ourself at Westminster the   day of in the   year of our reign.

In case of Removal.

VICTORIA, &c. To the council of   , greeting : For-asmuch as   , esquire, late one of our coroners of your county, is so much occupied in doing our divers businesses in your county, that he hath not leisure to exercise those things which belong to the office of a coroner in the same county, as we certainly understand, we have removed him from that office :—We command you, &c. [*as above*].

Or thus : Forasmuch as we have received information, from worthy testimony, that   , esquire, late one of our coroners of your county, is so infirm and broken with old age, that he is not able to exercise those things which belong to the office of a coroner in the same county, we have commanded him, the said   , to be removed from that office :—Therefore we command you, &c. [*as above*].

---

7. *Writ de Coronatore exonerando.*

VICTORIA, by the grace of God, of the United Kingdom of Great Britain and Ireland, Queen, defender of the faith. To the council of   greeting : Forasmuch as we have for certain understood that C. D., one of our coroners of your county, was appointed coroner for your county in the year   , that he is about to quit the county, and to reside at a distance therefrom, and therefore cannot perform the duty of a coroner in your county :—We command you, that without delay you remove the said C. D. from the office of a coroner in your county. Witness ourself at Westminster, the eighteenth day of June, in the sixteenth year of our reign.

Or thus : VICTORIA, &c. To the council of   greeting : Forasmuch as we have for certain understood that C. D., of   , in your county, esquire, one of our coroners of your county, was appointed a coroner for your county in the year   : That on the   day of   last, a certain information was exhibited against him for certain misdemeanors alleged to have been committed by him in his office of one of the coroners of your county, on which he was tried at the last Shropshire assizes, when a verdict was found for the Crown, the jury at the same time stating, that there was no proof before them of his having received any bribe, and that he is also subject to severe rheumatic attacks ; and, from the above circumstances, he considers himself incapable any longer to perform the duty of a coroner as he ought to do :— We command you, that without delay you remove the said C. D. from the office of a coroner in your county. Witness ourself at Westminster, the '   day of   , in the year of our reign.

---

8. *Treasure Trove.*

Somerset, to wit. An inquisition indented, taken at Crowcombe, in the county aforesaid, on Friday the 19th day of September, in the 9th year of the reign of our Sovereign

Lord George the Second, by the grace of God of Great
Britain, France, and Ireland, King, defender of the faith,
&c., and in the year of our Lord 1735, by and before me,
George Cary, gent., one of the coroners of our said Lord the
King, within and for the said county, upon making inquiry
of certain treasure trove, lately found in the mansion-house
of Thomas Carew, of Crowcombe aforesaid, esquire, within
the manor of Crowcombe Bickham, in the said county, by
virtue of my office, and of the statute in that case made and
provided, upon the oaths of A. B., C. D., &c. [*naming the
jurors*], good and lawful men of the county aforesaid, who,
being charged upon their oath, and having heard evidence
upon oath produced to them, do say, that in or about the
month of June, in the year of our Lord 1724, Thomas
Parker, of Gittisham, in the county of Devon, joiner, in
pulling down the said late mansion-house of Thomas Carew,
Esq., aforesaid (he, the said Thomas Parker, being employed
by the said Thomas Carew, therein), did then and there find,
hidden in a vacant place in the wall of the said late mansion-house, certain parcels of old silver coin or old silver
monies, contained in several bags, amounting together, in
the whole, to the value of £700 and upwards sterling, of
current monies of this realm, and that the said Thomas
Carew is [and at the time of the said finding was] the reputed
lord of the said manor, and as such entitled to the several
royalties thereof, as appears by the several ancient records
and court rolls to the said coroner and jurors produced in
evidence. And the said jurors do further say, that the said
Thomas Parker then and ever since, to the time of the taking
of this inquisition, concealed his finding the said old silver
coin, or old silver monies, from the knowledge of the said
Thomas Carew; and the said jurors do further say, that the
said Thomas Parker is now in full life, and living at Gittisham aforesaid: In testimony whereof, as well I, the said
coroner, as the jurors aforesaid, have hereunto severally set
our hands and seals, the day, year, and place first above
mentioned.[1]

Another Form.

Town of Cambridge, to wit. An inquisition indented, taken
at the house commonly called or known by the name of the
Eagle Inn, situate in the town of Cambridge, in the county
of Cambridge, the fourth day of February, in the seventh

---

[1] This inquisition, extracted from Umfreville, was settled by Mr. Justice Chapell, then King's Serjeant.

year of the reign of our Sovereign Lord George the Fourth,
by the grace of God of the United Kingdom of Great
Britain and Ireland, King, defender of the faith, and in the
year of our Lord one thousand eight hundred and twenty-
six, before me, Aaron Chevell, gentleman, one of the
coroners of our Lord the King, for the town aforesaid, upon
the oaths of A. B., C. D., E. F., &c. [*naming the jurors*], good
and lawful men of the town of Cambridge aforesaid, who,
being sworn and charged to inquire on the part of our said
Lord the King, of and concerning certain treasure, lately
said to be found within the said town, upon their oath say,
that, on the third day of June last, one hundred and ninety-
five pieces of gold coin, in all weighing thirty-four ounces
five pennyweights, and of the value of one hundred and
thirty pounds and three shillings, of lawful money of Great
Britain; and three thousand five hundred and ten pieces of
silver coin, in all weighing two hundred and eighty-nine
ounces and fifteen pennyweights, and of the value of seventy
pounds and five pence halfpenny, of like lawful money, were
found by William Smith and Stephen Woodcock, being
labourers then in the employment of James Howell, of the
said town, bricklayer, hidden in the ground under the site of
an ancient house or building, situate in Benet-street in the
said town; and which said pieces of gold or silver coin were
of ancient time hidden as aforesaid, and the owner whereof
cannot now be known: And the jurors aforesaid, upon their
oath aforesaid, do further say, the said pieces of gold and
silver coin were deposited, and now remain in the custody of
Thomas Mortlock, of the said town, banker; which said
pieces of gold and silver coin, I the said coroner have taken
and seised into his Majesty's hands: In witness whereof, as
well the aforesaid coroner as the said jurors, have to this inquisition put their hands and seals on the day and year, and
at the place first above written.

9. *Judgment in Outlawry.*

A. B., being five times called to answer to our Sovereign
Lady the Queen, according to the tenor of this writ, and not
appearing, the coroners of this county, by virtue of their
office, do pronounce him outlawed [*or if the defendant be a
woman*, " do pronounce her waived "].

10. *Certificate of necessity for Appointment of Deputy Borough Coroner.*

Borough of —— to wit. Whereas, J. B., coroner for the
said borough, has satisfied us that he is under the necessity

of absenting himself from the said borough for weeks
[*or*, that he is at present ill, and unable to execute the duties
of his office], we do, therefore, certify that it is necessary
that a deputy coroner be appointed to act for the said
borough during the absence [*or*, illness] of the said J. B. and
no longer.

Witness our hands and seals this   day of

——— Mayor.

or ——— } two justices of the said borough.

---

11. *Indictment for not taking an Inquest.*

The jurors for our Lady the Queen, upon their oath present, that on the   day of , in the year , one
R. F. was drowned in a certain pond, and that the body of
the said R. F. at &c., lay dead, of which C. D., gentleman,
afterwards, to wit, on the   day of , in the year
aforesaid, then being one of the coroners of our said Lady
the Queen for the county aforesaid, had notice; nevertheless, the said C. D., not regarding the duty of his office in
that behalf, afterwards, to wit, on &c., to execute his office
of and concerning the premises, and to take inquisition of
our said Lady the Queen, according to the laws and customs
of this realm, concerning the death of the said R. F., unlawfully, obstinately, and contemptuously did neglect and
refuse; and that the said C. D. no inquisition in that behalf
hath as yet taken, against the peace, &c.

12. *Indictment for Extortion.*

The jurors for our Lady the Queen, upon their oath present, that C. D., on &c., then being one of the coroners of our
said Lady the Queen, for the county of , by colour of
his said office, unlawfully and unjustly did demand, extort,
receive, and take of and from one A. B. the sum of 50s. of
lawful money of Great Britain, for and as his fee for executing and doing of his office aforesaid, to wit, upon the body of
one R. F., who, on the day and year above mentioned, was
slain by misadventure, and there lay dead, to the great
damage of the said A. B. against the form of the statute in
that case made and provided, and against the peace of our
said Lady the Queen, her crown and dignity.

13. *General Order for Burial.*

I, the undersigned, coroner for the   of   , do hereby authorize the burial of the body of   which has been viewed by the inquest jury. Witness my hand this day of

A. B., Coroner.

---

14. *Warrant to Summon Jury.*

To the constables of the several parishes of   ,
     , and   , in the county of   .
———— to wit. By virtue of my office, these are in her majesty's name to charge and command you, that on sight hereof you summon and warn twenty-three good and lawful men of your several parishes, personally to be and appear before me on   the   day of   instant, at ten of the clock in the forenoon, at the house of   , called or known by the name or sign of the   , in the said parish of   , in the said county of   , then and there to enquire of, do, and execute all such things as shall be given them in charge, on behalf of our sovereign lady the Queen, touching the death of R. F. And for so doing this is your warrant. And that you also attend at the time and place above mentioned, to make a return of those whom you shall have so summoned. And further to do and execute such other matters as shall be then and there enjoined you. And have you then and there this warrant. Given under my hand and seal, this   day of   , one thousand eight hundred and

C. D., Coroner. (L.S.)

---

15. *Precept.*

———— to wit. By virtue of a warrant to me directed, under the hand and seal of C. D., gentleman,   coroner for this   , you are hereby required, charged and commanded, on sight hereof, to summon and warn six able and sufficient men of your parish, personally to be and appear before him the said coroner, on the   day of   instant, at ten of the clock of the forenoon precisely, at the house of   , known by the sign of the   , in the parish of   , in the said   of   , then and there to inquire, on her majesty's behalf, touching the death of R. F. And that you attend at the same time and place, to make a return of the names of those you shall summon, and not depart without

leave. Hereof fail not at your peril. Dated this   day
of   , one thousand eight hundred and
                                 Yours, &c.   H. S.;
        Constable of the said parish of   , in the said
        To the constables of the parish of   ,
            in the said   of

---

16. *Summons to Jurymen.*

———— *to wit.* By virtue of a warrant under the hand
and seal of C. D., gentleman, coroner for this   , you are
hereby summoned personally to be and appear before him as
a juryman, on the   day of   instant, at ten of the
clock in the forenoon precisely, at the house of Mr.   ,
known by the sign of the   , in the parish of   , in
the said   , then and there to inquire, on her majesty's
behalf, touching the death of R. F., and further to do and
execute such other matters and things as shall be then and
there given you in charge and not depart without leave.
Hereof fail not at your peril. Dated the   day of   ,
one thousand eight hundred and   .
                                 Yours, &c.   H. S.,
            Constable of the said parish of
        To Mr. E. B. of the parish of   , in the
        of   , carpenter.

---

17. *Return of Coroner's Warrant.*

The execution of this warrant appears by the schedules
thereto annexed.
    The answer of   .

---

18. *Proclamation.*

You good men of this county [*or*, liberty, *as the case may
be*] summoned to appear here this day, to inquire for our
sovereign lady the Queen, when, how, and by what means
R. F. came to his death, answer to your names as you shall
be called, every man at the first call, upon the pain and
peril that shall fall thereon.

19. *Proclamation for default of Jurors.*

You good men who have been already severally called, and have made default, answer to your names and save your fine.

---

20. *Oath to be administered on the Voir dire.*

You shall true answer make to all such questions as the court shall demand of you. So help you God.

---

21. *Affirmation of Juror.*

I, A. B., do solemnly, sincerely, and truly affirm and declare that the taking of any oath is according to my religious belief unlawful ; and I do also solemnly, sincerely, and truly affirm and declare that I will [*as in Form* 2].

---

22. *Proclamation for the Attendance of Witnesses.*

If any one can give evidence on behalf of our sovereign lady the Queen, when, how, and by what means R. F. came to his death, let him come forth, and he shall be heard.

---

23. *Oath of Witness.*

The evidence which you shall give to this inquest on be half of our sovereign lady the Queen, touching the death of R. F., shall be the truth, the whole truth, and nothing but the truth. So help you God.

---

24. *Affirmation of Witness.*

I solemnly promise and declare that the evidence given by me to this inquest [*as in Form* 23.]

---

25. *Oath of Interpreter.*

You shall well and truly interpret unto the several wit nesses here produced on the behalf of our sovereign lady the Queen, touching the death of R. F., the oath that shall be administered unto them, and also the questions and demands which shall be made to the witnesses by the court or the jury concerning the matters of this inquiry, and you shall well and truly interpret the answers which the witnesses shall thereunto give, according to the best of your skill and ability. So help you God.

26. *Summons for a Witness.*

———— *to wit.* Whereas I am credibly informed that you can give evidence on behalf of our sovereign lady the Queen, touching the death of R. F., now lying dead in the parish of , in the said county of : These are therefore, by virtue of my office, in her majesty's name, to charge and command you personally to be and appear before me, at the dwelling-house of , known by the sign of the , in the said parish of , at six of the clock in the evening, on the day of instant, then and there to give evidence and be examined on her majesty's behalf, before me and my inquest, touching the premises. Hereof fail not, as you will answer at your peril. Given under my hand and seal this day of , one thousand eight hundred and

C. D., Coroner. (L.S.)

To A. B., C. D., &c.

27. *Warrant against a Witness|for Contempt of Summons.*

———— *to wit.* Whereas I have received credible information that A. B., of the parish of , in the said [county] of , builder, can give evidence on behalf of our sovereign lady the Queen, touching the death of R. F., now lying dead in the said parish of , in the [county] aforesaid; and whereas the said A. B. (having been duly summoned to appear and to give evidence before me and my inquest, touching the premises, at the time and place in the said summons specified, of which oath hath been duly made before me), hath refused and neglected so to do, to the great hindrance and delay of justice : these are therefore, by virtue of my office, in her Majesty's name, to charge and command you, or one of you, without delay, to apprehend and bring before me , coroner for the said , now sitting at the parish aforesaid, by virtue of my said office, the body of the said A. B., that he may be dealt with according to law: and for so doing this is your warrant. Given

under my hand and seal this   day of   , one thousand eight hundred and

C. D., Coroner. (<small>L.S.</small>)

To all constables and other her majesty's
officers of the peace in and for the county
of   , and also to E. F. my special
officer.

-----

28. *Commitment of a Witness for refusing to give Evidence.*

˙ —— *to wit.* Whereas I heretofore issued my summons
under my hand, directed to A. B., requiring his personal
appearance before me, coroner for the said   of
at the time and place therein mentioned, to give evidence,
and be examined on her majesty's behalf touching the death
of R. F. then and there lying dead; of the personal service
of which said summons oath hath been duly made before me ;
and whereas the said A. B. having neglected and refused to
appear, pursuant to the contents of the said summons, I
thereupon afterwards issued my warrant, under my hand
and seal, in order that the said A. B. by virtue thereof, might
be apprehended and brought before me, to answer the premises ; and whereas the said A. B. in pursuance thereof
hath been apprehended and brought before me, now duly sitting by virtue of my office, and hath been duly required to
give evidence and be examined before me and my inquest,
on her majesty's behalf, touching the death of the said R. F. ;
yet the said A. B. notwithstanding hath wilfully and absolutely refused, and still doth wilfully and absolutely refuse,
to give evidence and be examined touching the premises, or
to give sufficient reason for his refusal, in wilful and open
violation and delay of justice ; these are therefore, by virtue
of my office, in her majesty's name, to charge and command
you, or one of you, the said constables, and others her
majesty's officers of the peace in and for the said county
of   , forthwith to convey the body of the said A. B. to
the gaol of   , in the said county, and safely to deliver
the same to the keeper of the said prison there ; and these
are likewise, by virtue of my said office, in her majesty's
name, to will and require you the said keeper to receive the
body of the said A. B. into your custody, and him safely
to keep in the prison until he shall consent to give his evidence and be examined before me and my inquest on her
majesty's behalf, touching the death of the said R. F., or
until he shall be discharged from thence by due course of
law. And for your so doing this is your warrant. Given

under my hand and seal this   day of   , one thousand eight hundred and   .

                           C. D., Coroner.   (L.S.)

To the constables and others her majesty's
officers of the peace in and for the said
county of   , and also to the keeper of
the prison at   , in the said county.

29. *Proclamation of Adjournment.*

All manner of persons who have anything more to do at
this court before the coroner for this   , may depart home
at this time, and give their attendance here again [*or at the
adjourned place*] on   next, being the   day of
instant, at ten of the clock in the forenoon precisely.—God
save the Queen.

30. *Proclamation at Adjourned Meeting.*

All manner of persons who have anything more to do at
this court, before the coroner for this   , on this inquest
now to be taken, and adjourned over to this time and place,
draw near and give your attendance ; and you gentlemen of
the jury who have been impannelled and sworn upon this
inquest to inquire touching the death of R. F., severally
answer to your names and save your recognizances.

31. *Recognizance of Jurors upon an Adjournment.*

You acknowledge yourselves severally to owe to our
sovereign lady the Queen the sum of ten pounds, to be
levied upon your goods and chattels, lands and tenements,
for her majesty's use, upon condition that if you, and each
of you, do personally appear here again [*or at an adjourned
place*] on   next, being the   day of   instant,
at ten of the clock in the forenoon precisely, then and there
to make further inquiry on behalf of our said sovereign lady
the Queen, touching the death of the said R. F., of whose
body you have had the view; then this recognizance to be
void, or else to remain in full force.   Are you content ?

32. *Summons for Medical Witness.*

Coroner's inquest at   , upon the body of
By virtue of this my order as coroner for   , you are required to appear before me and the jury at   on the   day of   , one thousand eight hundred and at   of the clock, to give evidence touching the cause of death of   , [*and then add, when the witness is required to make or assist at a post-mortem examination,* and make or assist in making a post-mortem examination of the body, with [*or,* without] an analysis, *as the case may be*], and report thereon at the said inquest.

(Signed)   Coroner.

To   , surgeon [*or,* M. D., *as the case may be*].

---

33. *Information of Witness.*

————— *to wit.* The information of J. S., of   , in the county of   , carpenter, taken and acknowledged on behalf of our sovereign lady the Queen, touching the death of R. F., at the house of M   , known by the sign of the   , in the parish of   , in the county [*or,* city, &c.] of   , on the   day of   , in the year of our Lord   , before me, C. D., gent., coroner for the said   , on view of the body of R. F., then lying dead within the said county [*or,* city, &c.].

This informant on his oath saith [*stating the evidence in the first person*].

Taken upon oath this   day of   , in ⎱ J. S.
the year of our Lord   , before me   ⎰

C. D., Coroner.

---

34. *Commitment for refusing to enter into Recognizances.*

—————, *to wit.* Whereas upon an inquisition this day taken before me, coroner for the said   of   , at the parish of   , in the said   , on view of the body of R. F., then and there lying dead, one J. S. was, by my inquest then and there sitting, charged with the wilful murder of the said R. F. ; and whereas one E. F., broker, was then and there examined, and gave information in writing, before me and my inquest, touching the premises, and which said information he the said E. F. then and there before me and my inquest duly signed and acknowledged, and by which said

information it appears that the said E. F. is a material
witness on her Majesty's behalf, against the said J. S. now
in custody and charged by my said inquest with the said
murder, and the said E. F. having wilfully and absolutely
refused to enter into the usual recognizance for his personal
appearance at the next   , to be holden at   , in and
for the said county, then and there to give evidence, on her
Majesty's behalf against the said J. S., touching the premises,
to the great hindrance and delay of justice : these are, therefore, by virtue of my office, in her Majesty's name to charge
and command you, or one of you, the said constables, and
others her Majesty's officers of the peace in and for the said
county, forthwith to convey the body of the said E. F. to the
gaol of   , in the said county, and safely to deliver the
same to the keeper of the said prison there; and these are
likewise, by virtue of my said office, in her Majesty's name,
to will and require you, the said keeper, to receive the body
of the said E. F. into your custody, and him safely to keep
in the said prison, until he shall enter into such recognizance
before me, or before one of her Majesty's justices of the
peace for the said county, for the purpose aforesaid, or in
default thereof, until he shall be from thence otherwise discharged by due course of law; and for your so doing this is
your warrant.   Given under my hand and seal this
day of   one thousand eight hundred and

C. D., Coroner.   (L.S.).

To the constables and others her Majesty's officers
    of the peace in and for the county of   , and
    also to the keeper of the   prison at   in
    the said county.

---

35. *Oath of Officer to keep the Jury until they are agreed upon their Verdict.*

You shall well and truly keep the jury upon this inquiry
without meat, drink, or fire ; you shall not suffer any person
to speak to them, nor shall you speak to them yourself,
unless it be to ask them if they have agreed upon their
verdict, until they shall be agreed.   So help you God.

---

36. *Certificate of the Finding of Jurors*

————, *to wit.*   These are to certify, that by an inquisition
taken before me, on view of the body of R. F., at the parish
of   , in the said county of   , bearing date the

day of   instant, the jurors in the said inquisition named
have found that C. D. justifiably, and of inevitable necessity
[*or as the case may be*], did kill and slay the said R. F.   Given
under my hand, this   day of   , one thousand
eight hundred and

C. D., Coroner.   (L.S.)

---

37. *Warrant of Apprehension.*

To all constables of the parish of   , in the county
   of   , and to all others her Majesty's officers
   of the peace within the said county.

———, *to wit.*   Whereas by an inquisition taken before
me, coroner for the said   of   , this   day of
   , at the parish of   , in the said county of   ,
on view of the body of R. F., then and there lying dead, one
   , late of the parish of   , in the said county, stands
charged with the wilful murder of the said R. F. : These are
therefore, by virtue of my office, in her Majesty's name, to
charge and command you and every of you, that you or some
or one of you, without delay, do apprehend and bring before
me the said coroner or one of her Majesty's justices of the
peace of the said county, the body of the said   , of whom
you shall have notice that he may be dealt with according to
law ; and for your so doing this is your warrant.   Given
under my hand and seal this   day of   , one thousand
eight hundred and

C. D., Coroner.   (L.S.)

---

38. *Commitment.*

To the constables, and other her Majesty's officers of
   the peace for the county of   , and also to the
   keeper of her Majesty's gaol of

———, *to wit.*   Whereas by an inquisition taken before
me, coroner for the said   of   , this day and year
hereunder mentioned, on view of the body of R. F., lying
dead at the parish of   , in the said county of   ,
G. H. stands charged with the wilful murder of the said R.F. :
These are therefore, by virtue of my office, in her Majesty's
name, to charge and command you, or any of you, forthwith
safely to convey the body of the said G. H. to her Majesty's
gaol of   , and safely to deliver the same to the keeper
of the said gaol ; and these are likewise by virtue of my said

office, in her Majesty's name, to will and require you the said
keeper to receive the body of the said G. H. into your
custody, and him safely to keep in the said gaol, until he
shall be thence discharged by due course of law, and for your
so doing this shall be your warrant. Given under my hand
and seal, the   day of   , one thousand eight hundred
and

C. D., Coroner. (L.S.)

39. *Warrant of Detainer.*

To the keeper of her Majesty's gaol of

———, *to wit.* Whereas you have in your custody the
body of G. H. ; and whereas by an inquisition taken before
me   , coroner for the said   of   , the day and
year hereunder written, at the parish of   , in the said
county, on view of the body of R. F. then and there lying
dead, he the said G. H. stands charged with the wilful
murder of the said R. F. : These are therefore in her Majesty's
name, by virtue of my office, to charge and command you to
detain and keep in your custody the body of the said G. H.
until he shall be thence discharged by due course of law;
and for your so doing this is your warrant. Given under my
hand and seal this   day of   , one thousand eight
hundred and

C. D., Coroner. (L.S.)

40. *Habeas Corpus.*

VICTORIA, &c., to the sheriff of   , and also to the keeper
of our gaol at   , in and for our county of   , or his
deputy, greeting : We command you that you have before
our right trusty and well-beloved . . . . . in our
High Court of Justice, immediately after the receipt of this
our writ, the body of   , being committed and detained
in our prison, under your custody (as is said), together with
the day and cause of his taking and detainer, by whatsoever
name the said   may be called therein, to undergo and
receive all and singular such things as our said Chief Justice
shall then and there consider of concerning him in that
behalf, and have you then there this writ. Witness, &c.

By the Court.

(*Indorsed on the back of the writ.*) The execution of this
writ appears in the schedule hereto annexed. The answer of
, sheriff.

---

41. *Return thereon.*

I, , of the county of , do humbly certify and
return to the Right Honourable . . . . . Chief Justice,
in the writ to this schedule annexed named, that before the
said writ came to me (that is to say), on the day of
, in the year of the reign of her present majesty
Queen Victoria, G. H., in the said writ named, was taken,
and in her majesty's gaol for the said county under my
custody is detained, by virtue of a warrant under the hand
and seal of C. D., Esquire, one of her majesty's coroners for
the said county, the said G. H., by an inquisition taken
before the said Coroner on view of the body of R. F., lying
dead at the parish of , in the said county, standing
charged with the killing and slaying of the said R. F., and
this is the cause of the taking and detaining the said G. H.,
which writ, together with his body, I have ready, as by the
said writ I am commanded.

---

42. *Certiorari to the Coroner.*

VICTORIA, &c. to C. D., Coroner for our county of
greeting: We being willing, for certain reasons, that all and
singular the inquisition, examinations, informations and
depositions taken by or before you, touching the commitment
of G. H. to the custody of the keeper of our gaol at
in and for our county of , for murder [*or*, manslaughter],
as is said, be sent by you before our right trusty and well-
beloved . . . do command you that you send
under your seal before our said Chief Justice, in our High
Court of Justice, immediately after the receipt of this our
writ, all and singular the said inquisition, examinations,
informations and depositions, with all things touching the
same, as fully and perfectly as they have been taken by or
before you, and now remain in your custody or power,
together with this our writ, that we may cause further to be
done thereon what of right and according to the law and
custom of England we shall see fit to be done. Witness, &c.
By the Court.

J. R

43. *Return thereon.*

The execution of this writ appears by the schedule hereunto annexed. The answer of C. D., one of the Coroners of our lady by the Queen for the county of   , within named, with the seal affixed.

---

44. *Notice of Bail.*

In the High Court of Justice, Queen's Bench Division.
The Queen *v.* C. D.

Take notice, that an application will be made in her Majesty's High Court of Justice, on   next, or so soon after as counsel can be heard, that the above-named defendant, then brought into court by virtue of a writ of *habeas corpus*, may be admitted to bail for his personal appearance at the next sessions of oyer and terminer, and general gaol delivery, to be holden in and for the county of   , to answer all such matters and things as in her Majesty's behalf shall then and there be objected against him, and so from day to day, and not depart the Court without leave; and the names and descriptions of the bail are A. B.. of &c., E. F., of &c. &c.   Dated, &c.

To X. Y., Esquire, Coroner for the county of   , and to L. M. [*the prosecutor*].

---

45. *To take up a body interred.*

————, *to wit.* Whereas complaint hath been made unto me , coroner for the said   of   , that on the day of this instant   , the body of one R. F. was privately and secretly buried in your parish in the said county, and that the said R. F. died not of a natural but a violent death ; and whereas no notice of the violent death of the said R. F. hath been given to the coroners for the said   , whereby an inquisition might have been taken on view of the body of the said R. F. before his interment, as by law is required; these are, therefore, by virtue of my office, in her Majesty's name, to charge and command you that you forthwith cause the body of the said R. F. to be taken up and safely conveyed to   , in the said parish, that I with my inquest may have a view thereof, and proceed therein according to law. Hereof fail not, as you will answer the contrary at your peril.

Given under my hand and seal the   day of   , one thousand eight hundred and   .

C. D., Coroner. (L.S.)

To the minister, churchwardens, and overseers [*or as the case may be*] of the parish of   , in the said county of

---

46. *Certificate for Fining an absent Juror or Witness.*

I, the undersigned C. D., coroner for the   of   *,* do certify, pursuant to the directions of the statute in that behalf made and provided, that a fine of   shillings is imposed by me on A. B., of   , for his default, after having been openly called three times, in not appearing and serving as a juror [*or,* giving evidence] upon an inquest now held before me at   in the said   , the said A. B. having been duly summoned as such juror [*or,* witness] upon the said inquest. Given under my hand, &c.

C. D., Coroner.

INDEX.

MUTUAL COMBAT,
  killing in, 171, 186

NEGLECT,
  of duty by coroner, 52, 63
  killing by, 158, 189

NEGLIGENCE,
  death caused by, 177, 193
  contributory, 193
  in mines, &c., to be reported to inspector, 126

NOTICE,
  of death to be sent to coroner, 6

OATH,
  of bailiff in charge of jury, 43, 238
  examination of coroner on, respecting accounts 97
  upon the *voir dire*, 34
  of jurors, 17, 223
  of interpreter, 33, 233
  of witness, 33, 233

OBSTRUCTION, 87

OFFICIAL CORONERS, 108

OUTLAWRY, 123

OXFORD,
  coroners of university, 103

PALACE. See *Queen's Household.*

PARCHMENT,
  when inquisition must be on, 83

PARENT AND CHILD,
  killing by one in defence of other, 213
  statutory duties of parents, 159

PARISH,
  definition of, 114

PETITION,
  for writ *de coronatore eligendo*, 67
  for division of county into districts, 118

POST MORTEM EXAMINATION
  when and by whom to be taken, 94
  where, 95
  fees for, 93
  no fee allowed for, unless made by order of coroner, 93
  on persons dying in hospitals, 94

THE END.

BRADBURY, AGNEW, & CO., PRINTERS, WHITEFRIARS.

4195

Chitty's Index to all the Reported Cases decided in the several Courts of Equity in England, the Privy Council, and the House of Lords, with a Selection of Irish Cases, on or relating to the Principles, Pleading, and Practice of Equity and Bankruptcy from the Earliest Period. Fourth Edition. Wholly Revised, Re-classified, and brought down to the end of 1883. Volume VII. Containing the Titles "Solicitor" to "Vendor and Purchaser." By HENRY EDWARD HIRST, Esq., Barrister-at-Law. Royal 8vo. 1888. Price 1l. 11s. 6d. cloth.

*** Vols. I., II., III., V., VI. and VII., price each 1l. 11s. 6d. Vol. IV., 2l. 2s. Vol. VIII. in the press.

Fisher's Digest of the Reported Decisions of the Courts of Common Law, Bankruptcy, Probate, Admiralty, and Divorce, together with a selection from those of the Court of Chancery and Irish Courts. From 1756 to 1883 inclusive. Founded on Fisher's Digest. By JOHN MEWS, assisted by C. M. CHAPMAN, HARRY H. W. SPARHAM, and A. H. TODD, Barristers-at-Law. In 7 vols. Royal 8vo. 1884. Price 12l. 12s. cloth.

*** Supplement for 1884, 12s. 6d.; for 1885, 1886, and 1887, each, 15s.

Dale and Lehmann's Digest of Cases Overruled, not Followed, Disapproved, Approved, Distinguished, Commented on, and Specially Considered in the English Courts, from the year 1756 to 1886 inclusive, arranged according to Alphabetical Order of their Subjects; together with Extracts from the Judgments delivered thereon, and a complete Index of the Cases, in which are included all Cases Reversed, from the year 1856. By CHARLES WILLIAM MITCALFE DALE and RUDOLF CHAMBERS LEHMANN, assisted by CHARLES H. L. NEISH and HERBERT H. CHILD, Esqrs., Barristers-at-Law. Royal 8vo. 1887. Price 2l. 10s. cloth.

*** *Forms a Supplement to "Chitty's Equity Index" and Fisher's Common Law Digest.*

Chitty's Archbold's Practice of the Queen's Bench Division of the High Court of Justice, and on Appeal therefrom, to the Court of Appeal and House of Lords in Civil Proceedings. Fourteenth Edition. By T. WILLES CHITTY, assisted by J. ST. L. LESLIE, Barristers-at-Law. 2 vols. Demy 8vo. 1885. Price 3l. 13s. 6d. cloth.

Chitty's Forms of Practical Proceedings in the Queen's Bench Division of the High Court of Justice.—With Notes containing the Statutes, Rules and Cases relating thereto. Twelfth Edition. By THOS. WILLES CHITTY, Esq., Barrister-at-Law. Demy 8vo. 1883. Price 1l. 18s. cloth.

Addison on Torts.—Being a Treatise on Wrongs and their Remedies. Sixth Edition. By HORACE SMITH, Esq., Editor of "Addison on Contracts," &c. Royal 8vo. 1887. Price 1l. 18s. cloth.

"**Upon a careful perusal of the editor's work, we can say that he has done it excellently.**"—*Law Quarterly Review*, April, 1887.

Addison's Treatise on the Law of Contracts.—Eighth Edition. By HORACE SMITH, Esq., Barrister-at-Law, Recorder of Lincoln. Royal 8vo. 1883. (In one thick vol., 1600 pp.) Price 2l. 10s. cloth.

Arnould on the Law of Marine Insurance.—Sixth Edition. By DAVID MACLACHLAN, Esq., Barrister-at-Law. 2 vols. Royal 8vo. 1887. Price 3l. cloth.

Williams' Bankruptcy Practice.—The Law and Practice in Bankruptcy, comprising the Bankruptcy Act, 1883; the Bankruptcy Rules, 1886; the Debtors Acts, 1869, 1878; and the Bills of Sale Acts, 1878 and 1882. Fourth Edition. By R. VAUGHAN WILLIAMS, W. VAUGHAN WILLIAMS, and E. W. HANSELL, Esqrs., Barristers-at-Law. Royal 8vo. 1886. Price 1l. 8s. cloth.

Lawrance's Precedents of Deeds of Arrangement between Debtors and their Creditors, including Forms of Resolutions for Compositions and Schemes of Arrangement under the Bankruptcy Act, 1883. Third Edition. With introductory chapters. Also the Deeds of Arrangement Act, 1887, with Notes. By G. W. LAWRANCE, Barrister-at-Law. 8vo. 1888. Price 6d. cloth.

Hall's Allotments Acts, 1887, with the Regulations issued by the Local Government Board, and Introductory Chapters, Notes, and Forms. By T. HALL HALL, M.A., Esq., Barrister-at-Law, Author of "The Law of Allotments." Royal 12mo. 1888. Price 7s. 6d. cloth.

Chalmers' Digest of the Law of Bills of Exchange, Pro- missory Notes, and Cheques. Third Edition. By His Honor JUDGE CHALMERS, Draughtsman of the Bills of Exchange Act, 1882, &c. Demy 8vo. 1887. Price 16s. cloth.

Stephen's Malicious Prosecutions.—The Law relating to Actions for Malicious Prosecution. By HERBERT STEPHEN, Esq., Barrister-at-Law. Royal 12mo. 1888. Price 6s. cloth.
" A reliable text-book upon the law of malicious prosecutions."—*Law Times.*

Lupton's Law relating to Dogs.—By FREDERICK LUPTON, Solicitor. Royal 12mo. 1888. Price 5s. cloth.

Archbold's Pleading and Evidence in Criminal Cases.— With the Statutes, Precedents of Indictments, &c., and the Evidence necessary to support them. Twentieth Edition, including the Practice in Criminal Proceedings by Indictment. By WILLIAM BRUCE, Esq., Barrister-at-Law, and Stipendiary Magistrate for the Borough of Leeds. Royal 12mo. 1886. Price 1l. 11s. 6d. cloth.

Castle's Law of Rating.—A Treatise on the Law of Rating. Second Edition. By EDWARD JAMES CASTLE, Esq., Q.C. Demy 8vo. 1886. Price 25s. cloth.

Carver's Law of Carriage by Sea.—A Treatise on the Law relating to the Carriage of Goods by Sea. By THOMAS GILBERT CARVER, Esq., Barrister-at-law. Royal 8vo. 1885. Price 1l. 12s. cloth.

Blackburn's Contract of Sale.—A Treatise on the effect of the Contract of Sale on the Legal Rights of Property and Possession in Goods, Wares and Merchandise. By LORD BLACKBURN. Second Edition. By J. C. GRAHAM, Esq., Barrister-at-Law. Royal 8vo. 1885. Price 1l. 1s. cloth.

Mitcheson's Charitable Trusts. — The Jurisdiction of the Charity Commission; being the Acts conferring such Jurisdiction, 1853-1883, with Introductory Essays and Notes on the Sections. By RICHARD EDMUND MITCHESON, Barrister-at-Law. Demy 8vo. 1887. Price 18s. cloth.

Shirley's Selection of Leading Cases in the Criminal Law, with Notes. By WALTER S. SHIRLEY, Esq., Barrister-at-Law, Author of ." A Selection of Leading Cases in the Common Law," &c. Demy 8vo. 1888. Price 6s. cloth.

Shirley's Leading Cases in the Common Law.—With Notes. Third Edition. By W. SHIRLEY SHIRLEY, M.A., Esq., Barrister-at-Law, North-Eastern Circuit. Demy 8vo. 1886. Price 16s. cloth.

Smith's Manual of Common Law.--For Practitioners and Students. Comprising the Fundamental Principles, with useful Practical Rules and Decisions. By JOSIAH W. SMITH, B.C.L., Q.C. Tenth Edition. By J. TRUSTRAM, LL.M., Esq., Barrister-at-Law. Demy 12mo. 1887. Price 14s. cloth.

Smith's Real and Personal Property.—A Compendium of the Law of Real and Personal Property, primarily connected with Conveyancing. Designed as a second book for Students, and as a Digest of the most useful learning for Practitioners. Sixth Edition. By JOSIAH W. SMITH, Q.C., and J. TRUSTRAM, LL.M., Barrister-at-Law. 2 vols. 8vo. 1884. Price 2l. 2s. cloth.

Pocket Law Lexicon.—The Pocket Law Lexicon, explaining technical words, phrases, and maxims of the English, Scotch, and Roman Law, to which is added a complete List of Law Reports, with

Lightning Source UK Ltd.
Milton Keynes UK
UKOW05f2357040117
291366UK00013B/323/P

9 781334 593550